David Boyle is a journalist who has written about new ideas in economics for the past decade in newspapers and magazines all over the world. He is the author of *Funny Money*. Since 1988 he has been the editor of *New Economics* magazine and he has also edited a range of other publications including *Town & Country Planning*. David Boyle is a fellow of the RSA and a well-known figure in organizations such as the New Economics Foundation. He has been a Winston Churchill Fellow and is a regular broadcaster on the future of money, the economics of cities and a range of other topics.

By the same Author
Funny Money: In Search of Alternative Cash

THE TYRANNY
OF NUMBERS

Why Counting Can't Make Us Happy

David Boyle

HarperCollins*Publishers*

For Joanna, Ben, Agatha and Frances

Flamingo
An Imprint of HarperCollins*Publishers*
77–85 Fulham Palace Road,
Hammersmith, London W6 8JB

www.**fire**and**water**.com

Published by Flamingo 2001
9 8 7 6 5 4 3 2 1

First published in Great Britain by
HarperCollins*Publishers* 2000

Copyright © David Boyle 2000, 2001

The Author asserts the moral right to
be identified as the author of this work

ISBN 0 00 6531997

Set in Meridien

Printed and bound in Great Britain by
Clays Ltd, St Ives plc

Acknowledgements

'Why are boys obsessed with numbers?' girl asks boy in Bill Forsyth's film *Gregory's Girl*, lying on their backs on the grass and gazing at the night sky. She was right to ask. Boys like numbers: there was a time in my life when I could list the statistics of British battleships until far, far beyond the tolerance threshold of Admiral Beatty himself.

So this book is partly an act of contrition to anyone unfortunate enough to hear me do so, but also an attempt to redress the balance a bit. Because, just as many of us imagine we are building a more feminine and caring world, the new place also seems to be underpinned by hard, unemotional and ultimately distorting statistics. I believe there's a contradiction here somewhere. I want to live where people can see beyond the figures to embrace complex truth.

This is intended as a polemic. I'm not against the idea of measuring, nor have I tried to write an academic critique of quantitative versus qualitative research – there's enough of them out there already, and I'm not qualified to write one. Nor is it intended as a critique of scientific method: I concentrate on the dilemma at its sharpest – with the business people, economists and politicians who are busy shaping our world. In short, this isn't a book about statistics, but a book about a pervasive blindness that I believe is creeping insidiously into the way we understand things.

I am enormously indebted to countless conversations about aspects of this labyrinthine subject with a range of friends and relatives on both sides of the Atlantic. I can't list them all, but they will recognize the discussions we had from these pages – and I hope it's a happy memory. I've certainly enjoyed it. I'd also like to acknowledge a debt to Theodore Porter's fascinating book *Trust in Numbers*, Robert Chambers' *Whose*

Reality Counts? and *The Dent Dictionary of Measurement* (Mike Darton and John Clark), where most of the bizarre units of measurement came from.

There are a number of others I'm ever so grateful to for specific nuggets of wisdom, help and advice, including Alan Atkisson, Clifford Cobb, Carol Cornish, Kate Cutler, Lesley Harding, Sue Holliday, Amanda Horton-Mastin, Sanjiv Lingayah, Serena and Tony Ludford, Alex MacGillivray, Mark Mackintosh, Rachel Maybank, Sara Murphy, Gill Paul, Alison Pilling, Peter Raynard, Melita Rogelj, Jonathan Rowe, Catherine Rubbens, Andrew Simms, Marian Storkey, Karen Sullivan, Mathis Wackernagel, Perry Walker, Gavin Yamey, Simon Zadek and everyone at the New Economics Foundation – for their patience, friendship and shared excitement over the years. And especially thank you to Edgar Cahn and Sarah Burns, whose inspiration will be obvious. And Ed Mayo, who read many of the chapters in draft, and made a series of incisive and sparkling suggestions which made the book much better than it otherwise would have been – and introduced me to e e cummings.

I am enormously grateful to my agent Julian Alexander, my editor Lucinda McNeile, to Lucinda Cooke at Lucas Alexander Whitley, and to Tamsin Miller and Cecilia McCullough at HarperCollins – and all the others responsible for making sure the book actually appears. Their brilliant advice and constant support has been one of the most luxurious aspects of writing it – writing anything, in fact.

The mistakes are of course all mine, but I couldn't have done it without them all. Their contribution is another excellent example of the unmeasurable.

Contents

While you and I have lips and voices which
  are for kissing and to sing with
who cares if some oneeyed son of a bitch.
  invents an instrument to measure Spring with?

e e cummings

Introduction

Still Life with Numbers

The renowned cosmologist Professor Bignumska, lecturing on the
future of the universe, had stated that in a billion years according to
her calculations, the earth would fall into the sun in a fiery death.
In the back of the auditorium a tremulous voice piped up. 'Excuse
me Professor, but h-how long did you say it would be?' Professor
Bignumska calmly replied, 'About a billion years.' A sigh of relief
was heard. 'Whew! For a minute there, I thought you said a *million*
years.'
Douglas Hofstadter, *Scientific American*, May 1982

There are no such things as still lifes.
Erica Jong

I

Mary Poppins was the first film I ever saw. I was six years, four
months old – let's measure it precisely. I remember trotting
as fast as I could beside my father along Whitehall, past the
Treasury and the other palaces of national calculation, to the
Haymarket. I remember the strange red torches and the
national anthem at the end. That's how it was in those more
deferential and innocent days before the hippies. And I
remember being completely blown away by the experience,
the songs of Julie Andrews and the idea that life should be a
little more magical than it was.

Within weeks I knew most of the lyrics by heart, though I
barely understood the words. Maybe, in retrospect, I was also
a little influenced by Mary Poppins' ridicule of George Banks –
Hollywood has recycled the name George Banks for pompous
boobies ever since – and his fascination for the kind of order
brought by numbers. 'They must feel the thrill of totting up

a balance book,' she sings to poor deluded George about his children:

> ... A thousand cyphers neatly in a row.
> When gazing at a graph that shows the profits up,
> their little cup of joy should overflow.

The irony is lost on him – as it was on me. And though Hollywood is still busily promoting the idea of magic, you would never catch them in this post-Thatcherite age making fun of profits or ridiculing the vital importance of calculation – still less the idea of cyphers neatly in a row. It's just too important to us all these days.

So I came away from the cinema determined to make sure I flung my tuppence away on some little old bird woman, rather than marvelling at the strange alchemy of compound interest if I put it in the bank. I was not going to be a George Banks. Yet here I am, 35 years later, with my pension and life insurance, living in a world completely overwhelmed by numbers and calculation.

It's the same for nearly all of us. There are personal calculations to be made each day, about investments, journey times, bank machines and credit cards. There are professional figures at work, in the form of targets, statistics, workforce percentages and profit forecasts. As consumers, we are counted and aggregated according to every purchase we make. Every time we are exposed to the media, there is a positive flood of statistics controlling and interpreting the world, developing each truth, simplifying each problem. 'Being a man is unhealthy,' said the front page of the *Evening Standard* recently, adding – like every similar newspaper article about statistics – the word: 'official.' As if we had been wondering about the truth all these years and, thanks to the counters, we now know. As if the figures are so detached that there is no arguing with them.

But of course we keep arguing. Just as the government keeps arguing despite its battery of benchmarks, quality indicators and league tables, as it struggles to hold back chaos like King Canute in front of the waves. We take our collective pulses 24 hours a day with the use of statistics. We understand life that way, though somehow the more figures we use, the great truths still seem to slip through our fingers. Despite all that calculating, and all that numerical control, we feel as ignorant as ever.

Mary Poppins might have been talking about me when she said that 'sometimes a person we love, through no fault of his own, can't see past the end of his nose'. She meant George Banks, of course, but I feel just as myopic myself. Life never keeps still long enough to measure anything important.

If you are said to be 'calculating', people could mean one of two things about you – both related and equally repellent. It could mean that you are constantly comparing what is best for you in any given situation. This is not a compliment. It implies something cold, fish-like and completely self-interested. But it could also mean you are someone who counts too much, someone who measures things but can't see the reality behind them.

There is something equally clinical about that, but disinterested rather than self-interested. A calculating person, in this sense, is someone for whom the world past the end of their nose is a foreign country. And although we have become exactly that with all our counting, and increasingly so, it can send a shiver down the spine when you come across extreme examples. Like the eighteenth-century prodigy Jedediah Buxton, in his first trip to the theatre to see a performance of Shakespeare's *Richard III*. Asked later whether he'd enjoyed it, all he could say was that there were 5,202 steps during the dances and 12,445 words spoken by the actors. Nothing about what the words said, about the winter of our discontent made glorious summer; nothing about the evil hunchback king.

Today, Buxton would probably be described as autistic. It is particularly horrifying to hear that his numbers turned out to be exactly right.

The story is funny now as then, but it is also faintly disturbing, and I have been wondering why this is. It could be that we see Jedediah Buxton as a fearsome symbol of the modern age, counting everything but seeing the significance of nothing. But I think it is deeper than that. There is something inhuman about it – not so much the ability to count, but the failure to be moved. We shiver, I think, at anybody with no emotions – as if they were completely amoral, like Dr Strangelove. We shrink from white-coated doctors too like cold calculating machines. Even doctors should be slightly fallible.

Even so, we encounter these 'calculating' machines almost every day. It's hard not to turn on the news without audibly tripping over one of them. Like the academic who refuses to pass judgement on any problem, however urgent, because there hasn't been enough research. Or the politician who is so obsessed with the polling figures that he can no longer trust his gut instincts. Or the social scientist who has laboriously proved with the use of statistics something which anybody else with an ounce of common sense knew already – that the death of a parent can scar a child for life, or that alcoholics have an unusually high depression rate. It's official, they say. Like the University of Michigan study which revealed that children who don't take exercise and eat junk food tend to be fatter. Or the recent research which showed that areas of high unemployment tend to have fewer jobs.

Then there are the familiar people who muddle up the numbers with the truth. Or, even worse, those who think you can change the truth just by changing the statistics. Don't forget those dismal agriculture ministers who urged the public to listen to the scientists over the safety of BSE beef (and really believed it) even though they were quietly suppressing the research of anybody who argued that it might not be safe to eat.

These are modern monsters, but none of us can completely escape the accusation. We're all tied up with figures, even if they are just cricket averages and lottery numbers.

Romantics and leftists traditionally say this is a bad thing. Romantics think that it reduces the individual to mere figures. Leftists think it's a kind of tyranny. They are both wrong in the sense that we do need to be able to count – but they are right too. The strange thing is that ratcheting up the calculations has often been done for excellent humanitarian reasons, driven by impeccably radical reformers. Of course in the history of the tyranny of numbers over life there are crazed scientists and Nazis with branding irons who stalk through the pages. This is no scientific history of counting, and there is no account of the great statistical pioneers like Herbert Spencer or Karl Pearson. Nor does it cover the byways of scientific research or IQ – or the people who really believed you could control individuals by counting them.

But counting was also a way of improving the world. Maybe they wanted to prove the existence of great inequality or disease, like Edwin Chadwick. Maybe they wanted to find a way of aggregating the national accounts to defeat Hitler, like John Maynard Keynes. Or maybe they wanted to force politicians to worry about people's happiness, like Jeremy Bentham. All the historic interludes I've chosen in this book fall into that category. They are people who – for the best of motives – brought forth the flood of numbers and calculations into the non-scientific parts of our lives.

It still is a way of improving the world. Are your schools not performing as well as they should? Then measure their results. Are you worried about the performance of a local council, a company, a great institution, a hospital? Send in the auditors, set some standards as benchmarks. You don't trust the professionals? Summarize their decisions in number form, send in the cost-benefit experts and keep your beady eye on them. It is the modern way. Numbers – like money – drive out the mysterious power of elites, the clubbable atmosphere of the professions, the we-know-best patronizing attitudes of those thick-set people with glasses and firm handshakes who used to lord it over our lives. We can control them if we can reduce their complex professionalism to numbers.

The trouble is that the numbers have proliferated, and it's sometimes hard to breathe – still less tell the difference between one statistic and another. It is difficult enough to remember your car registration number, PIN number, home, work and mobile phone numbers all at the same time. It's almost enough to make you coldly calculating.

II

If you want to watch people who go further than that – people who try to measure things which can probably never be measured – then come with me for a moment to the closing minutes of a libel action at the Law Courts in the Strand, London. The jury has decided that when a national newspaper described a respectable lady as a prostitute – when she was no such thing – they had clearly 'lowered her in the estimation of right thinking people,' which is one legal definition of libel. But what kind of damages should she be given?

The amount awarded is a decision for the jury, and the judge is not allowed to even hint at a figure. He cannot suggest to them that the average pay-out might be £10,000 or £500,000. His half-moon spectacles perched on the end of his nose, he turns to the jury box. 'Imagine if you will,' he says, 'a small flat in Battersea. Or perhaps a semi-detached in Maida Vale. Or maybe a penthouse apartment in Mayfair . . .'

And so he goes on. Did the humiliation the woman received deserve the flat, the house or the penthouse? Or something else? How could you start to measure such things? But the jury played safe and plumped for the house, and who can say whether they were right or not? 'If this is justice, I'm a banana,' said the editor of *Private Eye* famously with damages of £600,000 awarded against him in the same court. Damages are notoriously difficult to judge, but sometimes you still have to try.

Libel damages are just one example among many. What makes this such a peculiar moment in the history of measurement is that in almost every area of public life, qualities like happiness, competence or loyalty are being picked over by hordes of radical accountants and politicians, visionary entrepreneurs and planners – desperately trying to find ways of being more effective in a competitive world.

Despite the proliferation of measurements, somehow the numbers are still not providing an effective lever. Why? Because, so often, you can't measure what's really important.

But it's all very well to say it is impossible: decisions still have to be made – and if you don't count what's really important, it gets ignored. It doesn't count. There are only so many resources, so doctors must compare the quality of life of a 70-year-old with heart failure against a suicidal teenager with a long history of depression. Planners have to compare the pleasure and disruption brought by a new 18-screen cinema with the contentment of keeping the site as a park. Investors have to compare a notoriously polluting oil company with a dodgy record in human rights with a tremendously successful Internet company with three employees and no profits.

It's impossible of course, but they have to try, because otherwise the wrong decision will be made or their rivals will steal an advantage. So they find themselves isolating something which *can* be counted. Then they measure, measure, measure, knowing that what they measure is alive and will not keep still, and suspecting that maybe – however much they count – they will not capture the essence of the question they are asking. Things have to keep static if you're going to count them: that's probably why the first statisticians were known as 'statists'. But real life isn't still.

How, for example, can businesses measure what they are worth, when value is increasingly ephemeral – encompassing things which go way beyond traditional balance sheets? How can we measure our national or local success when our measuring rods are so inadequate, and yet so important to our politicians? Yet without measuring rods, it is hard to know whether we are making any progress.

But if politicians have a difficult time, it is nothing to what is happening in the business world, as managers struggle to find ways of measuring customer loyalty, brand reputation or staff morale. And as they do so, Internet companies which have never made a profit and which sell intangible products, rush past them up the Wall Street indices. When the balance sheets of a company like Microsoft show assets worth only 6 per cent of its stock market value, they need to find an answer.

It's all a bit like a computer game. What really matters can't be counted, but it's a much worse situation than that. If you make the attempt but measure the wrong thing, it isn't just wasted effort. It can destroy everything you've worked for. Like the school league tables that make teachers concentrate on getting borderline pupils through at the expense of their weaker classmates. Or the hospital waiting lists that fell because only quick simple problems were treated. It's a familiar story, just as unemployment statistics bear no relation to the number of people who actually want to work. It all comes down to definitions: governments prefer to count people claiming benefits rather than unemployed people. To count things, you first have to define them in measurable ways, and magically the system can manipulate the figures by narrowing the definition.

This amounts to a kind of crisis. We need answers, but we also know that what is most important to our lives simply can't be pinned down like a still life. We can't measure happiness directly, any more than we can measure God or measure life, but we can measure some of its symptoms, and some of the symptoms of its absence. Which is why a city like Seattle started measuring success by the number of vegetarian restaurants, or why Strathclyde started measuring success by the number of golden eagles. It is why schools are trying to measure their pupils' self-esteem, why investors are measuring the ethics of their investments – and why companies like Toys Я Us and Shell are pouring resources into measuring the knowledge and contentment of staff, communities and stakeholders.

A century and a half ago, the followers of the philosopher Jeremy Bentham were dashing around the country in their stagecoaches to measure everything they possibly could – from the health of slum inhabitants to the religious feelings of children – coming home with tables of figures with which to challenge the world. Now there is a new generation of iconoclasts who are determined to solve the measurement problem. You don't see them at work. They are safely behind their calculators or drawing up tables of comparison in just the same way. This book is about them, because – like scientists reaching into the unknown – they may change our lives for ever.

III

What we can't do is leave things as they are – all of those numbers are making us misunderstand things. They make us ignorant of the world past the ends of our noses, measuring things means defining them and reducing them. Still life is dead life. In fact, in Italian, still life is *'natura morta'*. We lose some of the magic in it. Every time a new set of statistics comes out, I can't help feeling that some of the richness and mystery of life gets extinguished. Just as individual stories of passion and betrayal get hidden by the marriage statistics, or the whole meaning of the Holocaust gets lost in the number 6,000,000. There is a sort of deadening effect, a distancing from human emotion and reality. Not much, but just enough for it to matter – like Jedediah Buxton trying to understand Shakespeare's masterpieces by counting the words.

Magic is about breaking out of categories, words and definitions, and I should declare an interest – I want a bit more of it. Measuring things takes away the childish sense of wonder where things are really possible. A serious-looking man with a white coat and clipboard – one of those disinterested people who counts a lot but feels little – will have to put me right, and tell me off for filling people's minds with airy-fairy nonsense.

But don't blame me. I was plummeted into this frame of mind as a teenager when I came across a poem by D. J. Enright called 'Blue Umbrellas', which in a few short lines summed up the poverty of definitions:

The thing that makes a blue umbrella with its tail –
How do you call it? You ask. Poorly and pale
Comes my answer. For all I can call it is peacock.

Now that you go to school, you will learn how we call all sorts
of things;

How we mar great works by our mean recital.
You will learn, for instance, that Head Monster is not the
    gentleman's accepted title;
The blue-tailed eccentrics will be merely peacocks; the dead
    bird will no longer doze
Off till tomorrow's lark, for the letter has killed him
The dictionary is opening, the gay umbrellas close.

Bizarre measurement No. 1

Guz

*(Middle Eastern measurement of variable length. One Guz =
27 inches in Bombay, 37 inches in Bengal, 25 inches in Arabia
and 41 inches in Iran.)*

....

Americans who claim to have been abducted by aliens: *3.7 million*

Speed of London traffic in 1900: *12 mph*
Speed of London traffic in 1996: *12 mph*

Average time US patients are allowed to speak before being
interrupted by their doctors: *18 seconds*

Chapter 1

A Short History of Counting

I

It was 12 September 1904. The Kaiser was on the throne, the
Dreadnought was less than a few rivets on the ground and
Freud was in his Vienna consulting rooms, thinking the
unthinkable. In Berlin, the unthinkable seemed to be becoming real.

As many as 13 of the city's greatest scientific minds were
convinced. The leading psychologists, veterinary surgeons,
physiologists – even the director of the Berlin Zoo – had come
away from the demonstration shaking their heads, worrying
slightly for their professional reputations. Yet they had just
signed the paper: the horse they had spent the day watching
was not responding to signals from its owner when it
demonstrated its considerable mathematical powers. Clever
Hans, in other words, was officially not a circus act. He really
was clever.

Clever Hans sounds like the title of a Grimm fairy tale or one
of Freud's more spectacular patients. Actually he was a horse
belonging to a retired maths teacher called Wilhelm von Ostein,
who believed passionately in its ability to do complicated multiplication and division – even fractions – tapping out the
answer with its hoof and manipulating sets of numbers up to

six decimal places. What's more, by converting his answers into numbers, Hans could also read, spell and identify musical tones. Zeros he communicated with a shake of the head.

Wearing a hard black hat over his streaming white hair and beard, von Ostein exhibited Hans in a northern suburb of the city every day at noon. He refused to take money for the show, rewarding Hans with a pile of bread and carrots for answering the questions of the daily audience who gathered around.

A leading biologist had become fascinated with the Hans phenomenon, and had invited the 13 eminent scientists – the so-called Hans Commission – to defend him and von Ostein from ridicule in the press. The commission recommended further study by a rising young psychologist, Oskar Pfungst. In the six weeks that followed, Pfungst had been severely bitten by Hans, von Ostein had withdrawn his horse in a rage, and (with a sigh of relief) modern science had cracked the mystery of the counting horse.

First of all, Pfungst noticed that Hans got excited if he could not see the questioner, and made strenuous efforts to see round his blindfold so that he could. They also found that the horse lost the arithmetical plot if he was asked questions that the questioners didn't know the answer to themselves. Clearly he must be responding to some kind of unconscious signal from the person asking the questions. When the implications of the blindfold experiment sank in, von Ostein exploded with fury at Hans, but the following day he had regained his ardent belief and took the horse away.

It was too late. Pfungst's report became a legend in experimental psychology. He argued, completely convincingly, that Hans was able to pick up the slight incline of the questioners' heads when they had finished asking the question and expected the answer to be tapped out. When Hans had reached the right number of taps, he was able to notice the tiny relaxation, the minute straightening up or raised eyebrow with which the questioners betrayed themselves, and he stopped tapping. Hans also tapped faster when he knew it was a long answer (a practice that added to his intellectual reputation) and this too, said Pfungst, he was able to deduce from tiny changes of facial expression.

Pfungst's own reputation was made, modern science had been vindicated – animals could not count. Von Ostein died a few months later. History does not relate what happened to Hans, but I'm not hopeful.

It was, of course, the dawn of the century of numbers. A hundred years later, we prove our humanity every time we open our newspapers with the mass of statistics on offer. Numbers are our servants, the tools of human domination. For centuries, counting was accepted as one of the key differences between human beings and animals. 'Brutes cannot number, weigh and measure,' said the great pioneer of quantification, the fifteenth-century cardinal Nicholas of Cusa. The arrival of a mathematical horse was a serious challenge to the numerical world view.

But 1904 was not just the year of Rolls-Royce and the *entente cordiale*, it was a moment of fantasy and wish-fulfilment. *Peter Pan* was on stage for the first time, British troops were taking the mysterious Tibetan city of Lhasa, and there was an absolute rash of 'clever' animals on offer, each one challenging the accepted view of numeracy as exclusively human. There was the English bulldog Kepler, owned by Sir William Huggins, which barked out its numerical answers. There was Clever Rosa, the so-called Mare of Berlin, and doyenne of the local music-hall stage. There was the clever dog of Utrecht, the reading pig of London, all forerunners of Babe in their own way. Pfungst despatched many of their reputations, but he was too old later to investigate Lady, the talking and fortune-telling horse of Virginia.

Lady managed to count and tell fortunes by flipping up letters on a special chart. Pfungst's biographer told the story of a colleague of his who had visited Lady to ask where his missing dog had gone. The horse spelled out the word DEAD. Actually, the dog turned up alive and well a few days later, and following Pfungst he gave his opinion – having studied Hans in such detail – that Lady had probably been able to sense the man's conviction that the dog was dead.

So we can all breathe a sigh of relief – animals can't count; numbers are safely human. But a century later, I still want to shake them all and say: 'Hang on a minute!' Here was a horse that was apparently able to read minds and spell correctly, never mind counting.

The accepted order of things is not absolutely safe, but we will never be able to set the clock back long enough to find out. Lady and Hans have long since gone to the knackers, and modern science is blind to strange phenomena like that. But the issue of counting and who is entitled to do so is still with us. Numbers have been in constant use for the past 6,000 years, but we have never quite resolved what they are. Are they intellectual tools for humans, invented by us for our own use? Or are they fantastical concepts, pre-existing in the universe before Adam, which we had to discover along with America and the laws of thermodynamics? Which came first: man or numbers? Are they available for any species to use or just an aspect of mankind? Are they real or human?

The consensus moves backwards and forwards through the centuries, and always with political implications. If numbers are a mysterious aspect of the universe put there by God, we tend to become subject to control and manipulation by accountant-priests. If they are a method by which humanity can control chaos, they become part of the tools of a techno-cratic scientific elite. The modern world is firmly in the second camp. We have rejected rule by priests in favour of rule by science. Measuring is something humans have invented for themselves, and animals – by definition – can't hack it. They might be able to spell or pick up astonishingly subtle body language, but it is important for our world view that they can't count.

The other view – that numbers have meaning in their own right – was represented by the Greek philosopher Pythagoras, in the sixth century BC, who was the great believer in the natural God-given beauty of numbers. For Pythagoras, numbers corresponded to a natural harmony in the uni-verse, as bound up with the music of the spheres as they are with calculations. Music and beauty were underpinned by numbers. The story goes that Pythagoras listened to a black-smith hammering away and heard the musical notes made by the anvil. He realized that they were generated by different lengths of hammer, and that there were perfect ratios of halves, thirds and quarters which generated perfect chords. They were the secret harmonies generated by the real numbers in nature. Another legend says that he learned about such things from the wisest people among the Egyptians and Phoenicians, and spent 12 years studying with the Magi after being taken captive and imprisoned in Babylon.

Numbers existed even before the universe itself, according to Pythagoras. But even that was too mild for St Augustine of Hippo, who declared that six was such a perfect number that it would be so even if the world didn't exist at all. 'We cannot escape the feeling,' said the mathematician Heinrich Hertz, 'that these mathematical formulae have an independent existence and an intelligence of their own, that they are wiser than we are, wiser even than their discoverers, that we get more out of them than was originally put into them.'

Numbers rule the universe, said Pythagoras and his followers. Anything less like irrational numbers was 'unutterable' and initiates were sworn to secrecy about them. According to his follower Proclos, the first people who mentioned such possibilities all died in a shipwreck. 'The unutterable and the formless must needs be concealed,' he said. 'And those who uncovered and touched this image of life were instantly destroyed and shall remain forever exposed to the play of the eternal waves.'

It was irrational numbers that eventually did for Pythagoras. When his descendants opened up a whole new world of paradoxes, irrationality, bizarre computations, negative numbers, square roots, then nothing ever seemed the same again. And although technocrats might breathe a sigh of relief about this evidence of the modern rationality breaking through, we may also have lost something from that sense of pre-existing perfection.

II

The tyranny of numbers over life began with the simple counting of things with marks on wood. You find notched reindeer
antlers from 15000 BC, well before Britain separated itself
from continental Europe. These methods lasted into modern
times, and were known in the English medieval treasury as
'tally sticks'. Tally sticks were finally abandoned by the British
civil service as a method of keeping track of public spending
as late as 1783. After that, the old ones hung around for a
generation or so, piled into the Court of Star Chamber until
they needed the room. Someone then had the bright idea of
burning them in the furnace that was used to heat the House
of Lords. The result was that the furnace set light to the panel-
ling and led to the conflagration in 1834 which burned down
the Palace of Westminster, and led to the world-famous monstrosity that we know today, complete with Big Ben and mock
Gothic.

A few more of these dangerous items were found during
repairs to Westminster Abbey in 1909, and they were put
safely into a museum, where they could do less damage.

Notches probably came before language. Prehistoric people
probably used words like 'one', 'two', 'three' and 'many' for
anything more complicated. In fact, sometimes 'three' might
mean 'many'. Take the French, for example: 'trois' (three) and
'tres' (very). Or the Latin: 'tres' (three) and 'trans' (beyond). A
tribe of cave dwellers was discovered in the Philippines in
1972 who couldn't answer the question 'How many people
are there in your tribe?' But they could write down a list of
all 24. But then counting is a philosophical problem, because
you have to categorize. You have to be able to see the similarity
in things and their differences, and decide which are important, before you can count them. You have to be able to do
Venn diagrams in your head. 'It must have required many
ages to discover that a brace of pheasants and a couple of days
were other instances of the number two,' said the philosopher
Bertrand Russell. But once you have grasped that concept,

there are so many other categories you have to create before you can count how many people there are in your tribe. Do you count children? Do you count foreigners who happen to live with you? Do you count people who look completely different from everybody else? Counting means definition and control. To count something, you have to name it and define it. It is no coincidence that it was the ancient Sumerian civilization, the first real empire, which developed the idea of writing down numbers for the first time. They had to if they were going to manage an imperial culture of herds, crops and people. Yet any definition you make simply has to be a compromise with the truth. And the easier it is to count, the more the words give way to figures, the more counting simplifies things which are not simple. Because although you can count sheep until you are blue in the face, actually no two sheep are the same.

The old world did not need precision. If Christ's resurrection was important, it wasn't terribly vital to know what the actual date was. Instead Europeans used numbers for effect – King Arthur was described as killing tens of thousands in battles all by himself. Modern politicians are the last remaining profession which does this, claiming unwieldy figures which they have achieved personally, and pretending a spurious accuracy by borrowing the language of statistics, when actually they are using the numbers for impact like a medieval chronicler. Nor were the numbers they used much good for calculation. Nowadays Roman numerals only exist for things which powerful people want to look permanent – like television programmes or the US World Series – but which are actually very impermanent indeed.

The new world needed accuracy and simplicity for its commerce. Although they were briefly banned by an edict at Florence in 1229, the new Arabic numbers – brought back from the Middle East by the crusaders – began to be spread by the new mercantile classes. These were the literate and numerate people – with their quill pens tracing the exchange of vast sums – plotting the despatch of fleets for kings, managing the processing of wool with the new counting boards.

And soon everybody was counting with the same precision. King John's Archbishop of Canterbury, Stephen Langton, had already organized a system of chapters and verses for the Bible, all numbered and meticulously indexed, which by the following century used the new Arabic numerals. Soon the new numbers were being used to measure much more elusive things. By 1245, Gossoin of Metz worked out that if Adam had set off the moment he was created, walking at the rate of 25 miles a day, he would still have to walk for another 713 years if he was going to reach the stars. The great alchemist Roger Bacon, who tried to measure the exact arc of a rainbow from his laboratory above Oxford's Folly Bridge, calculated shortly afterwards that someone walking 20 miles a day would take 14 years, seven months and just over 29 days to get to the moon.

It's a wonderful thought, somehow akin to Peter Pan's famous directions for flying to Never Never Land, 'turn right and straight on till morning'. But it was a different time then, when space was measured in the area that could be ploughed in a day and when time was dominated by the unavoidable changes between day and night. There were 12 hours in the medieval day, and 12 hours in the night too, but without proper tools for measuring time, these were expanded and compressed to make sure the 12 hours fitted into the light and the dark. An hour in the summer was much longer than an hour in the winter, and actually referred to the 'hours' when prayers should be said.

Nobody knows who invented clocks, though legend has it that it was the mysterious Gerbert of Aurillac, another medieval monk who spent some time in Spain learning from the wisdom of the Arabs, and who, as Sylvester II, was the Pope who saw in the last millennium. He was said to be so good at maths that contemporaries believed he was in league with the Devil. It was not for 250 years that clocks arrived in the mass market, but once they had, you could not argue with their accuracy. From the 1270s, they dominated European townscapes, insisting that hours were all the same length and that trading times and working times should be strictly regulated. Counting in public is, after all, a controlling force, as the people of Amiens discovered in 1335 when the mayor regulated their working and eating time with a bell, attached to a clock.

Clocks had bells before they had faces, and were machines of neat precision, as you can see by the fourteenth-century one still working in the nave of Salisbury Cathedral, with its careful black cogs swinging backwards and forwards, the very model of the new medieval exactitude. Soon every big city was imposing heavy taxes on themselves to afford the clock machinery, adding mechanical hymns, Magi bouncing in and out and – like the one in Strasbourg in 1352 – a mechanical cockerel which crowed and waggled its wings.

Where would they stop, these medieval calculators? Scholars at Merton College, Oxford in the fourteenth century thought about how you can measure not just size, taste, motion, heat, colour, but also qualities like virtue and grace. But then these were the days when even temperature had to be quantified without the use of a thermometer, which had yet to be invented. They must have been heady days, when the whole of quality – the whole of arts and perception – seemed to be collapsing neatly into science.

Renaissance humanity was putting some distance between themselves and the animals, or so they believed. Anyone still dragging their feet really was holding back history. Some dyed-in-the-wool conservatives insisted that people know pretty well when it was day and night, and when the seasons change, without the aid of the new counting devices. But anyone who thinks that, said the Protestant reformer Philip Melanchthon, deserves to have someone 'shit a turd' in his hat. The new world of number-crunchers had arrived.

III

To really get down to the business of measuring life, two important ideas about numbers were still needed – a concept of zero and a concept of negative numbers. But to emerge into common use, both had to run the gauntlet of the old battle lines about numbers drawn across medieval Europe. Then there were the adherents of the old ways of the abacus, whose computations were not written down, and whose ritual movements as they made their calculations were inspired by the old wisdom of Pythagoras. The new computations were all written down. They had no mystery. There was something open and almost democratic about them, and they needed no priests to interpret them. Calculation was no longer a mysterious art carried out by skilled initiates.

And the big difference between them now was zero. Its arrival in Europe was thanks to a monk, Raoul de Laon – a particularly skilful exponent of the art of the abacus – who used a character he called *sipos* to show an empty column. The word came from the Arabic *sifr*, meaning 'empty', the origin of the word 'cypher'. Either way, the old abacus could be put away in the medieval equivalent of the loft.

Inventing zero turns numbers into an idea, according to the child psychologist Jean Piaget. It's a difficult idea too: up to the age of six and a half, a quarter of all children write $0+0+0 = 3$. But once people had begun to grasp it, they tended to regard zeros with suspicion. Division by zero meant infinity and infinity meant God, yet there it was bandied around the least important trade calculations for fish or sheep for everyone to see. Even more potent were the objections of the Italian bankers, who were afraid this little symbol would lead to fraud. It can, after all, multiply other figures by ten at one slip of the pen.

So zero was among the Arabic numbers banned in 1229. But the enormous increase in trade because of the crusades and the activities of the Hanseatic League meant that something of the kind was needed. Italian merchants increasingly used zero as an underground sign for 'free trade'. Bootleggers and smugglers embraced the idea with enthusiasm. Like the V sign across the continent under Nazi tyranny, zero became a symbol of numerical freedom, a kind of medieval counterculture.

What normally happens with countercultures is that they get adopted by everyone, and that's exactly what happened here. Soon everyone was using zero quite openly and adding and subtracting happily using a pen and ink. Soon the abacus had died out so much that it became a source of fascination. One of Napoleon's generals was given one in Russia when he was a prisoner-of-war, and he was so astonished that he brought it back with him to Paris to show the emperor. Don't let's dismiss the abacus completely, though. In occupied Japan in 1945, the US army organized a competition between their automatic calculator and skilled Japanese abacus-users. The abacus turned out to be both quicker and more accurate for every computation except multiplication.

The people of Western Europe resisted negative numbers for much longer. They called them 'absurd numbers', believing they were futile and satanic concepts, corresponding to nothing real in the world. Now, of course, our lives are dominated by them, because the debts they represent correspond to positive numbers at the bank. Debt opened the way to negatives via the world-shattering invention of double-entry bookkeeping. This may not have been the brainchild of a friend of Leonardo da Vinci, a Milanese maths teacher called Fra Luca Pacioli, but it was Pacioli's destiny to popularize it. The writer James Buchan described his method as a 'machine for calculating the world'. It was one of the 'loveliest inventions of the human spirit', according to Goethe. It could work out, at any moment, when your complex deals were profitable, allowing you to compare one deal with another.

Pacioli was a Franciscan who knew all about profit. He had special dispensation from the Pope (a friend of his) to own property. 'The end and object of every businessman is to make a lawful and satisfactory profit so that he may sustain himself,' he wrote. 'Therefore he should begin with the name of God.' Pacioli and his followers duly wrote the name of God at the beginning of every ledger. Before Pacioli, traders tended to give any fractions to the bank. After Pacioli they could record them. They could grasp at a glance where they stood while their cargoes were on the high seas, or while they waited two years or more for them to be fabricated into something else. They could make them stand still to be counted.

A Neo-Platonist, fascinated by Pythagoras and his ideas of divine proportion, Pacioli filled his book with other stuff like military tactics, architecture and theology. He chose a potent moment to publish it: the year after Columbus arrived back from discovering America. But despite his Pythagorean roots, Pacioli provided the foundations for a more complex idea of profit and loss, of assets and liabilities, making all of them clearly measurable. His critics feared he had abolished quality altogether. All that you could put down in the double entries were quantities – numbers of sheep, amounts of wool: there was no column for qualities like good or bad. The numbers had taken over, simplifying and calculating the world in their own way.

'If you cannot be a good accountant, you will grope your way forward like a blind man and may meet great losses,' said Pacioli, the first accountant. He explained that it was all a matter of taking a piece of paper, listing all the debit totals on one side and all the credit totals on the other. If they add up and there's a profit – the result is happiness, he said, sounding like a Renaissance Mr Micawber. If not, you have to find out where the mistake is – as millions of frustrated amateur accountants have been doing ever since.

Within three centuries, accountants had developed into the professionals you called in after bankruptcy, a kind of undertakers for the business world, which is why the Companies Act of 1862 which regulated such matters became known as 'the accountant's friend'. 'The whole affairs in bankruptcy have been handed over to an ignorant set of men called accountants, which was one of the greatest abuses ever introduced into law,' said Mr Justice Quinn during a bankruptcy case in 1875. By 1790, the Post Office directory for London lists one accountant. By 1840 there were 107 of them and by 1845 – right in the middle of the railway boom – there were 210, ready to assist cleaning up the mess in the financial collapse the following year. Maybe they were even responsible for the rash of suicides in London in 1846; maybe they helped prevent more. We shall never know. Either way, it was just the beginning for the accountants. By the turn of the century there were over 6,000 in England and Wales. Now there are 109,000, but – as far as I know – no counting horses left at all.

IV

Pacioli and his spiritual descendants have helped to create the modern world with its obsession with counting, and the strange idea that once you have counted the money, you have counted everything. There is a hard-headed myth that numbers are serious and words are not – that counting things is a rigorous business for a serious man's world. 'When you can measure what you are speaking of and express it in terms of numbers, you know something about it,' said the scientist Lord Kelvin. 'When you cannot express it in terms of numbers your knowledge of it is of a meagre kind.'

Armed with this attitude, Lord Kelvin dismissed radio as pointless, aeroplanes as impossible and X-rays as a hoax, so we might wonder if he was right. But is my knowledge really of a meagre kind? Can I express something about myself in numbers? If Lord Kelvin's successors managed to express my entire genetic code in numbers, would they know me better than I do myself when I can do no such thing? Well, in some ways, maybe they can – but I doubt it. Any more than the Nazis could know anything about the victims in concentration camps by branding a unique number on their arms.

We are more than branded now. We are in a world obsessed with numbers, from National Insurance and interest rates to buses, from bank balances and bar codes to the cacophony of statistics forced on us by journalists, politicians and market-eers. They seem to agree with Lord Kelvin that it provides us with a kind of exactitude. Actually it is exact about some of the least interesting things, but silent on wider and increasingly important truths.

We have to count. I've used piles of statistics in this book. Not counting is like saying that numbers are evil, which is even more pointless than saying that money is evil. We need to be able to count, even if the results aren't very accurate.

'Without number, we can understand nothing and know nothing,' said the philosopher Philolaus in the fifth century BC, and he was right. But 25 centuries after Philolaus, the French philosopher Alain Badiou put the other point of view, and he was right too: 'what arises from an event in perfect truth can never be counted'. Both Philolaus and Badiou are right. The more we rely on numbers to understand problems or measure aspects of human life, the more it slips through our fingers and we find ourselves clinging to something less than we wanted. Because every person, every thing, every event is actually unique and unmeasurable.

This is the paradox. If we don't count something, it gets ignored. If we do count it, it gets perverted. We need to count yet the counters are taking over our lives. 'The measurable has conquered almost the entire field of the sciences and has discredited every branch in which it is not valid,' said the French poet Paul Valery. 'The applied sciences are almost completely dominated by measurement. Life itself, which is already half enslaved, circumscribed, streamlined, or reduced to a state of subjection, has great difficulty in defending itself against the tyranny of timetables, statistics, quantitative measurements and precision instruments, a whole development that goes on reducing life's diversity, diminishing its uncertainty, improving the functioning of the whole, making its course surer, longer and more mechanical.'

There was a time when numbers had significance beyond just 'how many', but we have lost the ancient understanding of numbers as beautiful and meaning something beyond themselves – the discredited and forgotten wisdom of Augustine and Pythagoras. We snigger patronizingly when we read St Thomas Aquinas's solemn injunction that 144,000 would be saved at the end of time. Though probably the last thing he meant was that literally 144,000 people would make it to heaven. To Aquinas, a thousand meant perfection, and the 144 is the number of the apostles multiplied by itself. 'I speak in parables of eternal wisdom, my honoured sir,' he might have said, like a character in Andrew Sinclair's novel *Gog*. 'I leave statistics to plumbers.'

The old way of looking at numbers means nothing to us now. The historian of the medieval mind Alfred Crosby called it the 'venerable model'. 'We sniff and cluck at its mistakes – that the earth is the centre of the universe, for instance – but our real problem with the Venerable Model is that it is dramatic, even melodramatic, and teleological: God and Purpose loom over all,' he wrote. 'We want (or think we want) explanations of reality leeched of emotion, as bloodless as distilled water.'

Bloodless one-dimensional messing can dismiss a horse so sensitive that it can read the faintest human gestures, just because it doesn't meet our narrow definition of intelligence.

Bizarre measurement No. 2

Momme

(Unit of mass in Japan used for measuring the size of pearls.
1 momme = 10 fun.)

Amount of time the average American spends going through junk mail in a lifetime: *8 months*

Amount spent by Americans every year breaking into broken automatic car locks: *$400 million*

Chapter 2

Historical Interlude 1: Legislator for the World

Nature has placed Mankind under the governance of two sovereign masters, pain and pleasure. It is in them alone to point out what we ought to do, as much as what we shall do.
Jeremy Bentham

There is nothing which has yet been contrived by man, by which so much happiness is produced as by a good tavern or inn.
Samuel Johnson, 21 March 1776

I

It was one of the strangest funerals ever held. Three days after his death on 6 June 1832, the body of the great utilitarian philosopher Jeremy Bentham (dressed in a nightshirt) was unveiled to his friends and admirers, gathered together at the Webb Street School of Anatomy in London. It was a stormy early evening, and the grisly occasion was lit by flashes of lightning from the skylight above, as Bentham's young doctor Thomas Southwood Smith began a speech which included a demonstration of dissection on his old friend.

Among the faithful were some of the great figures of reform from the immediate past and future, the radical tailor Francis Place and the future sanitation reformer Edwin Chadwick in the shadows. In their minds, we might imagine, was a sense of enormous achievement – two days before, the Great Reform Act, which had been the focus of all their hopes, had been given Royal Assent. There might also have been the occasional less welcome echo from Mary Shelley's Gothic novel *Frankenstein*, published 14 years before, as Southwood Smith's scalpel glinted in the candlelight – with all its warning for the Godless who meddle with the untouchable moments of birth and death.

They might also have been wondering whether this was the right way of remembering their hero. Dissection was then regarded as such an appalling end that it was handed out as an extra punishment for the murderers who normally found themselves cut open in this room. Southwood Smith the former preacher managed to keep his voice steady, but his face was as white as the corpse's. Bentham's funeral guests would have reassured themselves that they were carrying out the details of his will, and that they were men of the new age of science, and could put aside those old-fashioned notions of superstition, emotion and shame.

Could those things be measured in Bentham's new political morality of 'utility'? The facts – yes, the rigorously logical facts – were that it was more 'useful' to dissect the philosopher's body than it was to bury it. And as Bentham had written himself, if you were going to have statues or portraits of him, it was more 'useful' to use the real thing, rather than let it go to waste in a coffin in the earth.

When Smith finished his work of cleaning and embalming, Bentham's body was to be an 'Auto-Icon', a modern monument and a more exact replica of the man than any artist could possibly achieve. It would be dressed in his own clothes, with his walking stick (which he used to call Dapple, after Sancho Panza's mule) firmly in his hands. It would remain in a glass case in University College, London, which he had done so much to turn into the reality of bricks and mortar.

The plan didn't go quite as expected. Despite Bentham's best endeavours to study the head-shrinking methods of primitive tribes, his own head shrivelled ghoulishly and extremely fast. A few years later, the college decided to replace it with a waxwork. The original was placed between his legs, from where it has occasionally been stolen. And there Bentham's Auto-Icon remains, wheeled gravely into important college meetings, and still on display to the professors and students of London University and anybody else who wanders in, together with some very un-Benthamite rumours about ghosts.

It was a fittingly scientific end to the life of the man who gave us the philosophical school of utilitarianism. Because it was Bentham who told us that what is good and right is what most promotes human happiness – not necessarily what it says in law or the Bible. And it was Bentham who launched the world's politicians on an increasingly determined set of calculations, so they can know what this 'good' is in any given situation.

The daily outpouring of figures and statistics that now so dominates our conversations began partly with Bentham, but he was also a symptom of his time. At the beginning of his life, as he stood with his father at the age of 12 to watch the coronation procession of George III, London was dirty, foul-smelling and dangerously brutal, with one congested bridge over the river. By the end there were eight bridges over the Thames and the streets were lit by gaslight, and steam trains – 'self-moving receptacles', as he described them – were beginning to change the shape of cities. What's more, his native land had experienced no less than 30 years of census returns and was about to start the compulsory registration of births, marriages and deaths. The number-crunchers had arrived. Some people even predicted it at the time. 'The age of chivalry is gone,' moaned Edmund Burke in the House of Commons. 'That of sophisters, economists and calculators has succeeded, and the glory of Europe is extinguished for ever.' And if one person could be blamed for that, you could probably waggle the finger at Jeremy Bentham.

Now almost two centuries have gone by since his death, you would have thought it might be possible to get more perspective on the man who did so much to create this aspect of the modern world. But that still seems impossible. Bentham, for all his mild manners and gentle unemotional ways, has inspired passionate feelings of distaste ever since. Thomas Carlyle described Bentham's contribution as a 'pig philosophy'. Karl Marx went even further, describing Bentham as 'the insipid, pedantic leather-tongued waste of the commonplace bourgeois intelligence of the nineteenth century'. Trotsky was immediately converted by reading his works at the age of 17, but later condemned Bentham's ideas as 'a philosophy of social cookbook recipes'. The humourless Nietzsche was even moved to verse to describe him:

> Soul of washrag, face of poker,
> Overwhelmingly mediocre.

Looking at Jeremy Bentham's face now, in the glass case, it does seem a little on the poker side. Even his clothes seem ludicrous, as if they have been borrowed from a Disney cartoon, and don't seem nearly dangerous enough to inspire such hatred. Nor do the stories of the old boy jogging from his home in Westminster to Fleet Street well into his 70s, about his ancient cat (whom he called the Reverend Dr John Langhorn) and his determined early-morning walks round the garden.

His works are impenetrable and his autobiography was bolwderized and put into an unreadable third person by his incompetent assistant John Bowring, so it is hard to get a sense of the man. The overwhelming impression is that here was a mild, vain, fastidious, pedantic, irritating obsessive, who never really lived a full life – hardly loved and barely lost – but who brought about a revolution which is still such an important part of our lives that he remains as ambiguous as ever.

II

Jeremy Bentham was born on 15 February 1748, the son of a successful City of London lawyer who provided him with such a miserable, monotonous and gloomy childhood that he put the attainment of happiness at the centre of his philosophy. His mother died when he was ten, and life with Jeremy's overbearing and demanding father meant no games and little fun. No other children were ever asked to the house.

Instead of embracing the law as his father intended, Bentham used his small allowance to spend his time reading the works of the philosophers David Hume and Claude Adrien

Helvétius. In them he found the basis for his philosophy – that you could estimate happiness from a number of different pleasures and that public 'utility' was the basis of all human virtue. Reading Helvétius during the 1770s, and walking a little way behind his family – you can picture their exasperation at this gauche and bookish adolescent trailing along after them – he asked himself: 'Have I a genius for anything?'

Adolescents ask themselves this question often. But to Bentham, the answer came like the Angel Gabriel appearing to Mary. He took the clue from the book he was reading, where Helvétius gave his opinion that legislation was the most important of earthly pursuits, an opinion widely approved by legislators the world over. 'And have I indeed a genius for legislation?' said the young Jeremy to himself. 'I gave myself the answer, fearfully and tremblingly – Yes.'

Enthusiastically, and already packing his mind with this sense of historic mission, he devoured as many of the works of moral and political philosophy as he could get his hands on. Tom Paine was starting to think up his *Rights of Man*, there was simmering discontent in the American colonies, and ideas were dangerous world-shifting things. Bentham flung himself in. But it was when he travelled back to Oxford to vote as a university MA in the 1768 parliamentary election, that he had his real breakthrough. He was rummaging through the small library in Harper's Coffee House, when he came across the pamphlet by the chemist Joseph Priestley, which included the phrase 'the greatest happiness of the greatest number'. Bentham let out a sharp 'Eureka!' and dashed out to make it his own.

It remains the phrase for which Bentham is best known. Priestley never used it again – he didn't need it, said Bentham – so he adapted it as the centre of his philosophy. And there it is, in the first page of the first work he ever published, *A Fragment on Government*: 'It is the greatest happiness of the greatest number that is the measure of right and wrong.'

Before Bentham (or so he believed) the laws of England and the morality on which they were based were a hopeless jumble of superstition, tradition, contradiction and privilege.

After Bentham there would be a clear logical reason for laws, and governments would know automatically what to do. It would no longer be a matter of balancing distrust of the people with fear, as Gladstone said later, but a simple piece of arithmetic. Government action, all action in fact, should be based on what would make most people happiest.

For the rest of his life, Bentham devoted most of his intellectual effort to working out how his Greatest Happiness Principle might become clear in practice. Borrowing the popular thinking of the time which classified diseases or the Linnean classification of plants and animals into families, he set about classifying pleasures to meet the strict demands of his legislative theory. By the end of his life, Bentham had defined 14 broad kinds of pleasure and sent a generation of followers and enthusiasts away to measure them.

'I wish I could return in six or seven centuries time,' he was fond of remarking, 'so that I can see the effects of my work.' 'Alas! His name will hardly live so long,' wrote the essayist William Hazlitt, putting his finger on the whole problem with utilitarianism in one neat sentence: 'There are some tastes that are sweet in the mouth and bitter in the belly, and there is a similar contradiction and anomaly in the mind and heart of man.'

But in spite of this put-down, Bentham has managed to remain famous for over a century and a half. For a long time, it didn't seem as if he would even achieve this. He was much better known abroad. Hazlitt was also right when he said that Bentham's fame was in inverse proportion to the distance from his house in Westminster. When the traveller and writer George Borrow found himself arrested in Spain, he was released from prison on the grounds that he shared a nationality with the man his captor called 'The Grand Bentham'. And when Bentham visited Paris towards the end of his life (an honorary French citizen after the Revolution) the lawyers at the courts of justice rose to receive him.

'The case is, though I have neither time nor room to give you particulars,' he wrote in 1810, 'that now at length, when I am just ready to drop into the grave, my fame has spread itself all over the civilized world.'

III

So what kind of man was the legislator for the world, the philosopher who thought you could calculate human happiness? Not a very worldly one. You know instinctively that anyone who calls his morning walks something as pompous as 'antejentacular circumgyrations' is likely to be pretty cut off from life. This after all was someone with sufficient mental space to have a pet name, not just to call his walking stick, but for his teapot (Dick) – and who probably never talked to women at all, except for his cook and housemaid. He was never once drunk, and fell in love briefly twice – but without obvious effect. He proposed to Caroline Fox in 1805. They never met again, but when he was 80, he wrote her a nostalgic letter saying that not a single day had gone by since then without his thinking of her.

He surrounded himself with luxuries of bread, fruit and tea, but he never read literature. He covered his walls with Hogarth prints, and happily wandered round and round his garden in Queen Square Place, Westminster, scrupulously dressed with his straw hat on his head.

He loved animals more than people. It somehow makes him a little more human and endearing to think of him encouraging mice to play in his office while he struggled to classify human experience (though it was difficult to manage their relationship with his beloved cats). But it hardly seems like the description of a man so fired with life that he could settle down and measure the unmeasurable passions. His putative ward and interpreter John Stuart Mill certainly thought so, and he knew him: 'He had neither internal experience, nor external,' Mill said of Bentham. 'He never knew prosperity and adversity, passion nor satiety; he never had even the experiences which sickness gives ... He knew no dejection, no heaviness of heart. He never felt life a sore and a weary burthen. He was a boy to the last.'

He pottered about his writing, enthusiastically starting gigantic projects of classification, the first chapter of which would turn out to be so voluminous that he would have to concentrate on that and abandon the rest. It was a pattern that continued for the rest of his life. He began by writing a long critique of the distinguished jurist William Blackstone, part of which came out in 1776, as *A Fragment on Government*. The rest was expanded and expanded and abandoned because it was out of control. Next there was the *Treatise on Punishments*. Only the introduction was ever near to being finished. The rest had once again expanded beyond control and had to be turned into a study on laws in general. And so on and so on, collating, noting in margins, packed with expletive and rage, then putting the papers aside never to be looked at again.

Luckily, according to the historian Leslie Stephen, he 'formed disciples ardent enough to put together these scattered documents as the disciples of Mahomet put together the Koran'. Even so, it was hardly enough to make him a bestseller. One reviewer in his lifetime described his style as 'the Sanskrit of modern legislation' and those were the days when nobody could understand Sanskrit. 'He has parenthesis within parenthesis, like a set of pillboxes,' wrote his erstwhile secretary Walter Coulson. 'And out of this habit have grown redundancies which become tiresome to the modern reader.'

Nor did the *Fragment* have the desired effect. He published it anonymously, and it was immediately pirated in Dublin, so that the first 500 copies were sold without any profit to him, but it did attract some interest as people in political circles wondered who the author was. Unfortunately for Bentham, he confided his authorship to his father to prove he was achieving something in his career. But his father was extremely indiscreet, and as soon as people knew the pamphlet had been written by a nobody, the sales collapsed.

It was the Panopticon that changed Bentham's life. This was his invention of an efficient, modern prison, build in the shape of a flower, with the prison keeper at the centre able to watch over all the prisoners at once. The governor would run the new institutions as profit-making concerns, which would use the prisoners as motive power for a range of inventions that would make a profit and at the same time 'grind the rogues honest'.

To Bentham the idea was a masterpiece of enlightenment. Because the new prison governors relied for their profit on the prisoners' health, it was in their interest to keep them healthy and well-fed. It was never built, so we shall never know whether the prisoners would actually have thanked him – as Bentham believed they would. But since he was intending to work them 14 hours a day with another hour on the treadmill for exercise, it's hard to believe their gratitude would have been overwhelming.

For the next 20 years, Bentham barraged the government with his plans, and with some effect. They even bought a site for it on Millbank, where the Tate Gallery stands today, but the final signature was frustratingly difficult to obtain. Bentham was so certain the money would come through that he sank at least £10,000 into the project as early as 1796, and he soon found himself on the verge of imprisonment for debt. Day after day he wandered the Treasury corridors, writing letters, his hopes rising when William Pitt was replaced as Prime Minister by Henry Addington, only to be dashed again. 'Mr Addington's hope is what Mr Pitt's hope was,' he wrote in despair, 'to see me die broken-hearted, like a rat in a hole.'

He asked everyone he could for help. 'Never was any one worse used than Bentham,' wrote the anti-slavery campaigner William Wilberforce. 'I have seen the tears run down the cheeks of that strong-minded man, through the vexation at the pressing importunity of creditors and the insolence of official underlings.'

In the meantime, he turned himself into a Professor Branestawm of crazy ideas. He tried to interest the Treasury in currency schemes (always a sign of mild instability) and speaking tubes. He suggested the idea of a train of carts drawn at speed between London and Edinburgh. He told the Americans they should build a canal across Panama, and suggested to the city authorities that they should freeze large quantities of vegetables so that there could be fresh peas available at Christmastime. Not content with that, he linked up with Peter Mark

Roget, later to write the first Thesaurus – a Benthamite project of classification if ever there was one – to invent what he called a frigidarium to keep food cold. He told the Bank of England how they could create an unforgeable banknote. He wrote widely in favour of votes for women and proposed, in unpublished writings, that homosexuality should be legalized, at a time when you could be hanged for sodomy. 'How a voluntary act of this sort by two individuals can be said to have any thing to do with the safety of them or any other individual whatever, is somewhat difficult to be conceived,' he wrote.

Absolutely none of these ideas was taken up. He had more luck with inventing new words. 'International' is one of his. So is 'codify' and 'maximize'. He had less success renaming astronomy as 'uranoscopic physiurgics'. Still less renaming biology as 'epigeoscopic physiurgics'. And his letters urging the government to rename the country 'Brithibernia' remained in the minister's in-trays. His attempts to reshape the cabinet also had to wait more than a century. He suggested that there should be twelve ministers: including one for education; one for 'the preservation of the national health'; one for 'indigence relief'; one for 'preventive service' (to stop accidents) and an 'interior communication minister' (transport). In fact he died the year before the government first voted any money to education at all.

The hopelessly old-fashioned shape of the government was probably why the Panopticon stayed stubbornly unbuilt. That is certainly what Bentham thought, even when a parliamentary committee took pity on him in 1813 and voted him £23,000 in damages, with which he paid off his debts. The Panopticon story is important here because it made him realize that the whole of government needed reform. If Lord Spencer could hold up the project for a generation, simply because it was near his London landholdings, then the whole system was corrupt. He needed a method of government to calculate right from wrong, rather than letting it fall to whoever happened to have the ear of the prime minister of the day. If the system of government could not see that it was in the general

interest to adopt his plan, then how could you construct a
system of government that would automatically want to
improve human happiness?

'All government is in itself one vast evil,' said the frustrated
philosopher, and set about doing something about it. So, with
a sigh of relief, he went back to writing his impenetrable prose.
And in 1802, it all came right. The Swiss publisher Pierre
Dumont at last managed to get him to agree to publishing
some of his work. By the time Dumont had finished with it,
it was even easy to read and was attracting attention in Paris,
Moscow and Madrid. This was the *Traités de Législation Civile
et Pénale*. It included crucial parts of Bentham's *Introduction to
the Principles of Morals and Legislation*, and it was the first of
many.

He soon found that although he had a good deal more
influence abroad than he did in London, he still had little
power. By the time he had sent out his constitutional code to
the revolutionary governments of Spain and Portugal, both
had succumbed to counter-revolution. He sent it in nine instal-
ments to the provisional government in Greece, with much
the same effect. His ideas were welcomed at first by Rivadavia
in Argentina and Bolivar in Columbia, though it wasn't long
before Bolivar was busily banning his works from the universities. His letter bombardment of Sir Robert Peel seemed to leave
Peel pretty cold. And the Duke of Wellington did not respond
to his promise that his name would be as great as Alexander's
if he took his advice on law reform. He had more success in
Italy because Cavour remained a fan. The Tsar Alexander even
sent him a ring, which he returned with the seal unbroken.
And thanks to Lord Macaulay, he did have an influence in
shaping the new laws of India. So he was increasingly optimistic. In a calculation reminiscent of those by his medieval fore-
bears, he predicted that his code would finally be adopted in
every country in the world in the year 2825, presumably
exactly a thousand years since he made the prediction. It was
a letter from Guatemala that same year which gave him the
title which stuck: 'legislador del mundo' – the legislator for
the world.

The idea of measuring happiness was central to almost everything he wrote. But when he began to consider exactly how the formula would work – something his followers had to tackle after his death – he fell back on the moderate thought that any kind of calculation was better than none. 'In every rational and candid eye, unspeakable will be the advantage it will have over every form of precision being ever attained because none is ever so much as aimed at,' he wrote. All you needed was the formula, and that meant calculating the pleasures and pains against their intensity, duration, certainty, rapidity, fecundity, purity and extensiveness. Simple!

From the start he realized that this principle, whatever it was called, depended on being able to measure the way people felt. 'Value of a lot of pleasure or pain, how to be measured', was the title of chapter 4 of his *Introduction to the Principles of Morals and Legislation*. He imagined that this was a simple proposition: 'who is there that does not calculate?' he asked airily, but the complete absence of any official figures made him think again. Where was the raw data? He asked the Bank of England how much paper money was in circulation. They didn't know. Neither had the Foundling Hospital any idea about the cost of living for paupers.

In a sudden burst of enthusiasm for figures, he persuaded the great agricultural reformer Arthur Young to use his *Annals of Agriculture* to send out a questionnaire about rural poverty. Young even wrote an encouraging introduction to it. Unfortunately, Bentham's enthusiasm got the better of him, and the questionnaire included no less than 3,000 questions. Not surprisingly, only a handful of answers ever arrived back at Queen Square Place.

And even if they had poured in, how could you compare these different pleasures and pains? You couldn't count the number of people affected by them and you certainly couldn't compare how much they were feeling them. What if slaves were happy – did that make slavery right? This was a difficult question for Bentham, who was a lifelong critic of slavery. And how do you compare the one person who gets a great deal of pleasure from building a multi-screen cinema on a well-known beauty spot with the thousands of people who are mildly inconvenienced? It's still an absolutely impossible question to answer satisfactorily.

Luckily for the utilitarians, there was an answer to some of these practical problems in the new 'science' of economics. You can measure it all with money, what Bentham called the 'only common measure in the nature of things'. Using money means you can find the zero point between pleasure and pain, he said. So Bentham plunged himself into all things economic, getting to know the pioneer economist David Ricardo and seeing the new economists as the intellectual force which would put his movement into practice.

Towards the end of his life he worried that people would think only the majority mattered if he used the phrase 'the greatest number'. He also worried that people would think only money had any value – 'a vulgar error' he said. By 1831, just a few months before his death, he had carefully reformulated what he meant: the optimal goal is 'provision of an equal quantity of happiness for everyone'. But that makes the calculations even more difficult to manage. Especially these days, when the happiest people in the world were shown to be the Mexicans (the poorest) and the most miserable are known to be the Americans (the richest).

What about beauty? If you convert morality into a pseudo-science, how do you recognize the great benefits of creativity? What about spirituality? Bentham had three pianos and loved music, but it was Cardinal Newman who pointed out that he had 'not a spark of poetry in him'. This was confirmed in a letter the philosopher wrote to Lord Holland. The difference between poetry and prose, he explained, is that – with poetry, the lines don't reach the margin.

This was the stick with which his critics have beaten him ever since. But he seems to have agreed with them with his great defence of the game of shove-halfpenny: 'Prejudice apart, the game of push-pin is of equal value with the arts and sciences of music and poetry.' Fripperies, fripperies.

IV

When Bentham died, on 6 June 1832, he was surrounded by 70,000 pieces of un-indexed paper. It was left to his adoring disciples to do something with them, the first task of the political utilitarians before they got down to measuring the world. And foremost among them was James Mill, one of those frighteningly dour and driven Scots pioneers who had driven the reputation of the country in the eighteenth century. From the time he met him in 1808, Mill was walking from his home in Pentonville to have supper with Bentham every evening. By 1810, the whole Mill family had moved into John Milton's draughty old house, which happened to be in Bentham's garden, but he soon discovered this was so unhealthy, he moved back out to Stoke Newington. It was over the question of whether he could accept Bentham's subsidy of his rent that the two eventually fell out. Mill needed someone to hero worship, and he found it in Bentham. Bentham needed followers and a driven mind to organize them. It was a perfect match. Rigid and stern though he was, Mill signed his letters to Bentham as 'your most faithful and fervent disciple'.

Soon the patterns of Bentham's days were set. Dictating as he powered round the garden early in the morning, – 'vibrating in my ditch', as he put it. There were very occasional meetings with visitors during the day. Then dinner was served progressively later to allow for more work, as Mill, Bowring and Chadwick ministered to his needs. At the end of the day there was an hour-long ritual, after which he tied on his night cap, gave his watch to his secretary, who then read to him, and after a strange ritual with his window, he leapt into a special sleeping bag of his own design.

It was a disturbing time, and as well as parliamentary reform, the talk was of education. Mill and Francis Place even started a school, which collapsed by 1816, only to be replaced by plans to build another one in Bentham's back garden. David Ricardo even donated £200 to build it, but Bentham began to realize what having his home overlooked constantly by schoolboys might mean, and the scheme was abandoned. Meanwhile, Mill was trying another educational experiment of his own – on his eldest son. His history of India, dry and stern, had appeared in 1817 and as a result he was made Assistant to the Examiner of Indian Correspondence, with a hefty salary of £800. By 1830, he had risen to the rank of Examiner. By then he had been using every spare moment from writing the book to concentrate on John Stuart Mill's education.

And so began a strange intensive indoctrination, which involved starting to learn ancient Greek at the age of three, with gruelling studies from 6 to 9 am and from 10 am to 1 pm every day. There were no holidays. There was no birching, but his father's sarcasm was almost as unpleasant. There was to be no mixing with other children – the young John wasn't even allowed to go to church. What he learned in the morning, he was expected to pass on to his eight brothers and sisters in the afternoon.

John could not exactly love his father tenderly, he said later in his *Autobiography*. He described him as 'the most impatient of men', and we can imagine what that simple sentence conceals. For the rest of his life, he confessed that his conscience spoke with his father's voice. But he certainly gave him a 25-year head start over his contemporaries, which must have helped him slip into the role of the great Liberal philosopher of the Victorian age. The only area of human knowledge that he was kept in ignorance of was Utilitarianism: this he had to choose for himself, his father decided. Mill Senior needn't have worried. When he introduced the idea to his 16-year-old son in a series of 'lectures' as they walked along, demanding an essay on the subject the next morning which would be re-written and re-written again, John Stuart was so enthusiastic that he formed his own Utilitarian Society. James Mill's friends and allies looked on in astonishment. There was no doubt that John was a prodigy, said Francis Place, but he would probably end up 'morose and selfish'. Unfortunately, he was right.

In 1820, just before he left for a life-broadening trip to Paris,

James Mill took his son for a grave walk in Hyde Park, and told him that his education would single him out, and this should not be a source of pride. It was because of his father's efforts and nothing to do with him. In fact, it would be disgraceful if he didn't know more than everybody else in those circumstances.

It is hard to warm to Mill senior, or any of the unemotional utilitarians. Bentham said that his sympathy for the many sprang out of his hatred for the few. James Mill despised passionate emotions, describing them as a kind of madness. He showed almost no feelings at all – except for one: he was quite unable to hide how much he disliked his wife. He 'had scarcely any belief in pleasure', according to his son. 'He would sometimes say that if life was made what it might be, by good government and good education, it would be worth having: but he never spoke with anything like enthusiasm even for that possibility.'

James Mill lived only a few years longer than Bentham. The dust he inhaled in his regular journeys to his country cottage in Mickleham gave him a serious lung haemorrhage in 1835, and he died on 23 June the following year, leaving it to his son John as the second generation to carry the baton for Utilitarianism. It was John who gave the movement its name: he found it in a novel called *Annals of the Parish* about a Scottish clergyman who warns his parishioners not to abandon God and become 'utilitarians'.

At 20 John Stuart Mill – regarded by both his father and Bentham as their spiritual heir – set to with a will to finish Bentham's *Rationale of Evidence* for publication. 'Mr Bentham had begun his treatise three times at considerable intervals, each time in a different manner, and each time without reference to the preceding,' he wrote. He spent months unpicking his crabbed handwriting, chopping his sentences up into manageable parts, and finally sending five volumes off to the printers. The following year he had a nervous breakdown or a 'mental convulsion' as the Victorians put it. The breakdown took the form of a series of doubts about the whole Bentham legacy.

'Suppose that all your objects in life were realised; that all the changes in institutions and opinions which you are looking forward to, could be completely effected at this very instant: would this be a great joy and happiness to you?' And an irrepressible self-consciousness distinctly answered, 'No!' At this my heart sank within me: the whole foundation on which my life was constructed fell down. All my happiness was to have been found in the continual pursuit of this end. The end had ceased to charm, and how could there ever be any interest in the means? I seemed to have nothing left to live for.

It was an important question and it seemed to fly in the face of everything that Bentham stood for, just as the harsh unemotional education that he had received at the hands of his father seemed completely inadequate to deal with it. If the question couldn't be answered, how could any calculation of pleasure come to any conclusion? Life seemed complex beyond anything Bentham could have imagined.

For much of the year, Mill could hardly work at all. Music was a relief, and so were the poems of William Wordsworth, who he was convinced had experienced something similar himself. But, still in the grip of Bentham, Mill worried about music. If there were only a limited number of notes, wouldn't the music run out? Can you calculate the potential number of pieces of music in the world? Experience shows that it is too complicated to count, just as you can't count the combination of possible poems by the 26 letters of the alphabet. But these are the fears of a Utilitarian who has looked into the abyss.

He never fully recovered. A decade later he had another collapse, and for the rest of his life he suffered from a nervous twitching over one eye.

With antecedents like Bentham and Mill, it is touching to think of John Stuart struggling to find some kind of emotional meaning. He found it by coming out of his reclusion to dine twice a week with Harriet Taylor, the intelligent wife of a wholesale druggist. Mr Taylor seems to have been generous enough to overlook whatever was going on between them. His family roundly condemned him for the relationship and he retired from the world completely, finding that any reference to her by anybody else made him overexcited.

Instead he wrote a book about logic, then his magnum opus *Political Economy*. And when Harriet's husband died in 1849, he married her. When she died in Avignon of congestion of the lungs, he was absolutely devastated, and bought a house there so he could spend half his time near his wife's grave. 'The highest poetry, philosophy, oratory, and art seemed trivial by the side of her,' he said. At last love had come to the Utilitarians. She probably enabled him to humanize the Utilitarian gospel. She certainly inspired him to write *The Subjugation of Women* in 1869, and his lifelong support for votes for women.

In 1865, he was persuaded back into public life to stand for Parliament for the Liberal Party. He agreed, on condition that he didn't have to canvass, spend any money or answer any questions about religion. His disarming honesty seemed to win him support. 'Did you declare that the English working classes, though differing from some other countries in being ashamed of lying, were yet "generally liars"?' asked a hostile questioner during a public meeting.

'I did,' he replied, to tremendous applause, and found himself elected with an enormous majority. And there he sat until he lost his seat to W. H. Smith the newsagent in 1868, small and slight with his eyebrow twitching, his weak voice hard to hear above the hubbub. Sometimes he would lose his drift during a speech and stand in complete silence for a moment, but his fellow parliamentarians listened with respect. It was Mill who first dubbed the Conservatives the 'stupid party'. On 5 May 1873, he walked 15 miles in a botanical expedition near Avignon, and died unexpectedly three days later. He was, in a real sense, the last of the line.

V

'All emotions were abhorrent to his cold, precise but admirably balanced mind,' wrote Sir Arthur Conan Doyle, introducing the great detective Sherlock Holmes to the public just over half a century after Bentham's death. You can point to other figures, from Victor Frankenstein to the Duke of Wellington, who provided role models for human beings as calculating machines – Wellington's dispatch from the battle of Waterloo was so modestly written that the American ambassador reported back home that he had lost. But it was Bentham the 'reasoning machine' who tried to strip morality and government of its emotional and traditional baggage, who made Sherlock Holmes possible, with his detailed knowledge of inks and papers.

'He was, I take it, the most perfect reasoning and observing machine that the world has seen . . .' went on Conan Doyle on the opening page of his first Sherlock Holmes story, 'A Scandal in Bohemia'. 'He never spoke of the softer passions, save with a gibe or a sneer . . . For the trained reasoner to admit such intrusions into his delicate and finely adjusted temperament was to introduce a distracting factor which might throw a doubt upon all his mental results.'

Holmes could use his delicate and unemotional brain to see through the complex fogs of London to the truth, just as Bentham wanted to be able to do with the confusing mists of government. Whether you can actually get to any truth coldly and calculatingly, certainly any truth worth having, is an issue we still don't know the answer to. The twentieth century has rehearsed the arguments backwards and forwards, balancing the respective claims of the so-called Two Cultures, and probably the twenty-first century will as well. Can science find meaning? Can scientists make any kind of progress without leaps of imagination? We still don't agree, but we do now live in Bentham's world. He didn't have the necessary figures to make his calculations; we are drowning in them. He could not see some of the moral consequences of his ideas; we have some of the more unpleasant Utilitarian creeds of the century etched on our hearts. But he made the rules.

Yet his creed was softened by John Stuart Mill, who rescued utilitarianism for the modern world, so much so that it is now the Western world's dominant moral creed, among government ministers just as it is among everyone else. He also recognized that Bentham may have been 'a mere reasoning machine' and said the same could have been said of himself for two or three years before he learned to appreciate the value of emotions – though there are still precious few of those in his *Autobiography*. Mill's repeated depressions showed him also that happiness must not be the conscious purpose of life, or paradoxically, it would slip through your fingers. Bentham would never have understood.

Bizarre measurement No. 3
Gry

(*A very small linear measurement proposed in England in 1813 that was intended to make all measurements decimal. 1 gry – 0.008333 of an inch. 'Gry' means literally 'speck of dirt under the fingernail'.*)

....

Number of times every year that hackers infiltrate the Pentagon's computer system: *160,000*

Average time people spend watching TV in the UK every day:
3 hours 35 minutes

Chapter 3

Elusive Happiness

I said to my soul, be still, and wait without hope,
For hope would be hope for the wrong thing; wait without love
For love would be love of the wrong thing; there is yet faith
T. S. Eliot, 'East Coker'

A scientist may explore the Universe, but when he comes home
at night, he doesn't understand his wife any better.
Simon Jenkins, *The Times*, December 1999

I

But suppose you get everything you want, wondered John
Stuart Mill at the start of his first nervous breakdown and his
rejection of Bentham's puritanical legacy: 'Would this be a
great joy and happiness to you?' And the irrepressible self-
consciousness distinctly answered, 'No!'

Mill's irrepressible self-consciousness definitely got it right.
The human psyche is too complex and far too fleeting to be
pinned down in quite that way. You can carry out Bentham's
calculations of happiness with incredible accuracy, you can
measure what you want precisely, but somehow the psyche
slips away and sets up shop somewhere else. Or as Gershwin
put it: 'After you get what you want, you don't want it'. While
Mill was locking himself into his bedroom, Samuel Taylor
Coleridge was coming to similar conclusions: 'But *what* happiness?' he said to the Benthamites with a rhetorical flourish.
'Your mode of happiness would make *me* miserable.' Mill was
having his collapse 30 years before Freud was even a flicker
in his father's eye, and the idea that human beings might
secretly want something different from what they think they
want was untested and unfamiliar. Yet Mill instinctively knew

that measuring happiness was just too blunt an instrument.

Generations later we make the same kind of discoveries ourselves over and over again. But we tend to solve the problem by measuring ever more ephemeral aspects of life, constantly bumping up against the central paradox of the whole problem, which is that the most important things are just not measurable. The difficulty comes because they can *almost* be counted. And often we believe we have to try just so that we can get a handle on the problem. And so it is that politicians can't measure poverty, so they measure the number of benefit claimants instead. Or they can't measure intelligence, so they measure exam results. Doctors measure blood cells rather than health, and people all over the world measure money rather than love. They might sometimes imply almost the same thing, but often they have little to do with each other.

Anything can be counted, say the management consultants McKinsey & Co., and anything you can count you can manage. That's the modern way. But the truth is, even scientific measurement has its difficulties. Chaos theory showed that very tiny fluctuations in complex systems have very big consequences. Or as the gurus of chaos theory put it: the flapping of a butterfly's wings over China can affect the weather patterns in the UK. The same turned out to be true for other complex systems, from the behaviour of human populations to the behaviour of share prices, from epidemics to cotton prices.

The man who, more than anybody else, undermined the old idea that measurements were facts was a Lithuanian Jew, born in Warsaw before the war, the son of a clothing wholesaler who found himself working for IBM's research wing in the USA. Benoit Mandelbrot is probably the best known of all the pioneers of chaos because of the extraordinary patterns, known as fractals, that he introduced by running the rules of chaos through IBM's computers. And he got there with a simple question that makes the kind of statistical facts the Victorians so enjoyed seem quite ridiculous. The question was: 'How long is the coastline of Britain?'

On the face of it, this seems easy enough. You can find the

answer in encyclopaedias. But then you think about it some more and you wonder whether to include the bays, or just to take a line from rock to rock. And having included the bays, what about the sub-bays inside each bay? And do you go all the way round each peninsula however small? And having decided all that, and realizing that no answer is going to be definitive, what about going round each pebble on the beach? In fact the smaller you go, to the atomic level and beyond, the more detail you could measure. The coastline of Britain is different each time you count it and different for everyone who tries.

There was a time when accountants were able to deal with this kind of uncountable world better than they are now. In the early days of the American accountancy profession, they were urged to avoid numbers. 'Use figures as little as you can,' said the grand old man of American accounting James Anyon, who came from Lancashire. 'Remember your client doesn't like or want them, he wants brains. Think and act upon facts, truths and principles and regard figures only as things to express these, and so proceeding you are likely to become a great accountant and a credit to one of the truest and finest professions in the land.'

Anyon had arrived in the USA in 1886, to look after the firm of Barrow, Wade, Guthrie and Co – set up three years before by an English accountant who realized that there was a completely vacant gap in the accountancy market in New York City. Unfortunately, the day he arrived, he was threatened with violence by the very large chief assistant, who had been secretly trying to take the enterprise over. The case ended up in the Supreme Court. Anyon survived the ordeal and 30 years later, he was giving advice to young people starting out in what was still a new profession. 'The well trained and experienced accountant of today . . . is not a man of figures,' he explained again.

But Anyon's successors ignored his advice, and for a very familiar reason. The public, the politicians and their business clients wanted control. They wanted pseudo-scientific precision, and were deeply disturbed to discover that accountancy was not the exact science they thought it was. Every few years, there was the traditional revelation of a major fraud or gigantic crash, and a shocked public could not accept that accounts might ever be drawn up in different ways. How could two accountants come to different conclusions? How could some companies keep a very different secret set of accounts?

This issue was brought up by Pacioli himself, who said that even in his day some people kept two sets of books: one for customers and one for suppliers. In the First World War, Lloyd George once remarked that the War Office kept three sets of casualty figures, one to delude the cabinet, one to delude the public and one to delude itself. Anyone reading the public accounts of some companies will realize this practice has life in it yet. But as the centuries passed, it has become more and more of an issue, and accountants have been on the front line of solving the resulting confusions. The Western world is now awash with consultants and accountants who will accept a large fee to come into your organization, measure the way you work, test your assumptions and your profits, or lack of them, measure the mood of your employees and customers, and tell the public.

The National Audit Office and the Audit Commission arrived in the world in the early 1980s and set to with a vengeance. The British Standards Institute organized a standard of quality, then called BS5750, which auditors could measure accountants' achievements by. Environmental quality standards followed, and the whole range now available across the world, US, European, global standards, and auditors behind each one – measuring, measuring, measuring. By 1992, environmental consultancy alone was worth $200 billion. Counting things is a lucrative business. Which is one of the reasons the private sector auditing firms, like Arthur Andersen, PricewaterhouseCoopers and KPMG entered such a boom period in the 1980s. By 1987, they were creaming off as many as one in ten university graduates. It is one of the paradoxes of the modern world that the failure of auditors is expected to be solved by employing more auditors. And the trouble with auditors of any kind (accountants or academics) is that they are applying numerical rules to very complex situations. They wear suits and ties and have been examined to within an inch of their lives about their understanding of the professional rules. But their knowledge of life outside the mental laboratory may not be very complete. Sometimes it's extremely sketchy. And when Western consultants arrive in developing countries with their clipboards, like so many Accidental Tourists, it can do a great deal of damage.

Just how much damage can be done by faulty figures has been revealed in an extraordinary exposé by the development economist Robert Chambers. The number-crunchers he described like innocents abroad, deluded by local elders in distant villages. Sometimes deliberately. As a result of what may have been an elderly insect-damaged cob, consultants convinced themselves during the 1970s that African farmers were losing up to 40 per cent of their harvest every year. The real figure was around 10 per cent, yet American aid planners diverted up to $19 million a year by the early 1980s into building vast grain silos across Africa to tackle a problem that didn't exist.

Then there was the UN Food and Agriculture Organization's notorious questionnaires in the early 1980s, which completely ignored mixed farms in developing countries. They only asked about the main crop, anything else was too complicated. As a result, production rates in developing countries seemed so low that multinationals believed they needed genetically-manipulated seeds to help cut famine. But then, as Emerson said, people only see what they want to see. That's the trouble with questionnaires.

'Professional methods and values set a trap,' says Chambers in his book *Whose Reality Counts?*:

> Status, promotion and power come less from direct contact with the confusing complexity of people, families, communities, livelihoods and farming systems, and more from isolation which permits safe and sophisticated analysis of statistics ... The methods of modern science then serve to simplify and reframe reality in standard categories, applied from a distance ... Those

who manipulate these units are empowered and the subjects of analysis disempowered: counting promotes the counter and demotes the counted.

Auditors deal in universal norms, methods of counting, targets, standards – especially in disciplines like psychology and economics that try to improve their standing by measuring. This is how economics transformed itself into econometrics, psychology transformed itself into behavioural science, and both gained status – but all too often lost their grip on reality. Sociologists tackled their perceived lack of 'scientific' respectability by organizing bigger and bigger questionnaires to confirm what people knew in their heart of hearts anyway. Even anthropologists, who need a strong dose of interpretation provided by the wisdom, understanding and imagination of a researcher on the ground, began to lose themselves in matrices and figures. Scientists have to simplify in order to separate out the aspect of truth they want to study – and it's the same with any other discipline that uses figures.

Often it's only the figures that matter, even when everybody knows they are a little dodgy. One paper on this phenomenon by the economist Gerry Gill – called 'OK the data's lousy but it's all we've got' – was a quote by an unnamed American economics professor explaining his findings at an academic conference. Which is fine, of course, unless the data is wrong – because people's lives may depend on it. 'Yet professionals, especially economists and consultants tight for time, have a strongly felt need for statistics,' says Chambers. 'At worst, they grub around and grab what numbers they can, feed them into their computers, and print out not just numbers but more and more elegant graphs, bar-charts, pie diagrams and three-dimensional wonders of the graphic myth with which to adorn their reports and justify their plans and proposals.'

Chambers found that there were twenty-two different erosion studies in one catchment area in Sri Lanka, but the figures on how much erosion was going on varied by as much as 8,000-fold. The lowest had been collected by a research institute wanting to show how safe their land management was.

The highest came from a Third World development agency showing how much soil erosion was damaging the environment. The scary part is that all the figures were probably correct, but the one thing they failed to provide was objective information. For that you need interpretation, quality, imagination.

'In power and influence, counting counts,' he wrote. 'Quantification brings credibility. But figures and tables can deceive, and numbers construct their own realities. What can be measured and manipulated statistically is then not only seen as real; it comes to be seen as the only or the whole reality.' Then he ended up with a neat little verse that summed it all up:

> Economists have come to feel
> What can't be measured, isn't real.
> The truth is always an amount
> Count numbers, only numbers count.

But the distinctions really get blurred when politicians start using numbers. Waiting lists up 40,000, Labour's £1000 tax bombshell, fertility down to 1.7, 22 Tory tax rises – elections are increasingly a clash between competing statistics. It's the same all over the world. Figures have a kind of spurious objectivity, and politicians wield them like weapons, swinging them about their heads as they ride into battle. They want to show they have a grasp of the details, and there is something apparently hard-nosed about quoting figures. It sounds tough and unanswerable.

But most of the time, the figures also sound meaningless. The public don't take them in, and they simply serve as a kind of aggressive decoration to their argument. But, as politicians and pressure groups know very well, a shocking figure can every so often grasp the public's imagination. In the UK, the best-known election policy for the 1992 general election – repeated in the 1997 election – was the Liberal Democrat pledge to put 1p on income tax for education. It sounded clear and costed, but it was the perfect example of a number being used for symbolic effect. It implied real commitment and risk: the 1p meant almost nothing. 'If relying on numbers didn't work,' said Andrew Dilnot of the Institute of Fiscal Studies in a recent BBC programme, 'then in the end a whole range of successful number-free politicians would appear.'

They haven't appeared yet. The problem for politicians is that they have to use figures to raise public consciousness, but find that the public doesn't trust them – and the resulting cacophony of figures tends to drown out the few that are important. The disputes of political debate have to be measurable, but they get hung up about measurements that only vaguely relate to the real world.

Take rising prices. You can't see them or smell them, so you need some kind of index to give you a handle on what is a real phenomenon. You can't hold them still while you get out your ruler, yet the ersatz inflation figures have assumed a tremendous political importance. We think inflation is an objective measure of rising prices, when actually it is a measurement based on a random basket of goods which has changed from generation to generation. In the 1940s, it included the current price of wireless sets, bicycles and custard powder. In the 1950s, rabbits and candles were dropped in favour of brown bread and washing machines. The 1970s added yoghurt and duvets, the 1980s added oven-ready meals and videotapes, and the 1990s microwave ovens and camcorders. It's a fascinating measure of our changing society, but it isn't an objective way of measuring rising prices over a long period of time.

II

'Oh the sad condition of mankind,' moaned the great Belgian pioneer of statistics, Adolphe Quetelet. 'We can say in advance how many individuals will sully their hands with the blood of their neighbours, how many of them will commit forgeries, and how many will turn poisoners with almost the same precision as we can predict the number of births and deaths.

Society contains within it the germ of all the crimes that will be committed.'

It's a frightening thought, just as it was frightening for Quetelet's contemporaries to hear him say it in the 1830s. But he and his contemporaries had been astonished by how regular the suicide statistics were. Year after year, you seemed to be able to predict how many there would be. There were the occasional bumper years, like 1846, 1929 and other economic crash periods, but generally speaking it was there. People didn't seem to be able to help themselves. Amidst a constant number of individuals, the same number would take it into their heads to murder as much as get married. Statistics were powerful.

Quetelet was among the most influential of the statisticians trying to solve the confusion of politics by ushering in a nice clean, unambiguous world, urging that we count things like the weather, the flowering of plants and suicide rates in exactly the same way. 'Statistics should be the dryest of all reading,' Bentham's young disciple William Farr wrote to Florence Nightingale, explaining that they could predict with some certainty that, of the children he had registered as having been born in 1841, 9,000 would still be alive in 1921.

To help the process along, Quetelet invented the dryest of all people – the monstrous intellectual creation, *l'homme moyen* or Average Man. Mr A. Man is seriously boring: he has exactly average physical attributes, an average life, an average propensity to commit crime, and an average rather unwieldy number of children – which used to be expressed as the cliché 2.4. But Average Man only exists in the statistical laboratory, measured at constant room temperature by professional men with clipboards and white coats. The whole business of relying on numbers too much goes horribly wrong simply because Mr Average is the Man Who Never Was – counted by people who know a very great deal about their profession or science but precious little about what they are counting. The Man Who Never Was measured by the Men Who Don't Exist. It's the first and most important paradox of the whole business of counting:

Counting paradox 1: You can count people, but you can't count individuals

Average Man belongs to the Industrial Revolution and the Age of the Masses, but we just don't believe most of that Marxist stuff any more. It belongs in the twentieth-century world of mass production, where people were transformed into cogs in giant machines, as pioneered by the great American industrialist Henry Ford – the man who offered his customers 'any colour you like as long as it's black'. Mass production and Average Man had no space for individuality. Figures reduce their complexity, but the truth *is* complicated.

Now, of course, you can almost have your car tailor-made. You can mass-produce jeans using robots to designs which perfectly match the peculiarities of individual bodies on the other side of the world. The days have gone when clothes issued by the military didn't fit, when you struggled to keep up with the speed of the production line, with your tasks individually timed for Average Person by the time and motion experts. And we can see more clearly how difficult it is to categorize these widely different individuals who make up the human race. But in the hands of a bureaucratic state, people who don't conform to the norm get hounded and imprisoned. Or, these days, social workers visit them and remove their children.

And after all that, when you get to know Mr Average, you find he has a bizarre taste in underwear, he has extraordinary dreams about flying through galaxies, and a hidden collection of Abba records. He wasn't average at all. Counting him in with other people ignores the real picture.

Counting paradox 2: If you count the wrong thing, you go backwards

Because it is so hard to measure what is really important, governments and institutions pin down something else. They have to. But the consequences of pinning down the wrong thing are severe: all your resources will be focussed on achieving something you didn't mean to.

Take school league tables, for example. When the Thatcher

government latched onto the idea of forcing schools to compete with each other by measuring the progress of children at three comparable moments of their lives, they were intending to raise standards. They probably have done in a narrow way. The trouble was that schools concentrated on the test results to improve their position on the tables, which was anyway pretty meaningless. That meant excluding pupils who may drag down the results, concentrating on the D grade pupils – the only ones who could make a difference in exam result league tables – to the detriment of the others. It meant concentrating on subject areas the school could compete in, never mind whether they were the subjects the children needed. And worst of all, it meant squeezing the curriculum to produce children that can read and write but are, according to National Association of Head Teachers general secretary David Hart, 'unfit philistines'.

Then there was the business of using hospital waiting lists as a way of measuring the success of the health service. Tony Blair's new government made an 'interim promise', which then hung around their neck like an albatross, to reduce waiting lists by 100,000. They did push the lists down, though painfully slowly. But the result was the emergence of new secret waiting lists for people just to get in to see the hospital consultant, before they were even allowed near a real waiting list. Quick simple easy operations were also speeded up to get the numbers down, at the expense of the difficult ones. And when the hospital league tables of deaths came out in 1999, consultants warned it would make administrators shy of taking on difficult complicated cases.

Governments and pressure groups latch onto the wrong solutions and then busily measure progress towards them. They thought that shifting to diesel fuel for cars would clean up polluted air and measured progress towards achieving it. Result: air full of carcinogenic particulate matter. They thought more homework for primary school children was the solution to underachievement and measured progress towards it. Result: miserable dysfunctional kids.

It has all the makings of a fairy tale. If you choose the wrong measure, you sometimes get the opposite of what you wanted. And any measure has to be a generalization that can't do justice to the individuals that are included.

Counting paradox 3: Numbers replace trust, but make measuring even more untrustworthy

When farmers and merchants didn't trust each other to provide the right amount of wheat, they used the standard local barrel stuck to the wall of the town hall, which would measure the agreed local bushel. When we don't trust our corporations, politicians or professionals now, we send in the auditors – and we break down people's jobs into measurable units so that we can see what they are doing and check it. If doctors hide behind their professional masks, then we measure the number of deaths per number of patients, their treatment record and their success rate, and we hold them accountable. When politicians look out of control, we measure their voting records and their popularity ratings – just as the TV commentators break down a sporting performance into opportunities, misses, aces, broken services and much else besides.

It wasn't always like that. Previous generations realized that we lose some information every time we do this – information the numbers can't provide. They realized, like James Anyon, that we could never measure what a doctor does so well that we could do it for them. They still have experience that slips through the measurement, so we still have to accept the word of the professionals to get to the truth. The British establishment used to be quite happy to accept the word of the professionals if they were 'trustworthy gentlemen of good character'. But from the outside, that trust looked like a cosy nepotistic conspiracy. And probably it was.

It was this kind of political problem which led to the growth of cost-benefit analysis. This was originally used by French officials to work out what tolls to charge for new bridges or railways, but it was taken up with a vengeance in twentieth-century America as a way of deciding which flood control measures to build. After their Flood Control Act of 1936, there would be no more federal money for expensive flood control measures unless the benefits outweighed the costs. Only then would the public be able to see clearly that there was no favouritism for some farmers rather than others. It was all going to be clear, objective, nonpolitical and based on counting.

Even so, the professionals clung to their mystery as long as they could, just as doctors fought the idea of scientific instruments that would make the measurements public and might lead people to question their diagnoses – the stethoscope was acceptable because they were the only ones who could listen to it. Even the US Army Corps of Engineers – in charge of the flood control analysis – tried to keep the mystery alive. 'It is calculated according to rather a complex formula,' a Corps official told a Senate committee in 1954. 'I won't worry you with the details of that formula.' It couldn't last. The more they were faced with angry questioning, the more their calculations had to be public.

But how far do you go? Do you, as they did for some flood control schemes, work out how many seagulls would live in the new reservoir, and how many grasshoppers they would eat, and what the grain was worth which the grasshoppers would have eaten? Do you work out what these values might be in future years? Do you value property when no two estate agents can name the same price? 'I would not say it was a guess,' one of their officials told the US Senate about property values. 'It is an estimate.' And after all that, it is economists who persuaded the US Secretary of the Interior, Bruce Babbitt, to start demolishing the dams their predecessors laboriously calculated.

So here's the paradox. Numbers are democratic. We use them to peer into the mysterious worlds of professionals, to take back some kind of control. They are the tools of opposition to arrogant rulers. Yet in another sense they are not democratic at all. Politicians like to pretend that numbers take the decisions out of their hands. 'Listen to the scientists,' they say about BSE or genetically-modified food. 'It's not us taking the decisions, it's the facts.' We are submitting these delicate problems to the men in white coats who will apply general rules about individual peculiarities. It is, in other words, a shift from one kind of professional to another, in the name of democracy – from teachers and doctors to accountants, auditors and number-crunchers. And they have their own secretive rituals that exclude outsiders like a computer instruction manual.

But when it comes to auditing the rest of us in our ordinary jobs, auditing undermines as much trust as it creates – because people have to defend themselves against the auditors. Their lives – usually their working lives – are at stake, and their managers will wonder later why the figures they spent so much to collect are so bizarrely inaccurate. And as we all trust the companies and institutions less, we trust the auditors less too.

Counting paradox 4: When numbers fail, we get more numbers

Because counting and measuring are seen as the antidote to distrust, then any auditing failure must need more auditing. That's what society demanded the moment the Bank of Credit and Commerce International had collapsed and Robert Maxwell had fallen off his yacht into the Bay of Biscay. Nobody ever blames the system – they just blame the auditors. Had they been too friendly with the fraudsters? Had they taken their eyes off the ball? Send in the auditors to audit the auditors.

If the targets fail, you get more targets. Take the example of a large manufacturer that centralizes its customer care to one Europe-wide call centre. After a while, they find that the customers are not getting the kind of care they were used to before. What does the company do, given that it can't measure what it really needs to – the humanity and helpfulness of their service to customers? They set more targets – speed answering the telephone, number of calls per operator per day. They measure their achievements against these targets and wonder why customers don't get any happier. 'People do what you count, not necessarily what counts,' said the business psychologist John Seddon.

Counting paradox 5: The more we count, the less we understand

Numbers are the international tools of scientists. They allow experts to 'speak one and the same language, even if they use different mother tongues', said the philosopher Karl Popper – whose libertarian beliefs made him enthusiastic about anything which could break down totalitarian regimes. The auditors look for measurements with no human content, like the metre, (one 10 millionth of the distance from the pole to the equator) in their search for pure objectivity. It is a scientific dream of the kind you often get after revolutions, in this case the French. Could taking decisions like this usher in an era of facts after all that political confusion? Answer: no.

This is because everyone would have to count in exactly the same way, in laboratory conditions, taking no account of local variation or tradition, so the figures are not as informative as they might be. Decisions by numbers are a bit like painting by numbers. They don't make for great art. When you reduce something to figures or the bottom line, you lose information, and the Tower of Babel comes tumbling down again.

This is an international language based on centrally imposed definitions and understanding. It's a kind of modern imperialism, with all the respect for local understanding of the glass towers of the international architectural style. Can we really believe the European Union was getting accurate comparisons in their recent mega-survey asking 60,000 people if they 'could make ends meet'? As if a German, a Greek and a Brit would all understand the same by that. When Pepsi had their slogan 'Come alive with the Pepsi generation' translated into Chinese, it was understood as 'Pepsi brings your ancestors back from the grave'. Microscopic differences in definition have big effects. It's chaos theory all over again.

But the paradox also works the other way round. When the Berlin Wall came down, the global exchange controls were swept away, and almost everything around the world could suddenly be measured in money. The process drives out tyrants, privilege and secrecy – just as money is supposed to do. But the real reason money has this effect is because it is a counting system: it's the numbers which count, not the money. So we have a parallel process which you might call the 'globalization of fact'. In a world without borders and without trust, everything must be translated into figures.

Counting paradox 6: The more accurately we count, the more unreliable the figures

Number-crunchers can't miss anything out if they're going to be absolutely precise. So you get a peculiar phenomenon when the cost-benefit experts spend enormous efforts getting a figure absolutely correct – only to throw something else in which is simply plucked from the air.

This has a long tradition, back to the French statistician Adolphe Jullien in 1844, who worked out precisely the cost of moving one unit of traffic on their new rail system. He finally came up with a wonderfully exact figure of 0.01254 francs per kilometre. But what about administration and the interest on capital? Ah yes, he says – but these were more difficult to assess, so he arbitrarily doubled the figure. Or the US Corps of Engineers who would spend months on the exact cost-benefit of new waterways they liked, then shoved in a notional $600,000 for national defence and $100,000 for recreation.

Many figures are an unusual amalgam of the precise and the arbitrary. It's like Lewis Carroll's story about the little boy who comes up with a figure of 1,004 pigs in a field. 'You can't be sure about the four,' he is told. 'And you're as wrong as ever,' says the boy. 'It's just the four I can be sure about, 'cause they're here, grubbing under the window. It's the thousand I isn't pruffickly sure about.'

Counting paradox 7: The more we count, the less we can compare the figures

'It has not gone unnoticed that crime has increased parallel with the number of social workers,' said the doyen of moral conservatives, Dr Rhodes Boyson, in 1978. He was speaking after the fearsome, bible-bashing Chief Constable of Greater Manchester James Anderton had made a challenging speech about crime figures for England and Wales. There had been

77,934 recorded crimes in 1900, he said. In 1976, there were 2,135,713. The country was horrified.

The *Daily Mirror* replied with a classic critique of these kinds of statistics: 'It is equally true that crime has increased parallel with speeches from Dr Boyson,' they said. All you can do with statistics is to show that trends tend to happen together. Nobody can prove that one rise caused another. The point is that Anderton's frightening figures looked scientific, unanswerable and objective – an absolute test of Britain's criminality.

They weren't. In 1900, the recording of crime was pretty informal, and different crimes horrified people. What would have been seriously violent now, might then just have been charged as a simple assault or drunkenness. Crimes against property, or against the aristocracy, really upset the late Victorians and Edwardians. But violence seems to have been regarded primarily as what the lower classes did to each other, and it concerned society less. These were the days when one in four London policemen was assaulted every year, and when the streets echoed to the antics of gangs like the Somers Town Boys or the notorious Manchester Scuttlers. And when policemen in particularly violent areas tried to make an arrest, they were liable to be surrounded by large threatening crowds shouting 'Boot them!'.

It used to be different then. And if you doubt it, you can read the complaints of the chaplain of Newgate Gaol while Bentham was calculating the world – that all the boys in prison kept a mistress. That includes those aged nine and ten. Simple figures can't possibly compare such different worlds. The past is a foreign country, as L. P. Hartley once said: they do things differently there.

Every generation believes that crime is getting worse. 'The morals of children are tenfold worse than previously,' the social reformer Lord Ashley told the House of Commons in 1843, using a bogus statistical style that would be much copied. At the same time, the communist pioneer Friedrich Engels had calculated that crime had risen over seven times, since the Battle of Trafalgar in 1805. A generation later, in 1862,

British society was horrified by the outbreak of 'garottings' – a kind of mugging by throttling the victim. By the 1890s, it was 'hooligans', hitting old ladies in the street and brandishing pistols – which were then available by mail order from the department store Gamages. Then there was the sudden 90 per cent rise in bag-snatching between the wars, made to seem worse because police statistics stopped reporting such thefts as 'lost property'.

The same thing happened with vandalism in the 1970s, when police figures stopped distinguishing between major damage and minor damage (defined as less than £20). When the distinction was ended in 1977, the minor offences were added to the list, and vandalism figures doubled in a single year. This added about 200,000 incidents to the total number of crimes in the UK – just before Anderton unveiled his statistics.

Counting paradox 8: Measurements have a monstrous life of their own

Stalin announced his first Soviet five-year plan in 1928, an enormous undertaking planned to increase gross industrial output by 235.9 per cent and labour productivity by 110 per cent. But don't be fooled by these figures, which were completely spurious. The fake precision was to lend a pseudo-scientific air to the whole enterprise. The actual effect of the plan was to reduce real per capita income by half, and starve millions on what Stalin referred to as the 'agricultural front'. Even so, he declared the first five-year plan a success 12 months early in 1932, and the second one started right away.

The figures were widely believed, even in the West. But not only were nearly all of the figures falsified (something you can do during a reign of terror) but they carried with them a terrible authoritarianism to try to force them to be true. Which is why strikes had to be redefined as 'sabotage', and why after 1939, employees had to be fired if they were once more than 20 minutes late for work. It was also why one in eight of the Soviet population was either shot or sent to a labour camp during Stalin's reign. Figures are frightening sometimes.

Counting paradox 9: When you count things, they get worse

In quantum physics, the mere presence of the observer in sub-atomic particle experiments can change the results. In anthropology, researchers have to report on their own cultural reactions as a way of offsetting the same effect. And once you start looking at numbers you keep falling over a strange phenomenon, which is that the official statistics tend to get worse when society is worried about something. For the sake of argument, I'll call it the 'Quantum Effect'.

Why, for example, did the illegitimacy figures shoot up only *after* the war babies panic in 1915? At the time of the panic, the number of illegitimate births was actually astonishingly low – and the number of marriages strangely high. After the panic, the illegitimacy rate suddenly increased. Why was the number of homes unfit for human habitation in the UK in 1967 (after the TV film *Cathy Come Home*) almost twice the figure for 1956 – despite over a decade of intensive demolition and rebuilding?

The garrotting scare in the 1860s was the same. The story began during the silly season in August 1862, and public horror got so bad that *Punch* advertised a range of fearsome neck-guards with metal spikes to protect your neck. But the increase in the crime statistics came immediately afterwards, once the Garrotters Act had brought back flogging for adults. The tragic death of Stephen Lawrence in a racist attack led to widespread concern about race attacks in London. But *after* the public inquiry on the subject in 1998, Metropolitan Police figures of race attacks leaped from 1,149 to 7,790 in one year.

It was the same with the sex abuse statistics. They toddled along in the UK at the 1,500-a-year mark until 1984, when an unprecedented wave of publicity on both sides of the Atlantic catapulted the issue to the top of the public agenda. Between 1984 and 1985, the National Society for the Prevention of Cruelty to Children reported a 90 per cent increase in reported cases. And in the following year they reported a similar rise. Child abuse campaigners would say that the actual rate of child abuse is never reflected properly in the statistics. They may well be right, the same would be true of the figures for racist attacks. All I am saying is that the actual statistics wouldn't have told you anything, except how strongly the public felt about it at the time. So often, the statistics start rising *after* the panic, rather than the other way round, as an eagle-eyed society tries to stamp out the unforgivable. That's the quantum effect.

It's difficult to know quite why the figures go up. Sometimes the definitions change to reflect greater public concern. Sometimes people just report more instances of it because it is in the forefront of their minds. Sometimes, maybe, what we fear the most comes to pass.

III

If you wander through the East End of London, you can still catch a glimpse of the best British example of political numbers having a life of their own. By the end of the Second World War, up to a third of all of the homes in Britain had been damaged, and almost half a million couldn't be lived in at all. The Attlee government failed to build more than 170,000 replacements a year, and it was the future Prime Minister Harold Macmillan who launched into the 1951 general election campaign, as Conservative housing spokesman, with a pledge to build 300,000 new homes a year.

There was nothing very unusual about this. Politicians have made statistical promises for generations, but Macmillan was different in that he actually achieved it. By reducing the building standards and cutting the space requirement by 10 per cent, there were 300,000 homes being built every year by 1953, and Macmillan had made his reputation as 'Supermac'.

But even in Britain, where there was barely a hint of Stalinism, numbers have a strange effect when they are wielded by politicians. Once the 300,000 new homes had been promised and achieved, no politician could dare achieve anything less. Soon a new white paper and government programme (called irritatingly enough, Operation Rescue) was planning to speed up the process by encouraging local authorities to demolish more homes. It was the beginning of so-called 'slum clearance', and soon the 'slums' – which would now be a gentrified gleam in an estate agent's eye if they had survived – were tumbling down. Subsidies were given to local councils to get the job done and soon 60,000 homes were being demolished every year.

To keep the replacements rolling, the new housing minister – Winston Churchill's son-in-law Duncan Sandys – changed the building subsidies to produce as many flats as possible in the new space. And so high-rise flats were born as a way of reaching the target. Sandys' successor Sir Keith Joseph went further, forcing councils to use the new industrialized-system building methods, which turned out, too late, to be substandard. The new flats were soon being condemned as damp, vandalized and impossible to let.

The Profumo affair ushered in a new Labour government in 1964, but the numbers stayed in the ether and the process speeded up, with a new election promise of 400,000 new homes a year. 'Why not rebuild the whole thing?' said their housing minister Richard Crossman, peering at a plan of Oldham. Soon a 1967 survey was showing that 1.8 million homes were unfit for human habitation – well over twice what the previous survey had shown a decade before. The quantum effect strikes again.

It wasn't long before Harold Wilson's ministers were enthusiastically discussing the possibility of building half a million new homes a year, and had pushed the annual number of demolitions up to 70,000. Britain's inner cities were being transformed from civilized though neglected streetscapes into concrete deserts. It was as if the numbers had blinded policymakers and professionals to the original humane reasons behind the target. Local communities found themselves ridiculed and strong-armed in the name of progress. 'We are dealing with people who have no initiative or civic pride,' said a leading planner from Newcastle. 'The task, surely, is to break up such groupings even though the people seem to be satisfied with their miserable environment.'

The power of political numbers was hard to turn back, and

it took the collapse of the brand new 22-storey Ronan Point in 1968 to begin to turn the tide. It turned out that the crucial joints holding it up had been packed with bits of old cardboard and cigarette ends, and high-rise was soon succeeded by the even less attractive neo-brutalist school of system-built low-rise flats, many of which are unfortunately still standing.

What had begun as a necessary and enlightened policy had been transformed into a fearsome machine with no human qualities. The bulldozer became a symbol of rampant state power. Many of the resulting monstrosities still hang like a millstone round our necks in the form of unpaid municipal debt, the interest for which we pay through our council tax. And all because of a target number which took control. Or, more precisely, because of counting the wrong thing. But then the number of new flats was easy to count. It was much harder to count the number of families feeling at home in well-balanced communities.

IV

After all this, you might be wondering why we count at all. Why do we do something so unpredictable? But numbers are still an absolutely vital tool for human progress. They mean we can begin to test new therapies, judge schools, hospitals and cities. They seek out the fraudulent or inefficient. They still give us some control over our unpredictable world. They can take us by surprise – and it's in that sense that most of the statistics are used in this book. It's just that they are not objective, nor the final answer, and we rely on them too much. All too often, policy decisions are taken on the basis of a single number which actually just symbolizes the question, while the truth scuttles away through our hands as we try to snatch it. To make a difference, we have to measure the ethereal, and nobody has told us how to do so.

Which brings us to the most difficult counting paradox of them all, and the reason why the difficulties in measurement are so important now. Unlike the others, paradox 10 is urgent:

The more sophisticated you are, the less you can measure.

This is true for politicians who try to measure the elusive source of 'feelgood' in their populations, and long for the days when they knew they could just measure wages. And it is true for the doctors who used to measure disease, but know there is some other kind of psychic health that allows people to recover from operations – but which they cannot count under the microscope. But it's most urgent for business.

Business leaders increasingly recognize that the key to success is realizing that their assets are intangible qualities which are extremely hard to measure directly – like knowledge, information or reputation. Count up the value of their fixed assets and you come up with a figure wildly different from the actual value of their company on the world markets. Microsoft is an extreme example. Its balance sheet lists assets that amount to only about 6 per cent of what the company is worth. 'In other words,' says the futurist Charles Leadbetter, '94 per cent of the value of this most dynamic and powerful company in the new digital economy is in intangible assets that accountants cannot measure.'

What's really important can't be measured. Perhaps we should call that the 'McKinsey Fallacy'. It may also be why the best things in life are still free. Yet if your competitors are going to try, then you have to try too. For politicians or business strategists, measurement is a growing headache. It isn't the perennial problem of the two cultures – arts and science will never agree on each other's primacy. Nor is it the clutter of numbers we live through day by day, though that can be misleading too. It's that we have reached a point where measuring things doesn't work any more. When you're in politics or business and you need to measure the unmeasurable in order to make things happen – and your career and our lives may depend on you being able to do so – then you have a crisis. It is a counting crisis.

The word 'crisis' is overused, especially by people who then launch into a stream of statistics, so I should use the word carefully. It certainly isn't the kind of crisis which commentators usually trumpet about, and isn't the kind campaigners can put on a graph – the crisis hasn't grown by 6 per cent since last February or dropped by three and a half miles – but it is a crisis nonetheless. It is that number-crunchers don't have the necessary tools for the new world.

Because of this, we have begun to see some of their methods changing, and strenuous efforts (some brave and exciting, some completely wrong-headed) are now being made to capture in numbers the kernel of truth. And sometimes, a few brave souls have been going further, to abandon the whole idea of numbers altogether and still try to measure the success of places, people and organizations. Their success or failure will determine the kind of world we live in in the new millennium.

In the meantime, we have to see through the fog to work out what's really important in life. The difficulty comes when numbers are used to reduce the sheer complexity of life to something manageable. And it was this fallacy which was tackled by Charles Handy, Britain's answer to the US management gurus, in a lecture he gave to the Royal Society of Arts in London in 1996, called 'What's it all for?'. He described this as the 'fallacy of the single criterion':

> Trying to find one number that is the sum of everything is misguided. There is never any one number that will actually explain success in life and we are foolish ever to think that it might be there. Money certainly isn't it. Businesses know very well that profit is not the only measure. Sensible organisations now have about 18 different numbers that they look at. Nevertheless, the myth pervades our society that if you are profitable you are successful. Or if you're in the public sector, then efficiency is what matters. But efficiency is not quite the same as effectiveness. You can have a very efficient hospital if you don't take in very sick people or people who are not going to get better, like the old ones. So you push them outside. You're efficient but you're not terribly effective. Looking for the one number has corrupted our society.

That sums up the paradox perfectly. The closer you get to measuring what's really important, the more it escapes you, yet you can recognize it sometimes in an instant. And while 18 numbers are clearly better than just one, there are dangers there as well, because number-crunching brings a kind of blindness with it. When we measure life, we reduce it.

Which is why Handy ended his lecture with a poem by Shel Silverstein, called 'The Magic Carpet', which warns about what happens when you measure life instead of living it:

> I revealed to you a magic carpet that will whiz you through the air
> To health and wealth and happiness if you just tell it where.
> So will you let it take you where you've never been before?
> Or will you buy some drapes to match and use it on your floor?

Bizarre measurement No. 4
Saros

(An astronomical cycle used for predicting eclipse. 1 Saros = 18 years, 11 days and 8 hours.)

Number of floppy discs BT believes can store a digital version of every experience in an 80-year life: **7,142,857,142,860,000**

Amount the death rate dropped during a month-long doctors' strike in Israel in 1973: **40 per cent**

Chapter 4

Historical Interlude 2:
Commissioner of Fact

'You are to be in all things regulated and governed' said the gentleman, 'by fact. We hope to have, before long, a board of fact, composed
of commissioners of fact, who will force the people to be a people
of fact, and of nothing but fact. You must discard the word Fancy
altogether.'
Charles Dickens, *Hard Times*

Think of what our Nation stands for . . .
Democracy and proper drains.
Sir John Betjeman

I

Jeremy Bentham was five years old and well into his Latin
studies when the House of Commons met for the first time to
decide whether to hold a census. It was 1753, and only a
matter of months since a furious mob had torn apart the centre
of London – enraged by the loss of eleven days to bring the
calendar in line with the Gregorian one used on the Continent.
Numbers mattered even just in the form of dates. Yet there
were actually very few accurate figures. Nobody in England
had the slightest idea what the population of the country was,
and the prevailing opinion was, with a typical kind of English
pessimism, that it was dropping like a stone. Counting people
seemed like a good modern idea, which would help the tax
authorities, and provide information on the number of
paupers. It might even help plan a local police force.

The man behind the idea was the former secretary of the
Prince of Wales and son of the Archbishop of Canterbury,

Thomas Potter, MP for St Germans – 'a man of more than middling abilities,' according to *Gentleman's Magazine*, 'and somewhat conceited of his own parts'. It might perhaps have helped the counting cause if Potter hadn't been a member of the orgiastic Hellfire Club – motto: 'Do as thou shalt wish' – but that was some months in the future, and probably nobody knew at the time. No, the bill was widely admired and showed every sign of being passed into law.

The fact that Britain did not become the first country in the world to hold a census, ceding that place to Sweden, was down to the sterling efforts of one man. Almost single-handedly, York MP William Thornton mustered enough votes to defeat the idea in a series of bravura performances that stand as a contemporary critique of statistical thinking. In the first division, he was the only MP voting against it. By the time it reached the Lords, he had so stoked up the opposition that they threw it out.

His main arguments were that this was a back-door attempt to bring in nasty French institutions like the police, and that official counting was a pointless activity that changed nothing and undermined the privacy of true Englishmen. It would also make parish officials much too powerful – just to molest every family in the kingdom for the sake of what he called 'political arithmetic'.

'Can it be pretended, that by the knowledge of our number, or our wealth, either can be increased?' he asked fellow MPs. 'And what purpose will it answer to know where the kingdom is crowded, and where it is thin, except we are to be driven from place to place as graziers do their cattle? If this be intended, let them brand us at once; but while they treat us like oxen and sheep, let them not insult us with the name of men.'

Quite so, and for good measure, Thornton promised to refuse to give any information to official busybodies. If the officer persisted, he warned, 'I would order my servants to give him the discipline of the horse-pond'.

It is easy to laugh from two and a half centuries later, in these days when we count almost everything. Yet there was something rather noble about Thornton's defence, boneheadedly English for all that in his powdered wig, yet strangely reminiscent of Euro-sceptic rhetoric at the end of the twentieth century. You can almost imagine modern politicians, like Thornton, quoting Cromwell with approval because he refused to speak to the French ambassador in French. To do otherwise would have introduced 'a conformity to their slavish constitution and modes of government,' said Thornton proudly.

By the second reading of the bill, he had a sizeable following cheering him on, as he imagined 'constables' visiting homes to write down people's age and gender, checking that when the form said 'women', they were actually proved to be women. You can imagine the shiver of horror down the backs of the crusty old MPs. 'We are to entrust petty tyrants with the power of oppression, in confidence that this power shall not be executed; to subject every house to a search; to register every name, age, sex, and state, upon oath; record the pox as a national distemper, and spend annually £50,000 of the public money – for what? To decide a wager at White's!'

Then as you read through his speeches in a dusty old tome edited by William Cobbett half a century later, there suddenly seems to be some sense in what he says. How can counting the population stop people leaving for America, as contemporaries were afraid they were doing? Why should press gangs create armies when volunteers would surely fight better? It was true when he said it, just as it is now. There is a long and noble tradition in Britain of suspicion of official interference, though it is constantly dragged out through history to justify the completely indefensible.

Consequently, the nation did not get its first census for nearly another half-century, by which time the argument about population had become even more pessimistic – but for the opposite reason. Under the influence of the Benthamite clergyman Thomas Malthus, public opinion was afraid that the working population was increasing very much faster than the available food. Now the fear was that there were too *many* people, but there was still no adequate way of finding out what the population was.

Malthus' solution was pure New Labour. Mothers should be told that, after a certain date, no new children would be given welfare. Clergymen should explain to couples what a bad idea it was to marry recklessly. And there should be a national system of education set up, along with a national system of savings banks. There are 20,000 Londoners, said Malthus, plucking another unsupported statistic from the air, who get up every morning without knowing how they will pay for their meals.

History hasn't been kind to Malthus. Cobbett ridiculed him as 'Parson Malthus' and neither his solution nor his nightmare ever came to pass. But the figures which he and Bentham had called for finally began to arrive at the turn of the century. The Napoleonic Wars meant that the government simply had to know what the food requirements of the nation were for the year ahead. The legislation for the first national census was drawn up by Bentham's step-brother Charles Abbott, the MP for Helston in Cornwall, and was rushed through parliament on New Year's Eve 1800. Three months later, a muddled and inaccurate census counted 9.168 million people living in England and Wales.

By the 1840s, official figures covered criminal statistics, hospitals, how much money was taken from drunks in cities, how many pubs had billiard tables and how many people were 'destitute of spiritual belief'. The new registers of births, marriages and deaths were immediately controversial. The Archbishop of Canterbury thundered against anything 'required to gratify the statistical fancies of some few philosophers'. *The Times* weighed in to support the wife of a Leicestershire labourer who refused to give details of her new baby to the local registrar, talking of the new figures as a 'tyranny leading to the violation of the decencies of domestic life'. She was found guilty but not punished.

Counting births also annoyed the Church of England, which was afraid that it would undermine the old idea of simply counting baptisms. Anything else threatened to put the non-conformists on an equal level with the established church. Counting deaths annoyed the Utilitarians. Of course, it was all very well knowing how many people had died, but little use if you didn't know why. And it was this issue which engaged the man who was probably the most influential counter of all, Edwin Chadwick. It was he who persuaded the government to get a question marked 'cause of death' included on the registration form.

Chadwick was then 36 and approaching the height of his powers. He had already made himself the mainstay of two vital royal commissions, and their hefty reports, each one packed with tables of figures, were largely his work. It was Chadwick's assistants who were being sent out across the country to count and collect not just numbers, but numbers that would create change. Not just statistics, but what Chadwick called 'moral statistics'. Chadwick was not just the first modern civil servant, he was also a pioneer of modern campaigning.

'Here and there, and everywhere were Chadwick's young crusaders, the assistant commissioners, scouring the country in stage-coaches and post-chaises, or beating up against the storm on ponies in the Weald, returning to London, their wallets stuffed with Tabular data so dear to philosophic Radicals,' wrote the great historian of the Victorian age, G. M. Young, describing the period. Everywhere also were the new inspectors. There were factory inspectors from 1834. Soon there were also prison inspectors, then school inspectors, railway inspectors and mines inspectors. The great architecture of official calculation, still in place to day, was taking shape – each inspector armed with definitions against which they tested the schools or factories, counting, tabulating and assessing.

II

Edwin Chadwick was the son of an unsuccessful businessman from Longsight, Manchester. He was born in 1800, just 24 days into the new century, into a household so obsessed with cleanliness that all the children were washed all over every day. 'The mainspring of Chadwick's career seems to have been the desire to wash the people of England all over, every day, in administrative order,' wrote G. M. Young. Cleanliness became Edwin's obsession right up to his death at the age of 90. It was the source of his success, but also the key to his unpopularity. 'There is nothing', said *The Times*, 'worse than being cleaned against your will.'

At the age of 23, Chadwick decided to become a barrister, and moved into his new home in the disreputable Lyon's Inn, now in the courtyard of Bush House on the Aldwych. He lived there for seven years, learning about criminals, prisons, slums and fever and supporting himself by writing about them – living in abject fear that his fellow students might find out what he was doing. His career as a barrister, like Bentham's, lasted as long as his first case. He was employed to defend a man charged with bigamy, but the more he investigated the case, the more convinced he was that the client was actually guilty. 'What's it to you?' asked the client. 'You only have to shake the wife's evidence.' Chadwick abandoned the case and never practised law again.

Instead he expanded his journalism. Almost the first friends he made were two of Bentham's acolytes, Southwood Smith and Dr Neill Arnott, with whom he wandered round the fever dens of London's East End. Soon he was consorting with the Utilitarians, as one of the select group of young men who used to read to Bentham and tuck him into bed at night. His new friends soon persuaded him that he should write about the lives of the poor. In true Utilitarian style, he hit on the snappy title *The Means of Insurance against Accidents, etc.*

In 1831, Bentham persuaded him to leave Lyon's Inn and move in with him. He described his relationship with the old philosopher as 'active friendship'. Although modern readers will construe all kinds of homosexual undertones, this was a period of passionate friendship between men, but there was no doubt that Chadwick was absolutely devoted to Bentham, nursing him through his last illness with intricate care. To the end of his life, Bentham was Chadwick's idol. He never allowed anyone near him even to make a joke at the expense of the philosopher's memory. 'Bentham was his ideal, his guiding star, and had called forth all the tenderness of his nature,' wrote Chadwick's daughter. History doesn't relate whether he ever made the trip to University College to look at his old friend in the glass case.

The two were alike in many ways. If he had a sense of humour at all, Chadwick's was ironic and cynical. He was a big man, unlike Bentham, with piercing eyes and a mane of brown hair over his shoulders, but he shared the same apocalyptic passion and hatred for anyone he saw as getting in the way of progress – in effect, anyone who disagreed with him. He despised literature and people who read books for amusement. He was an obsessive, a bore in the century of really serious bores, and possibly at any other time apart from the 1830s, he would have been sidelined as a crank. But in the atmosphere of the day, with the new railways streaking into the distance, the Reform Bill discussed in Parliament, the agitation over the employment of children in factories, and a sense that science and figures could change the world, Chadwick's moral energy and determination could take him to the top.

There are two kinds of economists, he told the Political Economy Club – one who hypothesizes and the other who reasons from facts. To change the conditions in which people lived, you had to have the facts and Chadwick was determined to get them. He borrowed the example of the prison reformer John Howard, who had famously gone round the gaols of Britain armed with a measuring tape, weighing scales and notebook. Chadwick was going to do the same – and the notebook was important. Because, as he so rightly saw, the figures alone were not enough. You have to be able to talk to people to interpret them. He would write it all down. Not just facts, but moral statistics.

In February 1832, he got his chance. Earl Grey's government announced a Royal Commission on the Poor Laws, and one of the commissioners – his friend Nassau Senior, a kind of economic adviser to the government – commissioned him to look at how the existing law worked in London. He was given £100 as a retainer.

With all the twentieth-century rhetoric about the Welfare State, we tend to imagine that being poor two centuries ago was unremittingly hopeless. It probably was, but the situation wasn't completely different from today. About one fifth of national expenditure went on welfare payments to the poor, and this was rising fast, which is not completely different from now. By 1833, one sixth of the population was dependent on some kind of public charity. The Poor Laws were administered by local agents who included among them the enlightened, the patronizing and the petty tyrants, just as they do today. The difference was that in those days there was no objective, no system and no central control. The Poor Law was run by 15,000 separate parishes, administered mainly by farmers and publicans, and none of them had to submit accounts.

Most intelligent political commentators believed, like Malthus, that the time had come to abolish welfare altogether. The two bishops on the royal commission certainly thought so, and – if it hadn't been for Chadwick – they probably would have recommended it. But under the influence of Bentham, Chadwick had other ideas. He conceived of a new system that would demand that paupers would have to live in a new network of workhouses in order to get relief. These would sustain them, but not be so comfortable as to actually attract poor people off the streets. They should be what he called 'uninviting places of wholesome restraint'. If the system worked, the first effect would be to increase employment and raise wages – or so he believed.

Writers like Dickens have painted an appalling picture of the workhouses as cruel and degrading places which most of them in fact became, but this wasn't quite the plan that Chadwick envisaged. He wanted separate institutions for different categories of people: hospitals for the sick, almshouses for the elderly, schools for the young, where the problems of each could be dealt with properly. That never happened. The inhumanity of the system, which so brought Bentham's ideals into disrepute, happened because all the inmates were lumped in together to save money. There was no thought of categorizing them, still less of helping them.

Even so, Chadwick remained more proud of the Poor Law Report than anything else he did. The figures collected by him and his fellow investigators filled 15 volumes. As soon as he had finished investigating London, he set off to look at Buckinghamshire, Sussex and Hampshire. That filled another volume, with a note at the end which said 'the remainder of Mr Chadwick's evidence will follow shortly'. But it grew and grew and ended up in a tin trunk, where it remained. Even without it, the summary report was a great success, selling 15,000 copies. The resulting new law was, said Chadwick later, 'the first great piece of legislation based upon scientific and economical principles'.

But before he had the chance to relax, the Home Secretary, Lord Melbourne, had sent him as one of three royal commissioners to the strike-torn cities of the north, to investigate the plight of children in factories, together with the indefatigable Southwood Smith. Their task was to put forward an alternative scheme for the government, to help them head off the popular head of steam behind Lord Ashley's Ten Hours Bill.

Chadwick set about interviewing his new assistants. He was not impressed. Most of them seemed to have been sent his way by politicians pulling strings for their friends and relatives. 'Why, I know Lord Althorp from having attended some of his family in Leamington,' said one assistant commissioner, when Chadwick asked him why he wanted the job. 'I was passing down the street accidentally the other day, when who should accost me but Lord Althorp, with "Hallo, Loudon, would you like to be on a commission?"'

Despite these frustrations, the assistant commissioners were sent on their way with a mass of questions for the factory owners, the children and their mothers. Was your first child born within a year of your marriage? How many children have you had stillborn? How many miscarriages? *The Times* was furious: 'Such a mass of impotent and stupid verbiage it has seldom been our fortune to face,' wrote their leader writer. The campaigners liked them even less. Workers were instructed not to give evidence to the assistant commissioners.

When they arrived in town, Chadwick's calculators were handed a written protest and faced a siege of children and parents around their hotel every night, singing the 'Ten Hours song:' 'We will have the Ten Hours Bill/That we will, that we will'.

Leaflets condemned 'heartless calculations'. 'If, instead of making us pay these men for the printing of these books, they had appointed a committee of old washerwomen and promised them a tea-drinking, and left them to decide whether children should work more than ten hours a day,' said the Ten Hours Committee, 'there should have been some credit due to them.'

But Chadwick outbid them. He proposed that no child under the age of nine should be employed. From the ages of 9 to 14, they should work no more than eight hours, and over 14 there should be no limit. And with this historic compromise under his belt, Chadwick hoped to be appointed as one of the three commissioners charged with the task of putting the new Poor Law into practice. It was to be a major disappointment.

III

The first meeting of the Poor Law Commission at Somerset House in London must have been a fascinating encounter. There they were, three completely unsuitable placemen and Chadwick. A crotchety Tory MP, Frankland Lewis, Shaw-Lefevre, a charmingly insipid former Cambridge blue, who had been so useless as an under-secretary that his clerks had laughed at him. And the banker George Nicholls who had so little sense of humour that – after watching Mozart's *Don Giovanni* – all he could exclaim was: 'What a shocking state of society!'

The minister had put Chadwick's name to the cabinet, but there was complete silence. His 'station in society' was not considered fit to be a commissioner. But Chadwick was taken aside by his patron, and offered the secretaryship; and promised that the role would have the status of a kind of 'fourth commissioner'. The trouble was that this special status was never written down or communicated to the others.

So the scene was set for a gigantic misunderstanding. The commissioners couldn't understand why their secretary was insisting on things and eventually sent him outside. Chadwick went but sent a message back in explaining that any meetings without him would be illegal. 'Mr Chadwick,' said an exasperated Lewis in the chair, waving a copy of the Act above his head, 'we have the authority to dismiss you.' And so Chadwick explained his special status to the meeting, and the Lewis mouth dropped further and further open. This was the high point of their relationship. It carried on downhill from there.

Chadwick's calculations led him to believe that the active head of the family needed to eat 2,252 calories a day. In theory it was impossible to stick to his limit *and* make workhouse meals less appetizing than ordinary meals labourers were used to outside, but in practice they rarely came close. Most of the new institutions – the 'bastilles', according to the populist opponents – insisted on ugly uniforms, short haircuts, ordered bells and religious services, rising at seven in summer and five in winter. If the inmates refused to work they were put on a diet of bread and water. The whole idea of the workhouse was soon a terrible stigma, and many paupers preferred to starve outside than subject themselves to it. Of the 149 paupers who applied for relief in the new workhouse in Cuckfield, Sussex on the first day of the snow, only six were prepared to face working the crank. Three more gave up after three days. There were rumours that workhouse gruel was ''nattomy soup', made up of poor children's body parts'.

Labourers in Suffolk burned down their local workhouse, but the real opposition came from the North of England. There were torchlight processions on the Yorkshire moors and a newspaper called the *Northern Liberator* suggested that Chadwick should be gibbeted. He began to get death threats. One of his assistant commissioners survived no less than three assassination attempts. In Todmorden, the poor rates couldn't be collected, and the special constables sent to collect them were driven out of town. In Huddersfield, factory workers broke down the doors of the workhouse and extracted the Poor Law 'guardians'. There were minor revolutions in Oldham and Rochdale and, in Bradford, an assistant commissioner was seized by the crowd who proceeded to drive out the troop of cavalry sent to rescue him. They controlled the whole town for a month.

Completely oblivious of the fact that he was now the most hated man in the country, Chadwick dashed to Manchester for a holiday – ignoring his host's requests that he come incognito. But he noticed nothing. Every smile and handshake convinced him he was on the right track and he came back to Somerset House reinvigorated – only to find himself increasingly marginalized by Lewis. But it was the local tyrants that finally ended Chadwick's term of office, when *The Times* investigated goings-on at the workhouse in Andover, under a particularly brutal individual called McDougal. They found the inmates were so starved that they fought over the bones they were supposed to be crushing for manure, some of which were said to be from the local churchyard.

But by then, Chadwick had discovered another interest. When Lewis had earlier handed his position over to his far more competent but equally hostile son, Chadwick had found himself completely sidelined. He had convinced himself that the main reason people became paupers was disease, and as he looked around for something to do, he came up with the idea of researching this phenomenon more fully. It was the most important decision of his life.

Among the various professions he had come to hate the most, engineers and doctors ranked near the top. He simply didn't believe doctors were able to cure disease. The only thing to do was to prevent it entirely – and that meant more counting. His faithful bloodhounds Southwood Smith and Arnott, together with Dr James Kay (later Kay-Shuttleworth), set off to get them. Southwood Smith's calculations astonished Chadwick: out of 77,000 paupers studied, 14,000 had been made poor by catching fever.

It was 1839, and Chadwick had just got married (unlike the

other Utilitarians, he made rather a success of it) and he was spoiling for the challenge. He printed 7,000 copies of the report out of his own pocket and got a friendly bishop to ask the House of Lords to set up a bigger inquiry. Two days later, Lord John Russell commanded the poor law commissioners to do so. The result was the *Report on the Sanitary Conditions of the Labouring Population*, one of the most important documents of the Victorian age.

The report shocked the public. One Tory minister, Lord Normanby, refused to believe it until he had been taken round Bethnal Green and Whitechapel personally by Southwood Smith. It was followed by Chadwick's voluminous research into burials and by the Royal Commission on the Health of Towns. As his years of powerlessness as poor laws secretary went by, he studied everything, from the medical police in Germany to the drains of Paris. His office in Somerset House, from which he refused to resign, was filled with bits of new designs for drains or American street-cleaning equipment. The figures poured in from his assistant commissioners on the ground, and from the 553 new district registrars.

It was a particularly dirty moment for Britain's cities. London had doubled in population in Chadwick's own lifetime so far. In the 1830s alone, the death rate in Birmingham had risen from 14.6 per thousand people to 27.2. Most buildings had no drains, and anyway it was illegal to link them up to the sewers. Cityscapes were pockmarked with great stinking pools of sewage and other filth. And the recent privatization of London's water companies had led to much road-digging as they connected and disconnected pipes to rival companies, but could still only provide water for three hours a day. Most houses in the big industrial towns had no privy and nowhere to wash clothes. Some houses were surrounded by six inches of excrement that you could only cross by balancing on a network of bricks.

Then there was the problem of burials. In places like Rotherhithe, there were now so many graves that each new one would expose more half-decomposed bodies, which would have to be chopped up with spades and burned. 'He who drinks a tumbler of London water has literally in his stomach more animated beings than there are men, women and children on the face of the Globe,' said the witty canon of St Paul's, Sydney Smith.

In Manchester – where the newly formed Statistical Society's house-to-house surveys had counted 15,000 people living in airless lightless cellars, Friedrich Engels had been finding something even worse: 'Masses of refuse, offal and sickening filth lie among the standing pools in all directions . . . A horde of ragged women and children swarm around here, as filthy as the swine that thrive upon the garbage heaps and in the puddles.' In the whole area, he wrote, there was one 'usually inaccessible privy' for 120 people.

The Royal Commission provided even more resources for research. Under Chadwick's direction, a letter was sent to the 50 towns with the highest death rates, together with an appendix of 62 questions. The assistant commissioners followed shortly afterwards to get some answers. Chadwick was in his element. 'My vacation has been absorbed in visiting with Mr Smith and Dr Playfair the worst parts of some of the worst towns,' he wrote happily to the Registrar-General. 'Dr Playfair has been knocked up by it and has been seriously ill. Mr Smith has had a little dysentery; Sir Henry de la Beche was obliged at Bristol to stand up the end of alleys and vomit while Dr Playfair was investigating overflowing privies.'

Working up to 12 hours a day, wearing out subordinates and almost never taking a holiday, Chadwick moved slowly towards his goal – making scores of enemies along the way. He was now fighting rearguard actions against other campaigners who thought the solution was better building regulations, engineers who disliked amateurs designing sewage systems, and doctors who thought it was a matter of preventing infection. Chadwick never believed in the idea of germs. Anyone who counts finds it hard to distinguish between causes and effects, and Chadwick was no exception. It was 'miasma' which caused disease and cleanliness was the cure. 'All smell is, if it be intense, immediate acute disease,' he wrote, and until his death he never doubted it.

By 1847, the first Public Health Act was making its way through Parliament to set up a General Board of Health. It turned out to be only just in time.

IV

In the months before the new law, Chadwick had been hurrying to get his reports out and to persuade the government to take over London's rival sewer commissions – useless squabbling bodies, some of them set up in the time of Henry VIII – knowing that a cholera epidemic was creeping across Europe. In the face of this looming catastrophe, and the outright hostility of the doctors and the press, he worked night and day to prepare his Nuisances Removal Act, giving special powers to the new board. As the MPs debated the bill, the first deaths were reported from Berlin.

He had one stroke of luck. 'He never asked a favour of his superiors that did not smack of ultimatum,' wrote one of his biographers, but at long last, Chadwick finally was given a superior he could work with. The evangelical campaigner Lord Ashley may have been given to pious exclamations and public prayer, but he had forgiven Chadwick for sinking his Ten Hours Bill – and became an enthusiastic ally as chairman of the board.

By the summer of 1848, the board was ready. No minutes were taken at meetings because of the urgency of sending out questionnaires and circulars. By September, the first case of cholera was reported in Sunderland. The traditional quarantine regulations, which Chadwick so ridiculed, were put into effect. Then on 28 September, his nuisance removal powers came into force for the first time, the superintendent of quarantine lost his authority, and Chadwick sent out his first house visitors to check out the filth. The doctors raged. *The Lancet* described Chadwick's behaviour as 'buccaneering piracy against medicine'.

The epidemic slowly withdrew, but by the following summer it was back with a vengeance. This time it covered the whole country, killing as many as 14,000 people in London alone. As it made its lumbering approach, on 5 July 1849, a fearful letter appeared in *The Times*. It came from part of the former Rookery of St Giles, near where New Oxford Street currently runs, where 2,850 people were squeezed into 95 houses in little over an acre. It was to be the front line of the new battle:

> We live in muck and filthe. We ain't got no privez, no dust bins, no drains, no water splies, and no drain or suer in the whole place. The Suer Company, in Greek Street, Soho Square, all great rich powerfool men, take no notice watsomedever of our complaints. The Stenche of a Gully-hole is disgustin. We al of us suffer, and numbers are ill, and if the Colera comes Lord help us.

It *was* a battle. Many of the Poor Law guardians and the parishes refused to carry out his expensive instructions. Orders to clean up cesspools went unanswered. In Whitechapel they even ordered doctors not to visit the sick. At Tooting's pauper school, where deaths in their crowded unventilated four-to-a-bed dormitories were running at 20 a day, they refused to remove the children. When Chadwick's medical inspector reported that the dormitories were built over a stagnant sewer ditch, he took the law into his own hands and sent a force of 50 navvies to put things right with pickaxes and scoops.

Even the instructions to close the overflowing graveyards were being ignored. Worse, the parishes were winning the court cases brought against them by the board. And the board's decision to use quicklime on the bodies caused riots and widespread rumours that doctors were poisoning the water supply to reduce the population. 'We must not parley,' wrote Ashley to Chadwick at the height of the action. 'The necessity for action is immediate, urgent, paramount to all law, right or interest. At once refuse to receive deputations, and direct law to act instantly. I will take any amount of responsibility.'

By the beginning of September, deaths had reached 2,000 a week and the system of house-to-house visits came back into effect. The inspectors found many homes where adults and children were blue in the face, dying in each room. The battle was also taking its toll on the board. With London emptied of anyone who could afford to leave, their officials were slowly succumbing to illness and exhaustion. Even Chadwick had collapsed with suspected cholera, and for two weeks alone in the office, Ashley struggled to run the operation by himself, praying each morning – reverting in Chadwick's absence to very un-Chadwickian language. 'We are now in the City of Plague,' he wrote in his diary, 'and still by God's love under his shield and buckler.'

When Chadwick returned, able to speak only in a whisper, it was to hear that the Treasury had refused to let him appoint more inspectors. That day 500 people died in London alone.

But it was becoming clear that the epidemic had broken and on 6 November, Queen Victoria issued a proclamation for general thanksgiving. This time, *The Times* was firmly on the side of Chadwick and the centralizers. 'The parochial officers did nothing – absolutely nothing,' they said reviewing the disaster:

> They left the graveyards festering – the cesspools seething – the barrels of blood steaming in the underground shambles – the great mounds of scrutch putrefying in the Bermondsey glue yards . . . They rejected the medical officer's counsel, even mutilated his reports and only in the fifteenth week of a mortality unparalleled for two centuries did they consent to the nomination of the domiciliary inspectors.

Their behaviour had paved the way for Chadwick's schemes for what *The Times* had previously dubbed 'French centralization'. With the epidemic over, he settled down to extending his powers over the dirtiest towns in the country, designing new drainage systems, testing alternative water supplies for London from Richmond, Windsor and Farnham – even hiring a barge to spray sewage from the Bridgwater Canal, as an experimental method of disposing of London's muck.

He set up the Health of Towns Association and launched a

campaigning publication (with his usual gift for the snappy title) called *Weekly Sheet of Facts and Figures*. And to fill its pages, across the country stalked his inspectors with their measuring rods and tables of data, recording the filth, testing it against the mortality statistics, interviewing the local doctors, and filing their reports back to Chadwick. 'The town is old, and is in as bad a condition as Whitehaven, and I don't know if I can say anything worse of it,' reported inspector Robert Rawlinson from Hexham. 'I am staying at the best Hotel in the town, but there is no watercloset, only a filthy privy at some distance, the way to it being past the kitchen. I have just been out in the dark and rain blundering and found someone in the place.'

And so on and so on as the resistance clamoured around him, until once again, it forced him from office. Opposition came again from the parishes, from the trade unionists – 'meat not sanitary regulations', they chanted – and from the slum landlords and property owners who resented the expenditure being demanded of them. It came from the Private Enterprise Society, which believed Chadwick was at the heart of a giant socialist conspiracy. And increasingly it came from the engineers, led by Robert Stephenson and Joseph Bazalgette, who had their own plans for much larger brick-built sewers.

Before the next epidemic had burned itself out, Chadwick and his colleagues would be turned out of the board, and poor old Southwood Smith would be sacked without a pension, at the age of sixty-six. Their downfall came at the hands of their new minister, the ex-officio president of the Board, Lord Seymour, the heir to the Duke of Somerset. In two years of office, Seymour came to only three meetings. And in July 1854, with cholera back in Britain, he attacked the board in the House of Commons. 'The whole thing is perfectly monstrous,' he said. 'Some engineer whom no one else would employ, or some medical man whom nobody would consult, would be anxious to have the Health of Towns Act applied to his district; he would then get a few signatures . . .' There followed other wild accusations – junkets to Paris, 'interfering with everybody and everything'.

A storm of hate crashed around Chadwick. 'Every county, town, and village may obtain universal health and a large income from the sale of sewerage on one condition,' said an anonymous diatribe in the magazine *Engineers and Officials*. 'Unquestioning, blind, passive obedience to the ukase, decree, bull, or proclamation of the autocrat, pope, grand lama of sanitary reform, Edwin Chadwick.'

And that was that. He was pleased to get a letter from Lord Palmerston thanking him for the 'indefatigable manner' in which he had performed his duties, until he discovered that Southwood Smith had received exactly the same letter. Chadwick got a pension of £1,000 a year. In the final 36 years of his life, he never had a proper job again.

V

The great cholera epidemic of 1848–9 was the high point of Chadwick's life. The problem was that, for all his figures, he had got the problem wrong. Not disastrously so: the epidemic broke out in the same house in Leith as it had in 1832, and in Bermondsey next to the same ditch. His measures were right, but for the wrong reasons. The germs he so ridiculed were in fact responsible, as Dr John Snow discovered when he ended the outbreak in Soho by removing the handle of the water pump in Broadwick Street. Only in their final epidemic despatch, on 18 September 1849, did Chadwick's Board of Health suggest that drinking water should be boiled. He never relented and clung to the idea that epidemics were caused by dirt to the end of his life

As he got older, he became duller and even more obsessed with drains. He was shunned by the debating societies the Victorians so enjoyed because he would keep bringing every discussion back to the same thing. 'Mr Chadwick, the subject is taxation, not drainage,' said the irritable chairman at the Political Economy Club. And when he ran across the French emperor Napoleon III in Paris, he addressed him as 'Sire' like a medieval courtier, and then lectured him about sewage manure. Then was offended not to get an invitation back the next day.

His most frustrating battle, to create a sewage system for London, was finally won by his enemies the engineers after the Great Stink in July 1858. The smell from the Thames was then so bad that the windows of the House of Commons had to be hung with sheets of lime. The MPs left in despair, having voted to let the Metropolitan Board of Works borrow £3 million to do what they liked with. As a result, it is now Bazalgette's gigantic brick sewers that form the Victoria Embankment.

Chadwick reverted to the traditional Utilitarian pursuit of developing crazy ideas. He set up committees to campaign on army health, telegraphs, firefighting, better paving and especially drill in schools. He campaigned for votes for women and for every school to have its own gym and swimming pool. He also tried to arrange to suck pure air from towers down to the polluted cities, to abolish spelling lessons in schools, and to train fire horses to leave their stalls and run to the fire engine as soon as they heard the alarm. He twice stood for Parliament, coming bottom of the poll.

He died on 6 July 1890, the grand old man of sanitary reform. 'I cannot tell you,' he told a reporter in his last newspaper interview a few months before, 'how strongly I believe in soap and water as a preventative of epidemics.' His legacy had been recognized with a knighthood a few months before his death, despite years of letter-writing to the government asking for a peerage. His obituary in *The Times* recognized that if he had killed in battle the number of people he had saved, he would have had a whole army of statues erected to him. He got precious little, considering that his friend Ashley got Shaftesbury Avenue named after him and had the statue of Eros in Piccadilly Circus erected in his memory.

Yet it was Chadwick who laid the foundations, not just of drainage, but of a sensible graveyard system, a dispassionate civil service, a system of local government and much else besides. More than anybody else he was responsible for the falling death rate, but also for the Victorian obsession with measuring things. Everything could be quantified. The government was doing it, and from the 1830s, the new statistical societies were sending out their amateur counters in house-to-house surveys of school books, bible ownership, religiosity, illness, house design, sleeping arrangements, crime and anything which appealed to them, publishing table after table in closely argued pamphlets and reports. 'The first and most essential rule of its conduct is to exclude all opinions,' said the first prospectus of the London Statistical Society. The new measurement only dealt with facts.

If you open the issue of *Illustrated London News* which described Chadwick's work on the Health of Towns Commission in 1848, you can find the precise number of Christmas parcels brought into London by railway (17,209), the number of children in the Clapton Orphan's Asylum (168), the length of the cane used to hit Queen Victoria on the head in Piccadilly (27 inches), the amount of tobacco imported (26 million pounds) and the number of Americans christened 'George Washington' in the previous half century (over 30,000). You can find the amount of rancid butter seized, the number of evictions in Galway, the number of potatoes eaten at the annual meeting of the Royal Agricultural Society, and on and on. It is the symptom of a scientific age, confident that it can control the chaos around it with the unrelenting application of facts and measurements.

But it went further than that. Since the invention of clocks, measurement was also a way of controlling an unruly population. 'It has been suggested to me that the Railway Timetable did much to discipline the people at large,' wrote the historian G. M. Young in a footnote. 'I think this is true.'

So do I. Measuring things even controlled people's emotions and dampened their spirits. Witness William Jacob, Comptroller of Corn Returns, speaking at an early meeting of the London Statistical Society: 'A more general diffusion of accurate knowledge regarding the state of public affairs would tend to check that excitement and party spirit which has often been created by misrepresentation or exaggeration, and has produced an annoyance to the government.'

In short, the Victorian population was inspected, preached

at and counted, and the very chief of the counters, fighting ancient prejudices, superstitions, tradition and emotion, was Edwin Chadwick. There was something almost naive about it all, like a child who obsessively counts the cows in a field or the wheels on a railway engine. 'Side by side with his powerful intellect there was much that was childlike in his disposition,' wrote Chadwick's daughter Marion in 1928. It was an interesting remark, given John Stuart Mill's description of Bentham as 'a boy to the last'. There was indeed something childlike about the idea that pleasure or utility, let alone the sheer complexity of life, could be subsumed into numbers.

There still is. And it was this issue that brought the greatest propagandist of the age into the argument. Charles Dickens shared many of the ideals of the Utilitarians – 'I saw 30,000 children hunted, flogged, imprisoned, but not taught,' he wrote in 1850 – and he was eventually persuaded to ally himself to Chadwick's cause, but he despised their obsession with facts, believing that dry definitions missed out the spark of humanity which make the difference. His novel *Hard Times* stands as a testament to the case against counting, as relevant today as it ever was. There was something of Chadwick in the monstrous figure of Thomas Gradgrind, hardware merchant and Utilitarian, the man who believes that only demonstrable countable facts are important. Yet you can define something precisely, count every attribute and measure it in every way, Dickens implied, and still not know much about it.

He describes how the warm-hearted circus girl Sissy Jupe is adopted into Gradgrind's dry as dust household. Sissy knows all about horses because she was brought up with them, but asked to define one in class and she finds herself tongue-tied and overshadowed by one of her more experienced fellow pupils. 'Quadrupud,' he says. 'Graminivorous. Forty teeth, namely twenty-four grinders, four eye-teeth, and twelve incisive. Sheds coat in spring; in marshy countries, sheds hoofs, too. Hoofs hard, but requiring to be shod with iron. Age known by marks in mouth . . .'

'Now girl number twenty,' said Gradgrind, turning back to Sissy. 'You know what a horse is.'

Bizarre measurement No. 5

Cat Unit

(Minimum fatal dose per kilogram of cat, an American method of standardizing pharmaceuticals in 1910.)

....

Proportion of cars on Albanian roads believed to have been stolen elsewhere in Europe (1997): *80 per cent*

Average time spent by British people in traffic jams every year: *11 days*

Chapter 5

The Feelgood Factor

By psychology's 'mortal' sin, I mean the sin of deadening, the dead feeling that comes over us when we read professional psychology, hear its language, the voice with which it drones, the bulk of its textbooks, the serious pretensions and bearded proclamations of new 'findings' that could hardly be more banal, its soothing anodynes for self-help, its décor, its fashion, its departmental meetings, and its tranquilising consulting rooms, those stagnant waters where the soul goes to be restored, a last refuge of white-bread culture, stale, crust-less, but ever spongy with rebounding hope.
Dr James Hillman, *The Soul's Code*

Where is the wisdom we have lost in knowledge, and the knowledge we have lost in information?
Dr Richard Smith, paraphrasing T. S. Eliot, in a *British Medical Journal* editorial, 1991

I

The psychologist Lesley Fallowfield sat through the final illness of her friend, who died of leukaemia in her early thirties, then blasted the medical profession for their failure to look at people's emotional needs. The therapy had been unsuccessful with unpleasant side effects, and to make matters worse, they could only communicate through a disconcerting plastic window. 'Thus one of the most intelligent, sensitive, warm and generous-hearted people I have ever known spent some of her final weeks cut off from physical contact with most of her family and friends,' she wrote. 'I am still haunted by the last conversation we had, when she asked why I had not tried to dissuade her from a therapy with poor chances of survival, but a high chance of destroying the quality of whatever life she had left.'

Medicine and psychiatry are worlds where measurement has taken over more than most. Doctors will wire you up to machines, just as they used to read the charts at the end of your bed. You can hear them shouting out the figures on *ER* as they push the patients into hospital on their trolleys. Psychiatrists will often now use their own psychometric diagnoses, sometimes without even looking you in the eye while they tick the checklists. Single symptoms, blood counts, heart rates can be measured. But taken together, the figures will always miss something out.

The problem is that – despite the fact that emotions can have an enormous effect on our immune systems – some doctors ignore them, except as irritating disease-causing complications, just as economists do, because they do not fall under the list of things they find it easy to measure. Yet distressing emotions have a similar risk to health as smoking or eating butter and greasy chips stuffed with cholesterol. We are five times more likely to develop cancer if we are stressed, twice as likely to get colds if we are anxious, and five times more likely to die after a heart attack if we are depressed. That's what the figures say, if we believe them.

Given that, asked an editorial in the *Journal of the American Medical Association*, don't medical ethics mean that doctors should at least try to get a handle on emotions? Instead, Lesley Fallowfield's search turned up what she called 'ludicrously narrow' definitions of quality of life in the medical profession. The Karnofsky Performance Index of 1947 developed a way of working out how many nurses you might need on a ward, which scores people's health between 100 and 0. If you get 0, you're dead. Breast cancer patients score 80, whether they are bouncing with enthusiasm or crippled with depressive illness.

There have been many more attempts since then, from the Functional Living Index to the Rotterdam Symptom Checklist. There are other methods of getting patients to sum up what they feel, from the 'SF-36 General Health Questionnaire' to the 'McMaster Health Utilities Questionnaire', but still doctors usually prefer to 'do something' rather than not – even if it might seriously undermine a patient's remaining quality of life. But then, if you believe the figures, medical students are more scared of death than average. Whose preferences are these analyses really measuring: the patient's, the doctor's or the health economist's?

If it's the health economists, they use QALYs – the so-called quality adjusted life years – which modern health economists use to work out who their scarce resources should go towards treating. But when you look more closely at the basis for the research, you wonder whether these are actually the kinds of trade-offs people make in their own minds. People would often actually trade a shorter life for better health. QALYS also tend to be based on interviews with relatively few patients, who are asked to rank different states of illness and what they feel about having them. Small differences in the sample make big differences in the policy. And in any case, who ever heard of the Fire Brigade or the lifeboats checking up people's QALYs before turning on the siren?

The counting obsession has caused the same crisis among doctors as it has everywhere else, as the supporters of 'evidence-based medicine' – cold hard measuring followed by logical diagnosis – slug it out with their critics. Trisha Greenhalgh, from the Royal Free Hospital Medical School in London, tells the story of 'Dr Jenkins' hunch', breaking off his Monday morning surgery because a mother called to say her little girl had diarrhoea and was behaving 'strangely'. He would never normally break off from a busy surgery. How could he know, using the available evidence, that the girl had meningitis? But she did. Maybe the word 'strangely' alerted him. Maybe he knew the family and they rarely complained. But it wasn't the cold facts and risks that told him, it was the story.

Medical students can write long learned essays about the risks and competing treatments for high blood pressure, but that's not enough, says Greenhalgh. 'When I ask my students a practical question such as "Mrs Jones has developed light-headedness on these blood pressure tablets and she wants to stop all medication; what would you advise her to do?", they are foxed. They sympathize with Mrs Jones' predicament, but they cannot distill from their pages of close-written text the one thing that Mrs Jones needs to know.' Who can blame them? Which of us can distill from the piles of research figures about health risks what we should embrace and what we should avoid?

There is a growing sense in medicine that you can't treat patients as if they were average risks, in the same way you can treat cattle or buy stock. You can't offset one risk with another: you have to listen to each patient as an individual, and get at the truth each time. Greenhalgh calls this listening to patients' stories 'narrative-based medicine'.

Of course doctors need to count. They need to confirm hunches and, of course, to make sure their drugs won't have weird side effects – which is why the average new drug requires 100 research projects, takes between twelve and twenty-four years to bring to market and costs at least £350 million to develop. Though you should remember that one of the other peculiarities of the quantum effect is that what you look for in research, you tend to find. But then doctors have been running up against the same mismatch of measurements as the economists have. People might be rich and healthy, so there shouldn't be anything wrong with them. But there was. They weren't happy.

But then, how do you measure happiness, either as a doctor or an economist? For one thing, it's so difficult to compare – especially when, according to one Danish study, 'the life of the average Dane is to a large extent confused, stressful, alienated and isolated'. For Dane, read 'most of us' – though actually, the massive Eurobarometer project found that 55 per cent of Danes were 'very satisfied' with life, compared to 10 per cent of French and Italians (and around a third of Brits).

For another thing, physiologically anyway, happiness and misery are not opposites. They are dealt with by different parts of the brain and have to be measured in different ways.

There's the problem of the Dutch proverb: 'an ounce of illness is felt more than a hundredweight of health'. Happiness and unhappiness are qualities that are so paradoxical that they slip through your fingers every time you get out the ruler. Take the example of the writer and concentration camp survivor Primo Levi, who described how people found something to sustain them emotionally even in Auschwitz. Even at their lowest point, with nothing to look forward to, he says, they told themselves they could stop it raining just by running over to the electric fence. That sense of choice in the face of such devastating adversity was sometimes enough to keep them going. It made them feel a little better knowing they could end it all. But try measuring happiness in that kind of laboratory. You can't. It's too human.

Statistics prove we are getting our measurements wrong, yet we should be suspicious of too many numbers. Both assertions are true. It's just that, even with these moral statistics sprinkled about, you have to keep your fingers crossed. The figures get worse the more we worry about them.

For example, what do we make of the statistics which say there are now five million Britons who will suffer from depression some time in their lives? Why, as Oliver James puts it, do 'winners in society now feel like losers?' Is it that depression is really increasing or is it that drug companies are looking for a market for antidepressants? The whole idea of antidepressants was nearly canned by marketing experts in the 1960s because depression was such a rare disorder. In those days, they were developing Valium to tackle anxiety instead. Now anxiety is unfashionable and we're awash with Prozac.

It was the same with obsessive compulsive disorder. In 1980, the estimates were that people obsessively washing their hands or checking their front door accounted for less than 0.01 per cent of the UK population. Now it's estimated at over one million people. Are these enormous shifts really to do with a tidal wave of misery? Or is it something to do with subtle marketing, journal supplements and conferences on the subject, sponsored by drug companies? Or is it because we have only just become sensitive enough to see what was always under our noses? Or is it again the peculiar effect, that what frightens society most tends to happen? Whatever it is, we would not necessarily learn anything from the statistics, but we can recognize an underlying sense of unease.

II

Happiness isn't just a problem for medical figures; it's a problem for politicians and economists. I heard this once in an unexpected *cri de coeur* from a British Home Office minister. Virginia Bottomley explained that up to 93 per cent of the British population now had colour televisions, washing machines and freezers. That covered people of all classes, paying their own way and on welfare. It was an extraordinary achievement, she said – adding suddenly and off-message: 'Why on earth isn't everybody happy?'

I noted it down on the back of an envelope. It seemed to go to the heart of the unease at the time, because the usual measurements of success, for politicians in particular, had let them down so disastrously. People were having two foreign holidays a year, their house prices were rising fast, but people just weren't happy. The political press dubbed what was missing as the 'feelgood factor'.

This elusive, unmeasurable, indefinable factor became one of the key issues of the early years of John Major's premiership in Britain. Commentators discovered, as if for the first time, the terrifying figures of feelbad. There were 10,000 calls a day to the child advice phone service Childline, rising divorce and male suicide rates – three out of four bodies fished out of the River Thames are men, and five men in the UK attempt suicide every day. Academics were also stalking the pages of the broadsheets talking about a crisis of parenting. 'Governments must encourage parenthood of the highest quality,' wrote the respected social scientist A. H. Halsey after the 1990 riots. But how? And how could it be measured?

People seemed to be so angry. It wasn't just stories like Marlene Lenick, who shot her husband with a .38 because he wanted to watch the Philadelphia Eagles match when she wanted to watch the news. People were also needy. Book-shelves bulged with the weight of self-help titles like *Feel the Fear and Do it Anyway*. And when the marriage guidance organization Relate opened an office in a GP's surgery in the middle of London's commuter belt, at South Woodham Ferrers in Essex in 1991, there was a sudden enormous demand for free 45-minute sessions with a psychologist for stress or loneliness. Within two months, the office had been so overwhelmed that it had to close altogether.

Maybe it was always thus. Maybe nobody had noticed before. But the emotional toll on the richest people in the world seemed to be landing most heavily on children, and that felt new. Suddenly one in 20 British children was suffering from depression or anxiety so badly they needed professional help – including one in 50 in primary schools. Between 1 and 2 per cent of all British schoolchildren had anorexia. As many as half the long-term absences of school-children from school were because they feel inexplicably tired all the time.

Then there were the diets. Suddenly girls of just eight or nine were worrying about their weight. The British Association for the Advancement of Science was told in 1996 that the girls most aware of diets also had the lowest self-esteem. Leeds University's Dr Andrew Hill blamed Sindy dolls and their ultra-thin bodies. 'Why pick on Sindy?' said a spokesman for the manufacturers Hasbro. 'An eleven and a half inch piece of plastic is not responsible for the ills of today's society.'

But who was? Step forward the three main contenders – school pressures, rising divorce rates and the consumer society.

Describing her affluent town in Connecticut as a place that expects children to do well, columnist Anne-Marie Sapsted went on to outline a school system which puts enormous pressures on children from an early age. This is a place where eight-year-olds have an hour's homework every night and formal tests in each area of school work every week – and where they have such busy diaries filled with CV-building after-school activities that 'windows' for play are often a week or so apart.

Which brings us to the second contender. A recent survey at Leicester University showed that up to 40 per cent of the students were suffering from depression. One counsellor said it was probably something to do with family breakdown. Many of them had absolutely nowhere of their own to go at the end of term.

The Divorce Reform Act 1969 ushered in a whole new era of relatively easy separations, and the number of divorces in the UK doubled over the next decade. In the USA, the chances of divorce for married couples was 67 per cent by 1990. A decade later, it now only takes 20 minutes to produce the papers needed for a divorce through the US QuickCourt interactive computer system. Divorce can have a devastating effect on children. Children of divorced parents are more likely to get into trouble, perform badly in school, get stress-related illness and get divorced themselves. When the novelist Joanna Trollope researched her novel *Other People's Children*, she said she had never come across so much hidden pain.

Which leaves us with the pressures of a consumer society. By the time they are seven, the average American child will be seeing 20,000 advertisements a year on television. By the time they are 12 they will have an entry in the massive marketing databases used by companies. And as corporations realize the spending power of children, so the efforts to get at their money increase. Advertising to children increased by 50 per cent between 1993 and 1996, with movies, sneakers and hamburger wrappers all linked together as part of the elaborate child marketing system. By 1997, partly thanks to Batman, Hercules and Star Wars, up to half the spending on toys went on those licensed from TV or films.

According to the poet Robert Bly, children have to develop such a powerful critical sense to resist all this wanting that they eventually turn it on themselves. No wonder they are miserable. The awful thing is that the different measures of success actually contradict each other on this. Society is 'successful' if you use the conventional measure – money. But there is more money around because of the break-up of family life. A Ford UK executive recently admitted that divorce boosts car sales. Broken families also need two houses instead of one, so it pushes up house prices. And the toy trade certainly benefits: many children need duplicate toys – one for each home. Some measures of success hide other kinds of failure.

The communitarian Amitai Etzioni tells the story of American truck driver Rod Grimm, delivering his lorry-loads from Los Angeles to Maine. His work keeps him on the road 340 days a year, so his wife moved into the cab with him, their friendships have been reduced to occasional encounters and their relationship with the daughter to a cellphone link. Yet the economic measures see all the money he's earning and register this as a success.

Despite all the measures of success which are dashing off the scale, showing that our children are richer, smarter and healthier than any generation before them, the present generation in the West is also more lonely, angry, miserable, aggressive and depressed. We demonstrate that mismatch with the use of figures – of depression, suicide and alienation – without which we would carry on, on our own sweet way regardless. When you break away from one solitary measure of success, you do get closer to the truth.

Maybe the number-crunchers will one day prove exactly where the problem lies, but I doubt it. Real problems about real people don't usually have one single root. And even if they do, you can measure the causes next to the effects – as we've seen – but it's extremely hard to disentangle them enough to see which is which. Not without falling back on good old-fashioned common sense and intuition.

The point is that fundamental problems like unhappiness can't be measured. They just have to be experienced. Or as the French novelist and aviator Antoine de Saint-Exupéry wrote in *The Little Prince*: 'It is with the heart that one sees rightly. What is essential is invisible to the eye.'

III

John Vasconcellos is one of the first to take the feelgood debate somewhere political, taking it a little further than the usual cliches about 'family values' – pioneering an attempt to measure what's really important. If lack of self-esteem lies behind a range of intractable social issues, he reasoned, how can we hammer out a political programme to do something about it? Nobody had asked the question before. Coinciding with the angst on both sides of the Atlantic about why people were wealthier but more disturbed, Vasconcellos' initiative has fed into a whole new way of thinking about how institutions like schools and prisons succeed; and how we can measure whether they do.

Vasconcellos is difficult to categorize. Some dismiss him as a refugee from the 60s – though he is also the elected representative of Santa Clara, including Silicon Valley, which makes him bang up to date. They dismiss him as a shaggy branch of the new age movement too, but as chairman of California's Ways and Means Committee (responsible for balancing the state's budget) he has also had to be pretty down to earth. The local media has always gone heavy on his appearance, more like a cross between a rock star and a drug smuggler, according to one magazine. 'I mean *worn* loafers,' wrote one interviewer about his shoes – this is a nation where politicians wear hairpieces and not a piece is out of place. 'I mean, I got a higher shine on my worn loafers than he's got on his loafers and the last time my loafers shined, the Village People were still going strong.'

Despite all that, Vasconcellos began as a good Catholic. 'I was the best Catholic boy in the entire world,' he says now. In his valedictory speech in college he promised to devote his life to furthering the work of Jesus Christ. It was the time of the film *Man of La Mancha*, of dreaming the impossible dream, just to add to the Don Quixote impression, and Vasconcellos set up the La Mancha Fund to beat the impossible foe.

The trouble was, he put it later, that he didn't like himself.

In fact, he had such low self-esteem that he lost the first election he ever fought, for eighth-grade president, by one vote. His own.

Even as a politician, he was having to go through a period of disillusionment. The same year he was elected also saw Ronald Reagan take the reins of power as Governor of California, with a remit to dismantle everything he held dear. Soon he was storming out of meetings at the California Assembly.

Throughout the 70s, he grew his hair – at one stage refusing to cut it for three years. He got angrier and went through periods of heavy depression. Then he suddenly found himself in a process he described as 'cracking open'. It was the start of a long struggle with himself under a protégé of the great humanistic psychologist Carl Rogers, the bioenergetics therapist Stanley Keleman. 'If I carry on we're going to open up your rage,' Keleman told him. 'It may end your political career.' But the political capital he had built up got him through. A committee of colleagues was set up to calm him down every time he exploded during a debate. When he went public about his personal demons, he became a national figure.

California was in crisis by the end of the 1980s. The voters were poised to cut back the state's budget, but the prison system was 175 per cent full and two out of three people arrested in Los Angeles were testing positive for cocaine. Drug abuse was costing $235m in medical expenditure, $4bn in lost work, $2bn in law enforcement, $235m in prisons and $280m in premature death – in California alone. And nobody seemed to have anything new to suggest on the subject beyond lower taxes, tougher sentences and family values. But even these weren't what they were. Not when half of California's children will soon live in a single-parent household before the age of 18, and when 8 per cent of them live in traditional families where the fathers work full-time and the mothers stay at home.

It didn't add up. This was the richest state in the richest country in the world: the normal methods of measuring such things didn't seem to provide any answers. But what if the problems were symptoms of something so fundamental that the measurements for it simply didn't exist? Vasconcellos consulted his friend the self-esteem guru Jack Canfield, later to become immensely successful by selling seven million copies of his book *Chicken Soup for the Soul*.

Together, they put together the proposal for an official task force about self-esteem, which would make the case of 'feelgood' as a personal and political issue, and suggest what could be done about it. The first attempt in 1984 passed through the California Assembly in Sacramento by 55 votes to 22, but while Vasconcellos was recovering from triple heart bypass surgery, it was defeated by the senate. The next year it got through both houses but was thrown out by governor George Deukmejian. 'I do not agree that the creation of an additional quasi-governmental body is the appropriate way to address this problem,' he said.

Next year, Vasconcellos was back, broadening the remit to include 'personal and social responsibility'. The senators nodded it through and he went to see the governor himself. 'Why not just hand it over to a university to study?' asked Deukmejian.

'Because by spending a few tax dollars, we can collect the information and get it out. If that helps even a few persons appreciate and understand self-esteem and how they can live their lives and raise their kids better, we may have less welfare, less violence and drugs, and that's a very conserving use of taxpayers' money.'

'I've never thought of it that way before,' said the governor, and signed it into law. The task force would have a budget the same as sending one person to prison for fourteen years.

In May 1988, Vasconcellos went to San Francisco for a brainstorming session with Scott Peck, author of *The Road Less Travelled*, and began advertising for task force members. A record number applied. They appointed an unusual mixture ranging from a gay therapist to a captain in the LA sheriff's office, the vice president of a poultry farm, a poet and musician and the chairman of the board of the Evangelical Free Church. They appointed David Brooks in the chair, co-author of *How to be Successful in Less Than 10 Minutes a Day*.

It ran into trouble with the media straight away. 'As if they needed to reinforce Sacramento's credentials as the kook capital of the world,' said the *San Francisco Examiner*. 'The taxpayers had the right to hope that such silliness left the state with Governor Moonbeam,' said one Republican assembly member, harking back to the great days of the semi-hippy governor Jerry Brown.

Nonetheless, the task force report *Towards a State of Self-Esteem* hit the streets on 23 January 1990. It hit the front pages right across the USA, dismissed by the Right as a waste of money and by the Left for obscuring the issues of poverty and deprivation, but it sold 60,000 copies. Similar task forces were set up immediately in Maryland, Louisiana and Illinois and in fifty of California's fifty-eight counties. Rhode Island senator Claiborne Pell drew up plans for a national task force on 'human resource development', which was withdrawn after a battering against it from the Christian conservatives.

The report wasn't signed by the whole task force. The evangelical refused unless the definition of self-esteem included the words 'accepting myself as the image-bearer of God', the gay therapist refused unless it included a model programme for lesbian and gay youth, and the turban-wearing yoga teacher refused unless it included some simple yoga exercises to reduce stress.

But the report was finally out, packed with figures and inspiring little quotations, and it had an effect. Slowly, fitfully, government attention shifted towards Vasconcellos' three Rs: responsibility, self-respect and relationships – especially in small ways. Hillary Clinton even began keeping toys around the White House in case anyone needed to bring their children to work. The self-esteemers began drafting new laws for California: teaching art and creativity in prison; setting up parenting classes; putting self-esteem at the centre of the school curriculum; measuring the success of institutions by the self-esteem they created. The governor refused to sign the new law tackling teenage pregnancy, but designated February 1992 as Self-Esteem Month.

'Self-esteem amounts to a social vaccine,' said Vasconcellos. 'It provides us with the strength not to be vulnerable to dropping out or getting pregnant too soon or getting violent or addicted. It's a new strategic vision for the development of human capital. We need to give people material things but also encouragement to become able to protect themselves and take charge of their lives.'

Similar ideas in the USA had already succeeded in reducing delinquency figures, even truancy and teenage pregnancies. Some states already believed they could save six dollars in welfare spending for every dollar spent backing self-help pro-grammes to boost self-esteem. There have also been some spectacular successes in schools, led by the superintendent of one schools district, in San Jose, which gave all pupils 40 minutes self-esteem training a week. Average attendance increased to 97.7 per cent and achievement scores shot up 10 per cent a year.

Self-esteem has become an American industry in itself. So why did the political movement for self-esteem not capitalize on its momentum? Maybe because of the difficulty with one of the task force's recommendations – the so-called California 'self-esteem czar' was never appointed. But then, as one local paper put it: 'Who's got a sense of self-worth strong enough to step into the role? Big enough to deflect an entire stable of gag-writers?'

John Vasconcellos remains as convinced as ever of the vital importance of self-esteem, but frustrated by the criticism and the problem of measuring it. Even so, the movement he had given birth to had worked, he said. 'Most people now take it for granted,' he said. 'It's aspired to, talked about, written about, designed into programmes for kids. It's become so wide-spread, in fact, that it has created a backlash. 'Every govern-ment programme in operation could be operated by people with self-esteem, who can maintain their self-esteem with dignity and courage, can cherish other people as individuals,' he said. 'I think the whole culture's going that way.'

It is true, as he says, that people are increasingly trying to take control of their own lives. But there remains the crucial problem of how to measure it. Because self-esteem is so funda-mental, it is extremely hard to get a measuring tape to it, and therefore hard to get it accepted in our hard-nosed culture. 'Isn't there a bottom line?' I asked him. 'Doesn't the government have to find out how to provide people with self-esteem?'

'The government doesn't bestow it,' he told me. 'The family is the crucible of self-esteem. The government's role is the assessment of institutions. But there is a *bottom* bottom line that is whether I have it. If I just talk about self-esteem and just measure it and never experience it, then I'll never appreciate it.' It's an exciting and innovative approach to take a leap at what's really important, knowing that it can't be measured. It means that, in the end – however much policy-makers may demand the figures, the fundamental question can only be measured intuitively. 'Do I have self-esteem?' is a pretty fundamental question, and one I answer differently for myself every time I wake up. That's the bottom line. The leap in the dark is to extend that to anyone else.

'Measuring it, knowing how it's destroyed and created, takes a lot more knowledge than we have so far, because there is so much involved in being a human being,' says Vasconcellos.

What made things even more difficult was that, as well as finding it hard to quantify and so almost impossible to measure how much self-esteem was being built in institutions like schools and prisons, there was also hardly any research being carried out on the idea. Worse, some academics brought out papers saying that self-esteem was the same as egotism. The report defines it as 'appreciating my own worth and importance and having the character to be accountable for myself and to act responsibly towards others'. When you're going to count something, it has to be defined. When it's as complex a definition as that, it's pretty hard to count.

Next the cartoonist Garry Trudeau – who had lampooned the task force for months – went public about research which showed that North Koreans were best at maths but thought they were the worst, while for Americans it was the other way round. Was US self-esteem actually getting in the way? Or are we defining it in the wrong way again? Then there were the seven professors the task force had commissioned. They admitted that the links between self-esteem and the social issues Vasconcellos had been committed to tackling remained unproven. However much they stacked up the statistics, and talked about common sense, they just couldn't prove that crucial link.

Vasconcellos defended the idea: 'Just because the causality chain is incomplete with regard to self-esteem, it does not mean that it is implausible.'

The problem of cause and effect keeps coming up when you rely too much on quantification. Are people on drugs because of low self-esteem, or is it the other way round? Four out of five studies show a link between self-esteem and teenage pregnancy – 'anti-social teenage girls don't get violent,' said Vasconcellos, 'they get pregnant' – but can you be absolutely sure they don't have low self-esteem *because* they're pregnant? Are the schoolchildren improving because of the self-esteem training or just because people are paying them more attention? Or even more centrally, are people successful because they have self-esteem, or do they just like themselves because they're successful? Once again, it has to come down to common sense and intuition.

Then two things happened to blunt the growth of the self-esteem idea. The first was the California budget crisis, after the electorate voted to seriously cut taxes. The second event was 'emotional intelligence'.

Daniel Goleman, a journalist on psychological matters on the *New York Times*, published his book with this title in 1995 and it was an immediate bestseller (selling getting on for three million copies around the world). Goleman tells the story of a elderly Japanese man on the Tokyo metro who calmed a large and aggressive drunk who was threatening the passengers. The last thing they saw was the drunk in tears, laying his head on the lap of the old man and telling him about his dead wife. 'That is emotional brilliance,' said Goleman.

America had bought into self-esteem in a populist way. Writers like Jack Canfield and Nathaniel Brandon had bestselling feelgood books out. Corporations were organizing humour workshops for their staff. There were even cartoons poking gentle fun at families standing outside in their gardens, feeling the warm night breezes instead of sitting indoors watching the final episode of *Falconcrest*. It has been enormously influential (though slightly embarrassing to Europeans) to have children wear T-shirts that say 'If it needs to be done, I'll be the one'. Even so, self-esteem bumper stickers can occasionally give you a jolt. 'Commit Random Acts of Kindness' even reached Britain.

What Goleman tried to do was to turn the toe-curling aspects of self-esteem into something respectable for policy think-tanks. *Emotional Intelligence* did just that. Emotional intelligence, he showed, helped people to work better. It meant they were able to defuse tension, deal with racial diversity, work in teams and handle criticism – at a time when many premature deaths are caused because young men are completely unable to deal with shame. But that wasn't all. Goleman argued that emotional intelligence also made you healthier. Breast cancer sufferers, for example, found that a weekly meeting of emotional support doubled their period of survival.

Lay self-esteem and emotional intelligence side by side, and you won't see much difference, but the advent of the latter drove out the attention self-esteem was getting. 'Culture has this curious awful fascination with novelty,' Vasconcellos told me, with a slight edge to his voice.

But the problems of measuring emotional intelligence are exactly the same as measuring self-esteem. And when Goleman talked about the concept of 'flow' – that sense of letting go in the moment, that sportspeople or artists feel at their most creative and victorious – it gets even more difficult. It may be possible to start measuring such states of mind with electrodes in the brain, but in practice it's not going to be an everyday tool to check each other's pulses. Let alone the success of our schools.

Then there is hope, which he describes as a crucial element of emotional intelligence. To measure hope, you have to define it, and Goleman does it like this: 'Believing you have the will and the way to accomplish your goals, whatever they may be.' Try putting a steothoscope up to that one. But then just because measuring what's really vital is extraordinarily hard, it doesn't make those elements any less important.

IV

'What we are doing is deeply political and seriously radical,' said Gloria Steinem, the leading feminist, dressed in what looked like leopardskin trousers. 'The truth is there is already at birth a unique fellow human being – someone with all the human qualities in a unique combination, which has never happened before and will never happen again. Any process of child-rearing which isn't devoted to finding out exactly who that child is, is not proper education. Emphasizing what goes in during education, rather than what comes out, will convince a child that in order to live safely, they must become someone else.'

It was the second international conference on self-esteem, and speakers from as far afield as Poland, Ukraine and Australia took the story on further. Steinem has been the most articulate modern promoter of self-esteem, describing the moment when she meekly accepted being thrown out of a hotel lobby before interviewing a celebrity because she was an unaccompanied woman – before going back the next day and clearly and confidently making things clear to the manager. She is also an exponent of a healthily un-pragmatic and non-Utilitarian social philosophy: that we are not all numbers and we all have something individual that counts. 'Most of all we have to have faith that everything we do matters,' she told us in Cambridge. 'And understand that the end doesn't justify the means.' Bentham wouldn't have liked it.

The conference was organized by the UK Self-Esteem Network, launched the same year as a similar but higher-profile organization. Antidote was founded by film journalist James Park. He had been advised by therapist Susie Orbach that, if he wanted there to be an organization working for more 'emotional literacy', he would have to start it himself. The economic case was already being made – legal costs related to marital breakdown in the UK come to £330 million, alcohol costs the country £2.4 billion, a third of all sick leave is related to anxiety and depression – but it somehow required a different kind of counting, they felt. They wanted to measure 'emotional and social well-being'.

'We keep on using economic data when it comes to talking about the causes of crime or well-being, when it really doesn't tell us anything,' he told me in their offices in London's Barbican. 'The idea is to bring the reverence for economic data down a few notches and show how little it actually reveals, and allowing emotional "indicators" to be used alongside.'

'But isn't that just swapping one set of bizarre measurements for another?' I asked.

'No, we don't want indicators for that. We want emotional indicators to give us a revised basis for hypotheses about what might be going on. It's not about saying that the reason why crime has gone up is that the emotional indicators have gone down by 0.2 points. That would be absurd. But at the moment, one element in the equation lacks the spurious credibility that the figures give it.' The really frightening thing about being director of Antidote, Park told me, was meeting economists who really couldn't see the point.

The problem for the self-esteemers is that they all suffer from the same very practical problem: how do you convince a world obsessed with measurements that you are right? 'If you don't measure it, it doesn't count,' said the economist John Kenneth Galbraith. It remains a problem, and it means that exponents of self-esteem as a basis for measuring the success of institutions will have to rely on convincing the world via gut feeling and shock value.

The reaction to media appearances on the subject by Susie Orbach herself was more convincing than any facts she brought to bear. No media interview with her can go by without reference to her authorship of *Fat is a Feminist Issue*, or the fact that she was Princess Diana's therapist. Having got past that – and putting the case for emotional literacy on a BBC panel discussion in 1996 – she was greeted by an assortment of columnists and politicians who reacted with a sniggering mixture of cynicism and alarm. 'We don't want to encourage people to let everything "hang out"!' said a Conservative former Home Secretary. You could almost hear his little shiver of revulsion. Somehow his reaction and her insistence that they were aiming for exactly the reverse was a better confirmation of her arguments than anything else she could have said.

But the message does seem to be getting through, despite the impossibility of measuring emotional literacy directly. Business is showing more interest than any other sector in the idea, and this is no coincidence. Nor is it just that Vasconcellos happens to represent the new emerging information economy from Silicon Valley, paying a critical role swinging them behind Bill Clinton in his original bid for the presidency in 1992. Because if politicians still insist on measuring school pupils in a one-dimensional way, then employers are increasingly looking for people a little bit broader.

They are learning that happy well-balanced staff are more productive. According to one study of UK manufacturing companies in 1999, in fact, corporate culture can make between 10 and 29 per cent difference in profits. Another study in Bell Laboratories in Princeton showed that their star performers were not those with the highest IQs but those with the most successful interpersonal strategies. That's the attraction of employing more women and it's why businesses are urgently researching how to build trust.

The full flowering of this idea is appearing – rather shockingly in its surprise value – in the courses run in American corporations by the British poet David Whyte. 'Continually calling on its managers for more creativity, dedication, and adaptability, the American corporate world is tiptoeing for the first time in its short history into the very place from whence that dedication, creativity, and adaptability must come: the turbulent place where the soul of an individual is formed and finds expression,' says Whyte in his book *The Heart Aroused* –

with the tremendous sub-title *Poetry and the Preservation of the Soul in Corporate America*. 'The sound and the fury of an individual's creative life are the elemental waters missing from the dehydrated workday.'

Poetry at work, art in prisons, stories in the surgery, they are all an alternative approach to the dry analysis of numbers. Their advocates say: 'Forget the numbers for a minute. How do we inject humanity and life back into this situation?' Their answers are intuitive, disturbing sometimes, and impossible to measure directly. They tend to exalt creativity as a way of liberating the best in people. They are what would, in other circles, be called 'holistic'. Everything they stand for rejects the idea of chopping problems up into neat pieces, measuring them and puzzling out what affects what.

VI

Blundering around in the fog while on holiday near the Santa Lucia Mountains in California in the early 1960s, the psychologist Abraham Maslow stumbled upon the retreat centre where, a decade later, Vasconcellos would bring the battling legislators from Sacramento for a naked soak in the hot springs. The Esalen Institute was then attracting theologians like Paul Tillich, therapists like Carl Rogers and mystics like Carlos Castaneda and was fast becoming one of the founding influences on the Summer of Love and the New Age movement.

It was an argument over Maslow that caused Vasconcellos and the new Governor Reagan to fall out over dinner the first time they met. And it was Maslow's relationship with Esalen Institute, before he died in 1970, that popularized his so-called Hierarchy of Needs – now the basis of a great deal of modern marketing. He argued that you can't just measure people's needs and desires – they have lots of different ones. They start with food and clothing, and then when those are satisfied, they move up the hierarchy to shelter. Then to needs like keeping up with the Joneses, and beyond that to some of the sophisticated consumers of today, in control of their needs for the lower steps of the ladder, who want fitness, education, self-improvement. Different aspects of their personality need different things at different times of their lives. There's no bottom line.

There's no bottom line with intelligence either, because there is more than one kind – the great discovery of the visionary educationalist Howard Gardner, whose 1983 book *Frames of Mind* pointed out something which now seems obvious. Measuring people's intelligence by IQ alone means almost nothing unless you measure their other kinds of intelligence too, and educate them to get what they need at different levels of Maslow's hierarchy.

The controversy over IQ has been raging for most of the past century, and in some ways it prefigured more recent versions of the same issue – that one number can't possibly measure the success of companies, nations or cities in any meaningful way. But IQ has a darker side which the other arguments don't share, catalogued in Stephen Jay Gould's book *The Mismeasure of Man*, because of the way the figures are used, as if it measured something fixed and unchangeable about people. As if IQ (which originally included questions about baseball players to people who spoke no English) could be used to rank classes or races. As if it could somehow measure 'worth': 'This will ultimately result in curtailing the reproduction of feeble-mindedness and in the elimination of an enormous amount of crime, pauperism and industrial inefficiency,' wrote Lewis Terman chillingly. Terman tested every US army recruit in the First World War, and went on to try measuring the IQ of long-dead scientists and artists by analysing the length of their entries in encyclopaedias.

The problem about IQ as a way of testing pupils is that it is supposed to be a fixed evaluation of their abilities. It doesn't tell teachers anything about what they can do to help the child. And it explains nothing about how it is often the children with high IQs who go to pieces, join mind-bending cults or hang themselves in their bedrooms. And it says absolutely nothing about emotions and the ability to handle them and use them.

If Erasmus was right in his medieval calculation that the ratio of emotion to reason is 24 to one (though that's not something you can measure either) it makes some kind of emotional education all the more vital.

'We have gone too far in emphasizing the value and import of the purely rational, of what IQ measures, in human life,' wrote Daniel Goleman. 'Intelligence can come to nothing when emotions hold sway.' Whatever Jeremy Bentham and Sherlock Holmes might have thought, the mind doesn't work at its best without being able to understand, filter and use emotions.

But even if the narrowness of schooling isn't very important in itself, there seems to be a good business reason for letting IQ quietly drop. Narrow measures of people aren't very useful any more. They never gave a very good picture, but the new economy has no place for people educated to sift facts and figures and nothing else. It needs imagination, empathy, creativity and the ability to work in groups. It doesn't need one-dimensional machines. And it certainly doesn't need narrow psychological or educational measurements, cooked up in a laboratory, which reduce real life to one irrelevant dimension.

Self-esteem, emotional intelligence, emotional literacy are all ways of measuring the success of schools, which don't reduce human individuals, and which can inject life, spirit and significance back into the business of education – and medicine too. They are all symptoms of a shift away from too many numbers, which amount to the first glimmerings of a new kind of ideology. The danger is that, once the number-crunchers get their hands on them, they are reduced again to technocratic and simplistic measures that leave the basic problems untouched. We can't escape from the basic problem, however much we might want to. There's no two ways about it: the best recruitment policy focuses on individual jobs and individual applicants. The best education policy focuses on each pupil individually. This may not be achievable in the short-term, but it will always be true.

The idea of tailoring education policy to every pupil seems like a revolutionary idea, but something similar has been going on in business for years with the idea of what business guru Martha Rogers first called 'mass customization' – that companies can customize products for each individual customer. Businesses are telling customers – as they say on the Levi-Strauss website: 'There's only one rule. Be original. Other than that, just be your self. Hopefully you're both.' Wouldn't it be so much more effective if school or prison management could give up all these aggregated numbers and do the same?

In the meantime, ideas like self-esteem have managed to escape from the old closed-minded ideologies of the past, which forced the facts to fit the frame, providing a structure which brings common sense to bear on the dead world of figures, so we can see patterns again. We may not be able to measure trust – or feelgood, or self-esteem – but we know what it is when we see it. That requires human institutions that make people happy in the round, and humans to run them. It doesn't need schools like factories that define learning in such a narrow way that it is sucked dry of all joy.

You can't measure these human attributes directly, but that doesn't mean they're not important. Quite the reverse: they are a different kind of bottom line altogether – one which doesn't reduce people or squeeze the truth. Or as Vasconcellos puts it: '*We* are the bottom line.'

Bizarre measurement No. 6
Cran

(*A British unit of measurement for fresh herrings. 1 cran = 37.5 gallons of fish.*)

....

Cost of an online marriage on internetmarriage.com: **$24.45** (an online divorce costs $8.15)

Number of times people have sex around the world every day: **120 million**

Chapter 6

Historical Interlude 3:
Social Copernicus

Things hang together in a perplexing tangle of causation beyond the possibility of unravelment. The moral question rests at the bottom. On it rests the economic; and on both is built up the standard of life and habit. Then all act and react on each other; and to be attacked, must be attacked together.
Charles Booth, *Life and Labour of the People of London*, Vol 16

The sign of a truly educated man is to be deeply moved by statistics.
George Bernard Shaw

I

It was an age where there was barely a Victorian who did not conceal about their person a microscope, butterfly net or measuring tape. And none more enthusiastically than the Bristol doctor John Beddoe, whose life's mission – begun while filling in the long periods between patients at his sparsely-attended practice – was to measure everyone's head. It was Beddoe's self-appointed task to track down the old 'races' of Britain, the Vikings, Belgae, Celts, defining their hair and eye colour and facial features and head shape, all marked down on little cards which Beddoe carried with him everywhere.

He began his method on a trip to the Orkneys in 1853 and his work culminated in the publication of *The Races of Britain*, involving 300 volunteers out measuring heads around the country on his behalf. But this was a peculiar example of the difficulties of relying too much on measuring. What do you say to a stranger before 'hold still while I just whip out my measuring tape'? Beddoe solved the problem in particularly disreputable pubs by starting arguments about who had the biggest head. The betting would become so heated that Beddoe would normally have to step in to settle the matter, and to note down his precious data.

The Victorians were obsessed with the size of people's heads, driven by the thrill of phrenology, beginning with Franz-Joseph Gall in 1825 – the idea that bumps on the skull corresponded with aptitudes. Coachloads of scientists left their heads to science, so they could be measured and compared, including Gall, whose brain turned out to be considerably smaller than his contemporaries'. As, incidentally, was Einstein's: brain size is another measurement that misses the point.

For most of Queen Victoria's reign, the nation was swept by crazes for measuring and collecting. After the publication of G. W. Francis' *An Analysis of British Ferns and their Allies* (1837), everyone was out collecting ferns. Or flowers after *Handbook of British Flora* was published in 1858 by George Bentham (Jeremy's nephew). Or insects after *Ants, Bees and Wasps* (1874) by the banker and popular scientist Sir John Lubbock – a man so impatient to get to his work table in the mornings that he invented himself a pair of elastic-sided boots. Whole coastlines were stripped of their wild flowers by marauding collectors. Whole nations of butterflies were pinned in glass cases, whole ants' nests transported to glass formicariums on green leather desks.

It was the great age of the amateur naturalist, coming to terms with the meaning of natural history by counting and measuring, like trainspotters trying to imbibe the meaning of railways by noting down the number of wheels in their notebooks. At the same time, scientists were pushing out the boundaries of numbers. People like Edward Stanley, counting the prayer books, literacy and religious attendance of his long-suffering tenants in Alderley. Or like Darwin's nephew Francis Galton as he battled for his new 'scientific priesthood'. Galton invented a series of hidden machines that could measure the dullness of meetings, by measuring the number of times a person fidgets.

And while the natural historians were busy counting species, their counterparts were busy doing the same process in Africa, mapping new geographies, measuring new rivers or – like the explorer John Speke on his 1860 expedition – measuring the precise size of the gigantic wives of the Ugandan king of Karagwe, who were too fat to stand upright.

It was the days of 'darkest Africa', or 'Dr Livingstone I presume' and the Gatling gun, and in the middle of all this, a new vista of measuring opened up under the very noses of the Victorians. 'As there is a darkest Africa, so also is there a darkest England,' said the founder of the Salvation Army, 'General' William Booth. 'With ease and celerity, could you send me to Darkest Africa or Innermost Tibet,' the writer Jack London told Thomas Cook in his best journalistic rhetoric. 'But to the East End of London, barely a stone's throw distant from Ludgate Circus, you know not the way!'

Then, as now, official figures left out the answers which many people really wanted to know about their cities, and the lack of knowledge grew to forbidding proportions. How many prostitutes were there in London, for example? Henry Mayhew, the great observer of London life, estimated it at 80,000. *The Lancet* in 1857 came up with a figure of one woman in 16, and one house in 60. Nobody knew. But towards the end of the century, the answers to this and many other questions about London were suddenly answered. And all because of a shipowner called Charles Booth.

In 17 volumes of detailed research, it was Booth who set about mapping what he called the *'terra incognita'* of London, working far into the night for 17 years in the belief that the structures of society were unravelling under the threat of social unrest. He counted poverty, jobs, books, bibles, pigeon-fanciers, morality – building up as complete a picture of London as ever has been produced. It was Booth who, with his small white beard and elongated body, wandered around every street in London in his homburg hat, as the contradictions about his life and role grew ever sharper. A conservative who laid the foundations of the Welfare State and old age pensions. A 'reverent unbeliever' who devoted years to the study of religious life. A number-cruncher with a deep and growing suspicion that counting was not providing him with the answers he needed.

II

How did a shipping magnate end up tramping the streets of London measuring poverty and pioneering sociology? It's an unusual shift, and not explained by a major change of direction, by war, politics or bankruptcy. It isn't the kind of thing you expect of captains of industry today, any more than you did in the 1880s when Booth was setting out – for a bet as much as for anything else – on his gigantic counting exercise. But probably the clues to his unusual life are in Liverpool, where he was born on 30 March 1840 at 27 Bedford Street, a terraced house with a garden at the back, near where the Anglican cathedral is now. Like Bentham and Chadwick, his mother died when he was young. Charles left school at 16 – his years of education seemed mainly to consist of doing drill in the police shed – and began work as an apprentice to the shipping firm Lamport & Holt.

He was soon running his own fur-trading business with his brother Alfred. Standing in front of a map of the world with his sister's in-laws, the Holts, Charles regarded the atlas like a medieval Pope dividing the globe. Don't go east, said Alfred Holt, because our shipping line is operating there. Go west from New York and we'll help all we can. With a new mania for figures, Charles went back to New York demanding that his brother send more and more facts about existing services between New York, Central America and the West Indies. He devised a way of summing up any given business situation in figures and, by 1865, had decided to invest the whole of their family capital into two new ships to service the ports of Para, Maranhem and Ceara in South America.

They cost £16,000 each and his sister Emily launched the first, the SS *Augustine*, with a bottle of champagne in Liverpool. At the age of 25, Booth co-owned his own shipping line. When he set sail for the first time, he left behind the rest of their entire staff in Liverpool – his brother Alfred Booth and the office boy – and set to with a will. Just seven years later, he was in such a state of mental and physical collapse, that he abandoned the business for Switzerland, unsure whether he would ever recover.

Of course he pushed himself hard, ruining the health of his business partners, and that must have taken its toll on himself. But the mystery of his breakdown probably has more to do with his complex personality and the contradictory feelings he had about religion and politics. He was deeply religious, but found it increasingly difficult to believe – Darwin's *Origin of Species* had been published when he was nineteen. And he had been influenced by the 'positivism' of his cousins – the idea that only the things you can count can exist: 'Science must lay down afresh the laws of life,' he said: like the Utilitarians, the positivists believed in starting with a blank sheet of paper. 'I feel assured that the principles of Positivism will lead us on until we find the true solution to the problem of government.'

He was also increasingly critical of the kind of smug middle-class philanthropy carried out by his neighbours in affluent Liverpool. Here he was influenced by his wife. Charles Booth was not born into the tradition of Utilitarian number-crunchers – he was married into it. Mary's father, Charles Zachary Macaulay, was secretary to the Board of Health – after Chadwick's departure – and Commissioner of Audit.

Booth was one who, as he put it, 'reaches the point of marriage slowly, with many misgivings'. And it took him three years to marry Mary, discovering in her an intellectual equal with decided and conflicting views of her own. Under her influence, he firmly rejected the prevailing view of poverty – caused by 'idleness, gluttony, drink, waste, profligacy, betting and corruption', according to the chairman of the Congregational Union. He couldn't help noticing that many of the despised poor led considerably more God-fearing lives than he did. He believed that wealth and success gave him obligations – his idea of business was to pay as much as he could and sell as cheap as he could, not the other way round. But what was he to do personally? He earned more money than he needed. Should he give it away, or would that make things worse? Should he pay more for his everyday food? Should he pay his workforce more? He and Mary steadfastly refused to put on the lavish dinner parties of their neighbours, limiting them to three courses only, but should they do more?

By 1873, the moral crisis was preventing him from sleeping. He didn't seem able to digest food. He dragged himself back from his breakdown in Switzerland and for the rest of the decade hovered between saving the business and complete collapse. He worked 12-hour days, living off vegetables and cider, staving off seasickness at sea by drinking champagne and reading Trollope. By the age of 40, the business was so successful that Booth was able to buy a luxurious country house – Gracedieu Manor in Leicestershire. Mary's cousin Beatrice Potter, who was to be so important in his life and – as Beatrice Webb – in all our lives in the next century, describes meeting him then for the first time.

> Nearing forty years of age, tall, abnormally thin, garments hanging as if on pegs, the complexion of a consumptive girl, and the slight stoop of the sedentary worker, a prominent aquiline nose, with moustache and pointed beard barely hiding a noticeable Adam's apple, the whole countenance dominated by a finely-moulded brow and large, observant grey eyes, sitting through meals occasionally picking at a potato or nibbling a dry biscuit

Beatrice was in the throes of a long and miserable affair with the radical Liberal politician, and mayor of Birmingham, Joseph Chamberlain. She was also suffering from what was clearly a family problem: nagging worries about the 'useless-ness of life'. With the depression in the 1870s and the influx of refugees from the famine in Ireland and the pogroms of eastern Europe, poverty was to become the key issue of the next decade.

Booth was always horrified by socialism, but he was fasci-nated by the debate. Then in 1885, the situation exploded.

The Social Democratic Federation – led by the radical Old Etonian journalist H. M. Hyndman – published a survey which showed that 25 per cent of Londoners were living in extreme poverty. It was inflammatory. Riots followed. Nobody had ever come up with that kind of statistic before, and the campaigning editor W. T. Stead threw the weight of the *Pall Mall Gazette* behind the story. Stead was one of the original investigative journalists, ending his life on the *Titanic*. At that moment, he was facing arrest for buying a 13-year-old girl for £5 in the back streets of Marylebone, to prove that white slavery was alive and well. There was little he wasn't prepared to do to shock conventional opinion.

Booth was absolutely outraged. Although he had never met him before (he never met his namesake William Booth either) he went straight round to Hyndman's house to tell him personally just what he thought of that kind of cheap incendiary sensationalism. What's more, he would prove that the 25 per cent figure was wrong. He would pay out of his own pocket to establish the truth. And in this way, just as those Conservative MPs in the 1980s took bets about whether they could live on unemployment benefit for a week, Booth was drawn into his life's work by a wager with a socialist.

The bet changed his life. Within a couple of decades, he was the most famous sociologist in the country, and his inquiry was so famous that all you had to do was put the words 'Mr Booth's Inquiry' at the top of a questionnaire, and people would fill it in. It was one of those moments when people stumble over their true purpose of existence.

III

Even at the beginning of his survey, Booth was getting suspicious of his old positivist friends. Unlike his predecessors, he could already sense that it wasn't enough just to count. He decided to approach the truth by mixing statistics with personal observation, to find the mid-point between quantity and quality. Figures 'mislead from want of due proportion or from lack of colour,' he told his even more sceptical friend Canon Barnett. Yet he was also determined that this should be a completely objective survey, measuring poverty without emotion, ideology or solutions. Only when the facts were absolutely clear might he come round to setting out any suggestions about what might be done about it. Booth's tragedy was that this mythical moment never quite arrived. He could never quite make up his mind.

Nobody turned up to the meetings of his Board of Statistical Research, which he had set up to oversee the project. So, with his assistant Beatrice (she was desperate for some kind of distraction from looking after her invalid father) they set up in his office off Gracechurch Street, struggling towards what would be a new foolproof method.

The breakthrough came in a letter to Beatrice from Chamberlain. Why not start by interviewing the school board visitors, he suggested – then check what they say about each family with door-to-door interviews, discussions with the police and with anyone else who could help. Booth embraced the idea immediately. The trouble was the size of the task. The population of London was then around four million and it looked as though he might be the only interviewer. 'The task was tremendous; the prospects of its completion so remote; and every detail cost time,' he complained, as he began to juggle the burgeoning project with his shipping line.

The pattern of his next 17 years was being set. He devoted the daytimes to business, eating fruit at his desk to avoid the effort of lunch and devoting the hour after dinner to his family – when he usually fell asleep. By 10pm, he was free to return to his hobby, sometimes walking the streets, sometimes writing up the statistics gathered by his assistants, constantly urged by his wife to limit this work to just three hours a day. Then at the end of the week, it was the long cross-country train journey back to Gracedieu, with so many candles perched along the carriage window sill to light his work that – more than once – he was mistaken for a travelling grocer. Then in the early hours of Monday, back to London. 'In the early chills of the morning, greetingless, fireless and breakfastless – I woke to find you gone,' wrote Mary to him as she settled back to her own role in the project: secretly vetting and re-writing every finished page of his reports. The most quoted paragraphs are nearly all hers.

The first interviews took place at 7.30 pm on 1 and 2 September 1886, as Booth sat with his pencil ready to put the first piece of order on the chaos that was London – speeded in his work by growing concerns about socialist agitation and the urgency of an answer. 'Against this method of agitators who class all the working classes together as starving millions I strongly protest,' he said. 'And I do so all the more that I am deeply in earnest in my desire that the conditions under which the mass of people live should be improved, as well as those who now suffer actual distress.'

It was an important distinction, between those who are really poor and those who have poverty thrust upon them by their hopeless husbands. He was especially ambitious to find out the part really played by drink in poverty as popular mythology claimed. But how do you define the poor people you need to count? To do so, Booth invented the idea of the 'poverty line'. He set this at 10 to 20 shillings a week for an average family of four or five people. This was 'primary poverty', poverty because you didn't have enough money. It was arbitrary, of course. A poverty line which really meant anything – as Booth realized – would have to be drawn individually for each family. And his definition has caused controversy ever since: these days we tend to measure 'standards of deprivation' set in the 1960s – a kind of relative poverty – which include people who can't afford a holiday, birthday party or the occasional meal out.

After eight months, he was able to do a paper for the Royal Statistical Society about Tower Hamlets. But to his astonishment, he discovered that Hyndman had been wrong. In fact, Hyndman had *under*-estimated the extent of poverty in London. Moving on to Hackney, he went back to the parish of St George's-in-the-East only to find it was even worse than he had previously thought. Even with Booth's narrow definition, 30.7 per cent of Londoners were living in poverty.

Drink was clearly a factor, but it wasn't the cause. It might even be the result of poverty: Booth was falling foul of the perennial problem for number-crunchers – an inability to work out what causes what. But in the whole of the East End, he reckoned that only about 14 per cent of poverty seemed to have anything to do with addiction to alcohol – and this had more to do with women than men. 'This latter phase seems to be one of the expected results of the emancipation of women,' wrote Booth.

Even more shockingly, he publicly praised those supposed dens of iniquity, the East End pubs – and did so from personal experience: 'Behind the bar will be a decent middle-aged woman, something above her customers in class, very neatly dressed, respecting herself and respected by them,' he wrote. 'The whole scene is comfortable, quiet and orderly.'

The first volume of *Life and Labour of the People of London* was published in April 1889, to a city building up to the Great Dock Strike. The first edition sold out quickly, and Beatrice was praised by the reviewers for her work describing life in the Docks and the Jewish community. 'The book is entirely without literary merit but contains information useful for philanthropists,' wrote *The Athenaeum*. Stead's *Pall Mall Gazette* described Booth as a 'Social Copernicus'.

His detailed house-by-house descriptions of streets had an enormous impact. There was Shelton Street, in Covent Garden, now the venue for boutiques and expensive bars, and then as now filled with young men drinking beer in doorways. But then it was the home to 200 families in forty houses, most living in rooms about eight foot square, and making a living selling flowers, fruit, chickens or vegetables at the nearby market by day, sleeping in beds curtained off at the side of the room by night. Though on hot nights, most would just sit fully-clothed in the least vermin-infested corner of the room. These are people like Eliza Doolittle from George Bernard Shaw's play *Pygmalion*. This is in his description of nearby Parker Street:

At No 19 on the ground floor there was a woman with two grown-up daughters, all looking hardened in sin. They would beg for a bread ticket as though they had not broken fast for days, but if refused would alter to a fiendish grin and the most fearful language would follow, the strength of voice and expression leaving no doubt as to the absence of food or ill-health. In the first floor lived the Neals. The man had been a soldier and now earns his living as a market porter; his wife was fast breaking up and his son, a tall fellow of twenty-two, appeared to be in rapid consumption; the daughter also grown-up, sold flowers in the street. All four lived and slept in this room. In the back room lived a family consisting of mother, a son of twenty, a daughter of twelve, and an old grandmother who looked eighty – who gets her living as a crossing-sweeper and gets a lot of food and coal tickets given. The mother sells in the streets but suffers from asthma, and the son a few months ago was at the point of death from the same complaint. The girl also looked in a wretched condition – patches of plaster protruding where the walls had been roughly mended, windows stuffed with rags or mended with paper – vermin everywhere.

Parker Street looks different now. No 19 is between the office for the Elite Model Agency and the theatre showing *Cats*, but has been replaced by a hideous late Victorian block of flats. History doesn't relate what the families felt – if indeed they ever discovered that their lives had been laid bare on the printed page.

IV

'We are very fond of each other,' Beatrice confided in her diary in 1887, well into the first year of working side by side with Booth. 'A close intimate relationship between a man and a woman without sentiment (perhaps not without sentiment, but without passion or the dawning of passion). We are fellow workers both inspired by the same intellectual desire.' But it was all about to change. If he had still not reached any conclusion about his figures, Beatrice had. She now believed in municipal workshops as a solution to low and intermittent wages. And, worse, she had met and secretly become engaged to a socialist: the frighteningly intelligent socialist Sidney Webb. 'A huge head and a tiny body', she confided in her diary.

The Booths couldn't stand him. Trying to avoid the awkwardness, Beatrice suggested to Mary that they ignore the engagement. Mary breathed a sigh of relief: 'You see Charlie and I have nothing in common with Mr Webb,' she wrote back. 'Charlie would never go to him for help, and he would never go to Charlie, so that it would not be natural for them to see each other. When you are married it will be different.'

But it wasn't. The rift grew and as Sidney and Beatrice embraced the new Fabian Society and set about making the next century in the image of dull, authoritarian socialism, and as Charles continued to agonize about coming to any sure conclusion, they and the Booths drifted further and further apart. It was the end of a fifteen-year relationship. 'When I strained it, I should have thought slightly, it broke – or rather I found that it was already broken,' wrote Beatrice later. 'Even today I have not yet fully recovered from my amazement and wonder at this fact.'

Booth didn't seem to notice. He was off on the second phase of his gigantic project, looking at the work and living conditions of Londoners. And although Beatrice wasn't there this time, Booth took her great lesson to heart. She had learned 'how to sweat' as a tailor's assistant in order to write about the rag trade. So when he divided the classes from A (underclass) to H (upper middle class), he set about sharing lives. He took lodgings in houses typical of classes C, D and E, to find out about life around the poverty line.

'CB went to live in the East End,' said Mary's diary baldly, hiding what an extraordinary thing this was to do in late Victorian England. He refused to disguise himself, but seemed accepted by his fellow lodgers as he caught fleas and filled his notebooks with details like the frozen garbage in the gutters. A man of his time, he seemed to feel no shame at all – no sense of apology for landing on them from his different station, as modern Booths would probably consider natural. One working class family he stayed with in Liverpool only discovered who he was when he suddenly invited them to work as caretakers at Gracedieu.

To match and check the poverty line, Booth introduced the idea of 'crowding', of not having enough space to live in, like the Neals in Parker Street. Striving for an objective system of measurement that he could apply to any city from New York to Calcutta, he applied it rigorously to London – 31.5 per cent of the city was crowded. Again, it was not an objective test. Just because people were richer, they might not choose to spend their money on more space. But he set about classifying streets in eight colours from black to yellow – with black lines to indicate 'vice' – and put them up on an enormous map of London 16ft by 13ft, still on display at the London School of Economics, and now available on the Internet.

Worst of all again was St George's-in-the-East with 48.9 per cent poverty and 57 per cent crowding, where 'the temptation to drink to excess . . . comes with especial strength'. Best on all measures was what Booth called 'happy, happy Hampstead'.

It was still a gigantic undertaking, as Booth and his assistants wandered back across every street, counting, classifying and bringing the information back. His work was now world-famous. He was in a unique position as a wealthy industrialist and leading expert on poverty and social conditions, but (to the exasperation of the Webbs) there was still no solution. Why did he not do a little less counting and a little more campaigning work for change? Yet at the end of volume 9, the message was the same: 'I shall still attempt no answer . . . in spite of the length to which it has attained, I have to ask once more the patience of my readers.'

He was increasingly influential. Seebohm Rowntree was confirming his figures in his detailed surveys of York and other researchers were copying his methods, but as the century ground towards its close, Booth was increasingly aware of the limitations of numbers. He felt as far away as ever from the truth of what was really important – the interplay of forces between good and evil. So he embarked on the third and final phase of his study, to uncover the moral and religious influences in London.

But measuring people's religion and morals was far more difficult, so for his latest project he would rely more on personal observation. This time, he would put aside numbers altogether. Enthusiastically, he wrote to the leaders of all the church denominations asking for their help. He had assistants set about interviewing every clergyman and social agency in London. The office piled up with pamphlets, annual reports, leaflets and parish magazines. Sunday after Sunday he spent in different churches, staying just long enough to get the feel of the proceedings then moving on to the next. For the rest of the week he would walk with the local police down every street. Then he would take the data back to the office and transfer it to colour codes on the wall map – scarlet for places of worship, black for pubs and places selling booze, blue for schools.

The problem was the usual one: cause and effect. Just because people went to church, did that make them better people? You could count until you were blue in the face, and still not work that out. 'Spiritual influences do not lend themselves readily to statistical treatment, and we have not attempted it,' he wrote in the first volume. 'The subject is one in which figures may easily be pressed too far and if trusted too much are likely to be more than usually dangerous. Our object, rather, has been to obtain truthful and trustworthy impressions.' How right he was.

But there was resistance to this kind of in-depth counting. The 1,800 religious interviews they carried out might take two and a half hours each or more. Some people were afraid his assistants would give their findings to the fearsome General Booth of the Salvation Army. Some just didn't like this kind of thing. 'Dear Sir,' wrote the Vicar of St Paul's, Herne Hill. 'As you have the consent of the Bishop of Rochester and Southwark I suppose I must consent to see your representative ... But I am weary and sick of the incessant "numbering of the people'' for one cause or another.' Thank goodness the poor man wasn't around a century later.

Booth's impressions were explosive. The advent of universal schooling seemed to have had a good effect on crime and on the relationship between pupils and teachers – teachers were no longer stoned by children in the street. Booth reported: 'The day was (says an old resident) when no cat would appear in the streets of Bethnal Green without being hunted and maltreated; now such conduct is rare.'

But otherwise the findings were a terrible slap in the face for the churches. He recognized that there were individual priests and ministers doing good work, but they were few and far between. Most mission work he described as having 'the character of galvanized activity without one spark of vitality'. And he reserved his special contempt for the Salvation Army, describing their threat of hellfire to the poor as 'the most awful example of theological savagery'.

He approved of the Quakers, Unitarians and Congregationalists for their social concerns and clear ethical demands. He disapproved of the Methodists and Baptists and evangelical missionaries: 'The admixture of Gospel and giving produces an atmosphere of meanness and hypocrisy, and brings discredit on both charity and religion,' he wrote. He found himself cheering on one needy old lady who steadfastly refused the Salvation Army's demands that she should 'turn to Christ'. 'I think she derived moral support from our presence,' he said, with evident relish.

He was already sceptical about organized religion by then, but he also found no evidence that it was helping improve people's condition – except as far as the people doing the charity work benefited. Christianity went with income tax, he said. If you were too poor to pay it, you seemed to be beyond the reach of any denomination. 'I try to do two things,' the Vicar of St Stephen's, North Bow told them: 'To teach men to fear God and honour the King. If I succeed in that, I don't think I can go far wrong'.

Very few people went to church, about 6 per cent in Hackney and 2 per cent in Hackney Wick, not so different from today. The Vicar of Camberwell explained that he divided his parishioners into three: '(1) The common or garden materialist (the great majority). On Sunday morning he copulates about ten times with his wife and reads *The Referee*. (2) The Superstitious who turn to Ritualism, and (3) The Devout, who in nine cases out of ten go to chapel.' Again, it's not so different a century later.

By the end of the religious series of volumes, his readers held their breaths, but Booth was as confused as ever. We need a prescription, said the younger sociologists. Hard at work in the Fabian Society, Beatrice Webb (as intense and as miserable as ever) was finally rejecting Booth's approach. Did Booth just want more and more facts, she and her associates asked? Why would he not just make up his mind? He decided on one last volume to pull the strands together, and it was eagerly awaited for the answers it might contain. But by the end of it, everything seemed to have been defined as consequences. There seemed no bright shining cause to blame and tackle. It was all effect.

'The dry bones that lie scattered over the long valley that we have traversed together lie before my reader,' he wrote in the final paragraph of the seventeenth and final volume, with a self-deprecating air of exhaustion. 'May some great soul, master of a subtler and nobler alchemy than mine, disentangle the confused issues, reconcile the apparent contradictions in aim, melt and commingle the various influences for good into one divine uniformity of effort, and make these dry bones live, so the streets of Jerusalem may sing with joy.'

When the volume was published, he was 1,000 miles up the Amazon opening the port of Manaus, so he couldn't hear either the singing or the sighs of disappointment.

V

Charles Booth had a physical breakdown two years after he finished the final volume in 1903, finding himself immediately afterwards a privy councillor and a member of the government's Tariff Commission. Yet he had come to one conclusion at least. He was convinced of the need for old age pensions, five shillings a week from the age of 65.

The figures seemed unambiguous. In Stepney, 32.8 per cent of the poverty was caused by simple old age. He raged against forcing old people into workhouses, envisaging a time when 'they can still remain members of the society to which they are accustomed, can still offer as well as receive neighbourly favours, mind a baby, sit up with a stick, chop firewood, or weed the garden. They are not cut off from the sympathies of daily existence, and their presence is often a valuable ingredient in the surrounding life.'

When he told the Royal Statistical Society his ideas in 1891, there was complete silence, and then so many people wanted to condemn him that they had to adjourn the meeting to another day. At the hostile follow-up in December that year, thick London fog came into the room and it was impossible to see who was speaking. 'Voice after voice emerged,' wrote Mary. 'All unfavourable, many whilst courteous almost contemptuous in their repudiation of so wild a project.' The massively influential Charity Organisation Society – Booth's sworn enemies for their patronizing philanthropy – called it the 'most outrageous and absurd scheme yet promulgated'. Yet his ideas were incorporated into the 1908 Pensions Act by the new Liberal Chancellor of the Exchequer David Lloyd George only 15 years later.

In the period between, and despite his health, he was appointed to the Royal Commission on the Poor Laws, and found himself once again sitting next to Beatrice Webb. But this was a different Beatrice to the woman he had collaborated with nearly 20 years before. Sidney had taken over a bunch of cranks called the Fellowship of the New Life and turned them into the Fabian Society, and together with people like George Bernard Shaw – and soon H. G. Wells – they were transforming it into a force which would mould the twentieth century. Beatrice had none of Booth's growing doubts. She and Sidney had also rejected his individualism, but they had embraced the idea of counting with missionary zeal. It was a fatal mixture.

The obsession with facts led to the foundation of the London School of Economics in 1895, and their own ten volumes of work on English local government – their major works alone amounted to five million words. It led Sidney into the cabinet in two governments and it led both finally to burial in Westminster Abbey. It was no coincidence that Sidney Webb had been the son of a radical accountant. But their collectivism also led them to a snobbish rejection of people – 'the middle class are materialistic, and the working class stupid, and in large sections sottish, with no interest except in racing odds,' wrote Beatrice in 1900. It led to the Labour Party's traditional determination to cling to central power – to high-rise flats, block votes and all the other abominations of state socialism. It led them to a fatal admiration for Soviet collectivization, defending Stalin at the height of his tyranny. 'They regarded the function of a statesman to bamboozle or terrorize the populace,' wrote Bertrand Russell about them. Their drab influence can still be discerned today – the very perversion of Bentham's ideals, yet founded on everything he wrote.

It was not a combination designed to appeal to Booth, who urged the Royal Commission to return to the principles of Chadwick's 1834 Poor Laws. He wanted the Commission to 'interfere' in the lives of his poverty-stricken class B – assuming that class A would then disappear of its own accord – so that the other classes could be left as free as possible. He called this 'limited socialism'; the Webbs wanted no limits. The petty intrigues among his fellow members infuriated him. He infuriated them by interviewing witnesses in intricate detail for five hours at a stretch, as if he was still doing his survey. In 1908, he went home in disgust and exhaustion.

By the end, Beatrice had organized an influential minority report – calling for state child care, labour exchanges, land reclamation and a national heath service, much of which came to pass – and a permanent Royal Commission Office to collect facts, which didn't. Booth refused to sign either report, and published his own evidence which described welfare payments as 'a perfect hotbed of deceit'. It was his last intervention in public life. He died at Gracedieu on 16 November 1916, three blood-soaked days before the official end of the Battle of the Somme.

It was a different world by then and Booth had been brushed aside by the twentieth century, rejected as old-fashioned and too much of a number-cruncher to change the world. But looked at almost a century later, he seems a much more modern figure than the authoritarian Fabians. He may have been paralysed by the contradictions in his own figures, but he was also too humane to draw conclusions which did not do justice to the fine mesh of individual differences. He could see the paradoxes in the poverty statistics. He could see they failed to communicate the whole truth about poverty. 'Their lives are an unending struggle and lack comfort,' he wrote about the poor he knew. 'But I do not know that they lack happiness.'

But at the time, he seemed inexplicably conservative in his indecision. 'To action I have never pretended and any claim on abstract thought I abandoned as a childish delusion,' he wrote sadly to Beatrice. 'So nothing is left for me but investigation.' He had no stomach for the new world.

The Fabian rhetoric, on the other hand, was depressingly simplistic. Individuals didn't count, but money did. 'The universal regard for money is the one hopeful fact in our civilization,' wrote Shaw in the preface to his play *Major Barbara*, the year Booth joined the Royal Commission. 'It represents health, strength, honour, generosity, as conspicuously and undeniably as the want of it represents illness, weakness, disgrace, meanness and ugliness.'

This kind of simple counting squeezes out individual differences, along with life, love and significance. It implies a narrow view of equality and the human spirit. Booth replied with what is an absolutely classic critique of counting. It is the perfect answer to Bentham:

> It is difficult for those whose daily experience or imagination brings vividly before them the trials and sorrows of individual lives, to think in terms of percentages rather than numbers. They refused to set off and balance the happy hours of the same class,

or even of the same people, against those miseries; much less can they consent to bring the lot of other classes into the account, add up the opposing figures, and contentedly carry forward a credit balance. In the arithmetic of woe they can only add or multiply, they cannot subtract or divide. In intensity of feeling such as this, and not in statistics, lies the power to move the world.

Bizarre measurement No. 7
Skot
(Unit of light, used in Germany during the Second World War to measure how much light people were showing through their blackout.)

....

Time that UK parents spend driving children to school: *1 million hours a year*

Proportion of British males who believe in aliens: *58 per cent*

Chapter 7

The New Auditors

Grown-ups love figures. When you tell them that you've made a new friend, they never ask you any questions about essential matters. They never say to you 'What does his voice sound like? What games does he love best? Does he collect butterflies?' Instead they demand 'How old is he? How much does he weigh? How much money does his father make?' Only from these figures do they think they have learned anything about him.
Antoine de Saint-Exupéry, *The Little Prince*

First comes fodder, then comes morality.
Bertolt Brecht

I

If football is the new rock 'n' roll, as they say, then information is the new money. Torrents of it flow across the world's computer screens every day. Information about value, facts, measurements, indices, all of it twitching the massive markets. It's information, rather than money, that makes the world go round and which lies behind the gigantic instantaneous fortunes of the Internet billionaires. That means global information flow can be particularly valuable.

The story goes back to 1959, which is when management guru Peter Drucker published his book *Landmarks of Tomorrow*. In it, he coined the powerful phrase 'knowledge workers' to describe the footloose, innovating people whose business is the manipulation of information or the creation of world-beating ideas. It is strange to think that within those four decades since Drucker's prediction, 'knowledge workers' have already come to make up over a third of the whole US workforce.

Drucker later described how one of the largest US defence

contractors did a survey in the 1980s to find out what kind of information was needed to do the job effectively. 'The search for answers soon revealed that whole layers of management – perhaps as many as six out of a total of fourteen – existed only because these questions had not been asked before,' he wrote. 'The company had data galore. It had always used its copious data for control rather than for information.'

It was a familiar pattern and it still is, because information and knowledge mean different things. You can have too much information. But apart from the US futurists who think our brains are about to explode with future shock, you can't possibly have too much knowledge.

There's another difference too. You can put information into figures, tables and graphs, but you can't necessarily do the same with knowledge. So most organizations and bureaucracies very much prefer the first kind. They call it 'data'. The other kinds of knowledge, often simply the kind of informal know-how which people exchange over coffee or a cigarette – but equally important to the bottom line – often gets ignored because it can't be measured. Often the people who hold it are first in the queue for downsizing.

A new fascination for measuring 'knowledge' and 'learning' is the latest in a century-long struggle by business to isolate what makes them successful in terms of figures. The pioneering time and motion studies in the early twentieth century measured efficiency, realizing how much know-how could improve the profitability of a factory. Armed with his stopwatch and clipboard, Frederick Taylor measured every movement and gesture on the assembly line, but he missed out a key asset. The time and motion experts had no interest at all in the knowledge, wisdom and skill locked up in the heads of their human cogs. Only in the knowledge of the men in white coats.

Half a century later, it was the advent of Total Quality Management, an attempt to measure quality by the American business guru W. Edwards Deming, which launched the modern business dash to measure the unmeasurable. Deming was also one of the first of what became a herd of trampling

American management gurus, but in those days he was ignored by his compatriots. Only the Japanese took any notice.

'Why is it that productivity increases as quality improves?' he asked on the first page of his book *Out of the Crisis*. It is hard to remember that, until recently, most Western companies were obsessed with how much it might cost to make sure their services and products were good enough – an affliction shared by most British governments to this day. They were afraid that too much effort put into improving quality would cut their profits. They ignored Deming's answers to his own question, which were: 'less rework' and 'not so much waste'. Yet the Japanese businesses which adopted them found that, just by counting these things differently, a whole world of greater profitability opened up.

His idea took flight after Japanese engineers studied the quality control literature from Bell Laboratories. Bell had seconded their engineers to General Douglas MacArthur's staff occupying Japan. And by 1950, every top management meeting in Japan had this 'less rework' mantra up on the blackboard behind them. So when Deming went out there the following year to give a lecture tour on his statistics, they were so pleased to see him, they created the Deming Award in his honour. It soon became the most coveted industrial prize in Japan.

Deming had a rival Total Quality Management guru, J. W. Juran. Both were understood only in Japan, and they managed to carry on the feud between them well into their late 80s. Perhaps this was because they were so similar: both grew up in tarpaper shacks, Deming in Minnesota, Juran in Wyoming – though he had actually been born in Romania. Both were influenced by the Bell Laboratories physicist Walter Shewhart, the man who turned statistical ideas into a manufacturing discipline. Both also rose to such eminence in Japan that they won the Order of the Sacred Treasure, Second Class. Goodness knows what you have to do for the first class.

Total Quality Management had given Japanese industry a powerful edge by the competitive 1980s, before a combination of Japanese banking mismanagement and the sheer economic power of Wall Street pushed the Americans back in front. By then, Western manufacturing had caught on. Toyota were implementing 5,000 quality suggestions a day from employees, but their rivals at Ford were offering over half their executive bonuses for contributions to quality. Sometimes, you will notice, it is hard even to describe these things without resorting to numbers.

The next big management idea was 're-engineering', which in practice meant sacking coachloads of staff, but in theory – according to one of its gurus, Michael Hammer – it meant making the company 'easy to do business with'. Trying to measure this elusive concept, which Hammer turned into the acronym ETDBW, led to a disturbing discovery for big manufacturers. They found that most orders went through 15 to 20 departments in the average American business before they were actually fulfilled. Each department provided an excellent opportunity for mistakes and delay. It was an expensive process too. One company found it cost $97 to fulfil an order for batteries worth just $3. One soft drinks company found that only 55 per cent of its invoices were correct.

So the stage was set for the latest twist in management thinking, and it looks as though the one who got there first was the Swedish business writer Kark-Erik Sveiby. Twenty years ago he was a partner in Sweden's oldest business magazine *Affarsvarlden*, having previously been a commercial manager at Unilever's Swedish toiletries company, and he was given the task of doing the magazine's books. This was difficult, because the magazine outsourced almost everything. They had almost no assets to put in the books, apart from their brand name, which Sveiby valued at one krona. 'I kept forgetting to put it in, so the books wouldn't balance,' he told *Fortune* magazine. 'Then I would reflect that our brand was really worth much more.'

Out of that thought emerged the Konrad Group, meeting on St Konrad's Day in Sweden and discussing how you might measure know-how in a company. Soon Japan's business guru Ikujiro Nonaka was studying how business can create knowledge, *Fortune's* columnist Thomas Stewart was starting to write about intellectual capital and the movement was beginning to grow.

As a result, Sveiby's insight has turned into a major business trend called 'knowledge management', and European companies are now spending about 5 per cent of their revenues on it. Bizarre and unexpected new job titles are popping up around the corporate world, with bizarre and unexpected salaries to match, like 'learning manager', 'knowledge engineer', 'intellectual capital controller' or 'chief knowledge officer'. Soon Coca-Cola was hiving off its tangible assets altogether in a bid to become just the sum of its brand and its management ability.

Thomas Stewart explained the problem they had. Under conventional accountancy, a company that dumps 100 delivery vans before they are worn out, has to record them in their books as a loss. But if they dump 100 employees they have trained, and who have bags of know-how and ideas about the company, they don't have to record it anywhere. In fact, they get lauded on Wall Street and their directors get even fatter pay cheques. The experience and knowledge of employees have no value on conventional measuring scales. Accountants have found it very hard to measure such things.

But they do have a value. Knowledge is wealth, in fact, which is why the old measurements don't work any more. Count up the value of companies' fixed assets and you come up with a figure wildly different from their actual value on the world markets. Securities analysts now believe that 35 per cent of market value of the stocks they follow is not covered anywhere on the balance sheets. 'How ironic,' says the American business professor Baruch Lev, 'that accounting is the last refuge of those who believe that things are assets and that ideas are expendable.'

Lev is an academic accountant who believes the whole profession is going to have to change, because the way we measure the economy is suddenly so out-of-date. His research shows that American business now invests almost as much in their intangible assets as they do in old-fashioned buildings and equipment. Microsoft is an extreme example. Its balance sheet lists assets that amount to only about 6 per cent of what the company is worth. 'In other words,' says the futurist Charles Leadbetter, '94 per cent of the value of this most dynamic and powerful company in the new digital economy is in intangible assets that accountants cannot measure.'

This is not just an interesting but useless theory. Knowledge may be intangible but it creates 'real' money. Microsoft created 21,000 millionaires among its employees in 1997 alone – and provided goodness knows how much wealth to its founder Bill Gates. Then there was the odd story of the media company DreamWorks SKG. It was formed with capital of just $250 million, but was mobbed by investors who quickly drove up its value to $2 billion, purely because of the intangible and unmeasurable value of its founders, Steven Spielberg, David Geffen and Jeffrey Katzenberg.

Now, if you were to take that intangible difference between the measurable and the unmeasurable, and put it under a microscope, what would you find? The first thing would be the mildly intangible – those legal fictions like intellectual property and copyrights – but let's put those aside for the moment, because they don't actually make up the gap. The rest is the seriously intangible, like the skills, capabilities and expertise of the workforce – or maybe even the team of outside consultants they have gathered round them – plus the value of the brand name and its future sales potential, and the reputation of the company.

Thomas Stewart defines intellectual capital as the sum of everything everybody in a company knows that gives it a competitive edge:

> It is the knowledge of a workforce. The training and intuition of a team of chemists who discover a billion-dollar new drug or the know-how of workmen who come up with a thousand different ways to improve the efficiency of a factory. It is the electronic network that transports information at warp speed through a company, so that it can react to the market faster than its rivals. It is the collaboration – the shared learning – between a company

and its customers, which forges a bond between them that brings the customer back again and again.

'Reputation, reputation, reputation,' exclaimed Othello, noticing something similar. 'I have lost the immortal part of myself, and what remains is bestial.' But how do you measure such things?

The short answer is that it is impossible, but that's not good enough for businesspeople who see their rivals making enormous profits simply from their ability to measure intangibles and sell them. Or to boost the value of their companies: Coca-Cola believes its brand name is worth $39 billion. And there are all those hi-tech companies which have never made a profit, like the Internet bookshop Amazon.com, but which still made its owners billionaires as the belief in their value shot them thrillingly up the Wall Street markets. Suddenly a website like @ Home was worth the same as Lockheed Martin, or the Internet share-trader E*Trade was worth the same as the giant American Airlines. The point was that, even if you couldn't put a value to your intangible assets yourself, the markets would measure it for you. Precisely.

As the old-fashioned measuring systems break down – those tried and tested columns invented by Fra Pacioli – the divisions between the real and the hyped begin to go fuzzy. If enough people believe it, the hyped can become real. 'Do you believe in fairies?' asks Peter Pan, and Tinkerbell recovers if the audience does. It's the same with the modern world of hi-tech stocks.

So measuring the unmeasurable matters, which is why there has been such a flurry of business gurus, all of them trying to corner the market by naming the missing factor. Should we call it 'intellectual capital' like Thomas Stewart, or 'working knowledge' like James Brian Quinn, or 'managing know-how' like Karl-Erik Sveiby? In fact three books came out with the title *Intellectual Capital* in 1997 alone. But they all agree on the main point. That easily measurable money is no longer the most scarce commodity in the world. Information, know-how, intelligence is – get hold of that and the money will pour forth. All the old-fashioned balance sheets could do was give a vague idea of what you might get for a company if you bought it, chopped it up and sold it. As one management writer said, you might as well say a human being is worth £1.90, because that is what our various chemical components might be worth.

And so it was that the Swedish company Skandia published the first annual report supplement on intellectual capital, and another Swedish company Celemi published the world's first audit of its intangible assets. Soon the idea had spread so completely to the US business world that they were convinced they had thought of it themselves, christening the whole phenomenon the 'new economy'.

'I have seen the new economy and it works!' exclaimed Vice President Al Gore. But it wasn't quite clear, even then, whether it does. The Dutch engineering business Kema put a price tag of over $400 million on its highly-intelligent staff, but then found that their $12 million profits in 1994 looked rather small in comparison. The board member responsible for IT joked that maybe they should file for bankruptcy. Other companies missed the point by sinking vast sums into their computer systems, then ignoring their staff altogether. The result was that their 'intellectual capital' often decided to look at the jobs pages, and drifted away.

ING Barings bank lost half of its most successful Taiwanese team when it just got up and walked out of the door to Merrill Lynch. This never used to happen in the good old days of measurable bricks and mortar. Suddenly an accounting problem became a serious personnel headache. There was the strange story of the sacking of advertising guru Maurice Saatchi from the company that bore his name. Saatchi forced the board to dismiss him, but he was followed out of the door by some key staff and two crucial accounts – Mars and British Airways. The stock halved in value, and the Saatchi & Saatchi shareholders found they actually only owned half of the company. The rest of the value had seeped away almost overnight.

'In the knowledge society,' writes Peter Drucker, 'the most probable assumption for organizations – and certainly the assumption on which they have to conduct their affairs – is that they need knowledge workers far more than knowledge workers need them.' If you can't measure your assets, you don't know where they are, then you may not notice when they disappear. It's not a healthy situation for a cut-throat company.

So what could they do? What they have done is to try to empower their workforce, open up information inside the company, and measure anything that moves, mining the tons of resulting data for patterns and strange parallels. And that's just the start when you are trying to measure what counts. Remember, urges the business manual *Blur*, 'every sale is an economic, informational and emotional exchange'. That means extending 'the emotional experience of your customers to every aspect of your organization'. If you thought intellectual capital was difficult to measure, try empathy.

Jeremy Bentham would be turning in his grave, if he had one. Yet businesses still have to make the attempt if they are going to measure their progress, and the difficult fact is they will probably find a way – and stake their future on it. What makes the new world of numbers different from the old is that no two companies, and probably no two people, would measure it in the same way.

II

Or try ethics. While the business world has carried on in their own sweet way looking at the bottom line figures, the profits and losses, the earnings per share, a whole sector of the financial services industry has emerged to measure companies in a different way. Not according to how much they make, but how nice they are (or how ethical) and then to invest in them accordingly. It's called ethical investment.

Ethical investment is suddenly trendy in financial services. Expensive conferences are held on the subject. Enormously expensive software is used to track the ethical performance of companies around the world. Rival tables are produced and pored over. Even Dow Jones has launched its own 'Sustainability Index'. And well over £2.8 billion is now invested ethically in the UK alone. Across the Atlantic, where 'Christian' investment goes into anti-abortion companies, they claim it is fifty times that.

The whole idea began with the investment fund Pax Christi during the Vietnam War, and grew from there via disinvestment in South Africa in the 1980s, into an industry which even the biggest pension funds have to take seriously. It also took strength from disastrous revelations of corporate greed, like *Exxon Valdez*. Or like the Bhopal disaster in 1984, when a Union Carbide toxic gas leak killed 2,500 people and injured 200,000 after misrepresenting its safety record. Now the British government has ruled that every pension fund must reveal not just its profits, but make an ethical 'statement of investment principles'.

It's a new world. Only a generation ago, General Motors chief Charlie Wilson (later US Defence Secretary) could say in public that: 'What's good for the country is good for General Motors, and what is good for General Motors is good for the country.' These days we don't see 'good' in such clear-cut, easily measurable, Utilitarian terms. Instead we try to give our lives more of a moral coherence, a kind of joined-up self-government, so that we don't spend our lives campaigning for the protection of tropical forests only to find our pension money is invested in logging companies. And we don't pray for peace, only to find our hard-won savings are invested in boosting Britain's arms exports to unsavoury regimes.

Quite what we do next is still argued about, but we start by measuring the moral efficacy of our investments. We ask about interest rates less and about human rights policies more. Then we invest in the companies with the cleanest or greenest record. It's rather a strange shift, especially for hard-nosed business people who had never looked anywhere but the bottom line before.

As the years have gone by, the fashions have changed. Should we be avoiding what's downright wrong or should we be seeking out the good and investing in it – or some strange combination of the two? The return of what they call 'positive criteria' – measuring the good in companies rather than the bad – has been steady over the past few years, with the UK ethical investment researchers EIRIS starting to screen companies according to their positive employment and environmental policies. In the UK, the massive £20 billion pension fund run by British Coal have adopted just such a policy – denying that it is anything more than hard-headed economic sense. 'Obviously if you are a major polluter, then that is going to cut into your future profits,' they said. British Coal have since been followed by the other two pension funds in the biggest three – BT's and the university lecturers.

As always, measuring something like ethics depends on how you define it. That has become the job of the 25-strong staff of the EIRIS, perched in their offices above the railway line at Vauxhall Station – their intensive meetings drowned out every few minutes by the roar of the Eurostar express dashing along underneath. It's their job to define exactly what we mean by human rights, or 'involvement in genetically modified food', and to scour the media for the growing bundles of stories where companies get caught out in 'unethical' activity. They get paid to do this because – now that the ethical investors are flexing their muscles across the world – then dumping an oil-rig on the bed of the North Sea (like Shell) can cost you a lot of money. So can teaming up with an American TV evangelist who vilifies homosexuals (like the Bank of Scotland).

This is the strange paradox of ethical investment. It began as a way for people to accept a lower return for their money because they were keeping their consciences cleaner. But now there are so many of them that the money seems to be going their way too. Generally speaking, and in the long term, ethical companies seem to perform just as well. There are now so many ethical investors that sustainable strategies can raise a company's share price by 15 per cent, according to the latest study. Two American academics worked out that winning an environmental award boosts your share price by an average of 0.82 per cent. Bribery or corruption accusations cut it by

2.3 per cent. That is, I suppose, as precise a measurement of the money value of morality as it's possible to get. But when an undercover journalist secretly filmed animal rights abuses taking place in laboratories owned by Huntington Life Science a few years ago, and showed what she shot on Channel 4, their share price slumped from 124p to 18p and stayed there.

In other words, ethics has gone from an obscure way of measuring corporate success to something as vital as it is undefinable. By 1998, there were fifteen companies in the FTSE 100 with over 5 per cent of shares owned by ethical investors. That's enough for serious leverage. In fact, it's probably enough to mount a takeover bid. So watch out, Abbey National, Vodafone, Railtrack and Severn Trent – the ethical corporate raiders may be coming.

So, with a collective shudder, the business world has begun to realize that the rules were changing. EIRIS is busy measuring their morality, and shareholder activists are irritating them with questions at their company AGMs, asking directors to justify their pay packets. 'Justify? Can you justify YOUR salary?' bawled an enraged Lord King, the former British Airways boss, at the 1999 AGM of a small company called Aerostructures Hamble of which he was nonexecutive chairman.

'With respect, sir,' said the questioner, the shareholder's representative from Abbey Life, 'this is not my AGM, it's yours.' Not surprising, perhaps, that some Japanese corporations have responded by hiring Yakuza gangsters to stop people asking difficult questions at shareholder meetings. It doesn't work because, slowly but surely, the secrets that traditional balance sheets ignore are coming out in the open.

There was the Chentex factory in Nicaragua from where, in 1997, Wal-mart, K-Mart and J. C. Penney were sourcing their jeans, where workers made 11 cents for making each $14.99 pair. There was also the Mexican factory subcontracted by Walt Disney where there was no drinking water – workers had to bring their own. The companies involved wouldn't have known, but it still all suddenly becomes public under the close attention of the new auditors. So does the truth about where our money is invested. Suddenly the Church of England found it was investing in the Playboy Channel, the Labour Party in the big GM food and arms companies, Shell in BP and BP in Shell. It's a strange shadowy world, where anti-smoking campaigners suddenly find their pension money is invested in Imperial Tobacco.

Hot on the heels of the ethical revolution is a demand for honesty, openness and standard definitions. No longer are coloured photos of smiling children in the annual report enough to demonstrate a commitment to charity or community investment. Ethical investors want to know how much, whether it works, what local people think, whether it's gender specific, and the answers all go into the league tables. It's an exhausting process to measure it, and even then there are some knotty problems.

Here's one. If a small company gives a large proportion of their profits to charity, and a large company gives much more – though it happens to be a smaller proportion of their profits – which of them is the most ethical? Ethical investors don't know the answer, though whole conferences and reports are devoted to finding out. Those of us familiar with the gospels might recognize it as the Parable of the Widow's Mite.

III

You don't manage a football team by looking at the score, says one management consultant. In the same way, it's not a very good way of managing a company if all you're doing is looking at one simple measure of success – the profit line. The world is now much more complicated.

Many companies still believe the only purpose for their existence is the one they measure and nothing else – shareholder value. Critics say that profit became the main corporate goal for companies only as recently as the middle of the last century, that the original purpose behind the charters for the East India Company or the Hudson's Bay Company was public benefit. Even a century ago, a robber baron like Cornelius Vanderbilt kept his profits secret. He kept all his figures in his head because he didn't trust anybody.

Since then, business writers would quote the old economic warhorse Milton Friedman with approval: 'A corporation's social responsibility is to make a profit.' Not any more. Even Henry Ford realized there was more to it than that. 'Business must be run at a profit, else it will die,' he said. 'But when anyone tries to run a business solely for profit . . . then also the business must die, for it no longer has a reason for existence.'

If you have well over half of your customers measuring your products by how ethical you are, then you are already living more in Ford's world than Friedman's. The old measures don't work: how can they when between 25 and 40 per cent of shoppers admit to boycotting unethical companies, and when 71 per cent of all French consumers would choose a child labour-free product even if it's more expensive? And if measuring everything by the bottom line worked – and corporations were the great hope for the world – then how come the world is in such a mess?

That still leaves us with the question of how we can measure these various ethereal qualities which seem to lie at the heart of business success. Either you try to put a price on them, like intellectual capital. Or you measure them all in a completely different way, like ethics. Both are impossible to do with any accuracy, which is why companies are trying to knit the whole equation together. What they need, say the Harvard business gurus, is a new kind of scoring system. They call it the Balanced Scorecard.

For some reason, most companies prefer to divide this score-card into three different measures. At Skandia it is human capital, structural capital and customer capital. Ben & Jerry's ice-cream has a three-part mission statement: economic mission, product mission and social mission. DuPont goes for shareholders, environment and society, and their rivals Dow Chemicals slips another one in unexpectedly, measuring four kinds of success: economic, environmental, social and health. For John Elkington of the influential London-based consultancy SustainAbility, it is what he calls a 'triple bottom line' – financial, environmental and social.

Elkington cut his environmental teeth by rescuing Egypt's largest delta lake from a series of massive development projects and spent the next decade or so writing some of the first corporate environment 'statements'. But it was his runaway bestseller *The Green Consumer Guide* in 1988 which made his name and reputation, and unexpectedly brought the big companies rushing to employ him – even though Monsanto and three separate sections of ICI were also trying to sue him at the same time. His follow-up *Supermarket Guide* was based on the answers to a 99-page questionnaire: the process of measuring the greenness of companies was beginning. Then in 1990, they produced a report on environmental 'auditing'.

'Within days, forty-five or fifty companies had called up saying "We'd like an environmental audit – by the way, what is an environmental audit?"' he said later.

That was the second bottom line, but what about the third one – the social dimension? Companies were already starting to measure some parts of their effect on society. Some were trying to measure their reputation. Some, like Marks & Spencer, were measuring their suppliers' creativity. Most were trying to measure customer satisfaction, though often the wrong bits – the booking staff were polite, but the train was still late. A social audit went even further, trying to measure the impact companies have on what are now generally described as their 'stakeholders' – which can include anything from neighbours to employees' families.

The audits were developed by a range of organizations and pioneers like Richard Evans of the ethical trading company Traidcraft and Simon Zadek of the London-based New Economics Foundation, known to its friends as 'NEF'. The result tended to be an extremely complex audit report, packed with numbers and measures, but no bottom line.

Shell was one of the key companies in the trend. They realized that, if their public antenna had been a little more sensitive, they could have predicted the outraged reaction to dumping the Brent Spar oil rig – including having bullets sprayed across their petrol stations in Germany. If they had worried a little more about what the world thought of them, maybe they could have prepared better against the execution of Ken Saro-Wiwa in Ogoniland. Nike was another: their 'Just do it!' slogan led to accusations about the conditions in their Asian factories. Nike responded by inviting in independent inspectors and social auditors, just as Shell did, and both began the painful process of peering in the mirror at themselves long and hard.

When the Shell Values Report was published, it carried this piece of unexpected corporate honesty in the front: 'We had looked in the mirror and we neither recognized nor liked what we saw. We have set about putting it right . . .'

Measuring your corporate success in terms of a social bottom line can be a laborious process. It sets yardsticks by which you can measure your progress, and then measures it – and that can mean judging your success by some unusual ideas. Like the ethnic diversity of your employees (Co-op), your wage differentials (Happy Computers), your spending on internal training (Body Shop), customer complaints (Ben & Jerry's), trust in the company (BP), number of employees dismissed for taking bribes (Shell). None of those will give a complete picture – in fact you might get more complaints if your reputation is high – but they are no longer the rigid business of looking at the profits and nothing else.

IV

I first came across Simon Zadek when he was at the NEF, developing the idea of social auditing to the point where it was suddenly embraced by the big accountancy firms. He wore, as always, a strange brown hat with a wide brim and talked with animation in frighteningly complicated sentences – like a cross between Indiana Jones and Professor Branestawm. By the end of the 1990s he had established the idea enough for his Institute of Social and Ethical Accountability to attract some of the biggest names in business to their annual conference. Over the same period, he spread inspiration and irritation in almost equal measure – he was even threatened with legal action at one stage for using the phrase 'social auditing' at all.

Trained as an economist, Zadek cut his auditing teeth with Coopers & Lybrand, working in developing countries with the World Bank. But he had also done a Ph.D. in the economics of Utopia. 'Science fiction writers know more about development than economists,' he told me. 'They take a systems approach without even thinking about it. In economics, all the emphasis is on simplication, but in fiction the whole emphasis is on nuance.'

Zadek's heroes were writers like Ursula LeGuin and Marge Piercy – and Jurgen Habermas, the unintelligible Frankfurt philosopher of ethics. He was also a Buddhist; he wasn't your average auditor. Still, there he was writing reports for the government of St Lucia, working with VSO and other development organizations. By 1992 he was at the NEF, working with the ethical trade organization Traidcraft Exchange and developing a method for audits without a bottom line, spelled out in their joint pamphlet *Auditing the Market*. 'In practice that was what we now understand a social audit to be,' he told me later. 'It means understanding how an organization thinks and breathes and acts, from the procedures it has and its inner thinking. It means looking at it not from one perspective but from many perspectives.'

You might say that social auditing relates to financial auditing rather as Picasso's modernistic paintings relate to classical ones. You have all the perspectives at once crowded onto the one canvas. This is 'cubist' auditing.

Simon Zadek wasn't the first ethical auditor by any means. There were methods called 'constituency accounting', developed by the radical accountant Rob Gray in 1973. There were ethical accounting statements developed in the late 1980s in Copenhagen. Even the phrase was coined by Charles Medawar when he launched Social Audit Ltd in 1971, a joint venture with the founder of the Consumers Association, Michael Young. There was also a collection of Marxist journalists called Counter Information Services who carried out a series of 'audits' in the 1970s. They didn't pretend to be unbiased. The CIS 'audit' of GEC had a photo of bomb damage on Vietnam on the front. Their report on Ford carried a big picture of the Spanish dictator General Franco.

Social audits have to be as objective as financial audits, of course. It's just not clear how. When Medawar carried one out on the Alkali Inspectorate, which was supposed to be checking things on behalf of the public, it proved to be such a secretive organization that auditing of any kind was impossible. But when they carried out a more co-operative audit on the Avon Rubber Company, the company withdrew their support. 'A detailed correction of the report would in our opinion result in a document as voluminous as the draft report itself,' they said.

How could social auditors be objective? You can't do it without the co-operation of the company, but if you co-operate can you be objective? But as so often, practical demands overrode the logical problem. 'I would love it if every shareholder of every company wrote a letter every time they received a company's annual report and accounts,' wrote Anita Roddick of The Body Shop in 1990. 'I would like them to say something like "Okay that's fine, very good. But where are the details of your environmental audit? Where are the details of your accounting to the community? Where is your social audit?"'

Where indeed? But by 1995, she had one of her own, conducted with Zadek's team at the NEF, and then a full-blown Values Report commissioned partly as a response to the transatlantic campaign against them started by the American journalist Jon Entine which accused them – bizarrely – of being 'the most evil company in the world'. The Body Shop's first social report *Measuring Up* meant interviewing nearly 5,000 people. It even involved Zadek flying out to New Mexico to ask the views of the Santa Ana Pueblo Indians who supply the blue corn for Body Shop's face washes. Then there was Ben & Jerry's, the hip ice-cream manufacturers from Vermont. By 1995, when they commissioned a social audit from NEF, they were turning over more than the entire Russian economy and giving away as much as 7.5 per cent of their profits to charity. They were hardly an average company. The results of both were impressive.

One of the great advantages of getting socially audited is that it can stop companies deluding themselves with their own public relations. But the other side of the coin is that it can be embarrassing to make the results public. When Ben & Jerry's received their report in 1995, it showed that employee morale (admittedly very high) had dropped during the year. It also showed staff complaining that the company's commitment to the Children's Defense Fund conflicted with their own struggles to juggle family and job.

The idea of social audits arrived just as companies had finished their massive clear-outs of staff – known as downsizing. They had flattened their hierarchies and outsourced their services, and found that their success now depended on building relationships of what Zadek calls 'intimacy, understanding and trust'. The old hierarchies didn't work any more, just like the old measurements. There was no hierarchy to order around, just relationships with outsiders or valuable staff. Social auditing seemed to be a way of measuring them.

Zadek's model was based on the idea that stakeholders have the right to be heard, which gives social audits a kind of objectivity which simple market research doesn't have. They deserve a voice in big organizations which affect them. So the auditors just go out and listen. They don't necessarily dig – just as conventional auditors were found to have overlooked the peculiar finances of BCCI or Robert Maxwell's pension funds.

Yet social auditing is still measurement. 'Five years ago, those organizations were completely blind,' says Zadek now. 'Certainly the more progressive companies now have a far better knowledge, far more sophisticated understanding, and therefore a far more sophisticated ability to explore into civil society before it becomes part of the problem – for them. What made us a Trojan horse for the business community was our argument that this is not an evaluation. It's helping you count what counts, we said. The sales pitch was – you've obviously got an asset because you want to manage it, and that's all we're doing.'

Of course that wasn't all the social auditors were doing at all, which may be why there is a continuing grumbling from the old guard, clinging to the bottom line. Suppliers also reported being fed up with being audited by their customer companies over and over again. One magazine editor even dismissed the intellectual capital gurus like Thomas Stewart as 'business Bolsheviks' for their 'justification of irrationally overvalued companies'.

'Why we bolshies want the market to be high, I don't know,' replied Stewart.

But does social auditing work? As Chairman Mao said about the effects of the French Revolution, it's too early to tell. But the early indications are that measuring how effective it is could be yet another nonrational, uncountable business. It works if companies approach it with honesty and enthusiasm. If they don't, it doesn't. And like any other counting system, it may not be that accurate.

Simon Zadek tells the story of the successful completion of a social audit for a leading South African company. At the end of the board meeting, the chief executive took him out onto the balcony to congratulate him for a job well done But social audits can't see the whole picture, he said. 'Every company has a killer story that they're not disclosing,' said the chief executive, looking out across the other corporate headquarters below. 'And just to prove it, I'm going to tell you what ours is . . .'

By 1999, social auditing was all the rage. Pricewaterhouse-Coopers was offering the service. KPMG had bought up The Body Shop's social audit department lock, stock and barrel – a prime example of buying intellectual capital – announcing that the social audit 'market' would soon be worth £20 million a year. One New York consultancy was reporting fifty inquiries a day from companies wanting social audits. Suddenly ethics were big business. 'In a pinch? Thinking about re-tooling your company's ethics training?' said a full page advertisement in 1999 from the Ethics Resource Center in Washington DC. Or,

as the PricewaterhouseCoopers advert put it: 'We'd like to be
ethical, aware and responsible. But what's in it for us?'

What's in it for us sounds like a contradiction when we're
talking about measuring ethics. The answer is that social auditing is about measuring your reputation – not according to
what it's worth to put it on the balance sheet – but to show
where it's wanting. It's not so much a matter of measuring
how organizations perform, it's about listening and distilling
what people say about you. It is as close to a way of measuring
without using numbers as it's possible to get. Charles Booth
would have loved it.

V

Business has faced the counting crisis by changing what they
count, and counting even more. They are taking their attention away from the bottom line just a little, but enough to
look at what they call the company's 'balanced scorecard'. In
doing so, they have shifted from narrow financial reporting
to something more broadly economic.

As long ago as the Companies Act 1985, companies were
told to calculate the value of their 'cumulative goodwill'. Most
ignore this on the quite reasonable grounds that it is impossible
to work out. But there is now a multiplicity of counting
systems to choose from. There is an 'emotional bonding'
measure to measure customer loyalty. There is 'lifetime value
modelling' to work out what customers might be worth
throughout their buying lives. There is Customer Value Management, lead indicators, lag indicators, Total Asset Utilization,
People Value-Added. Even Calculated Intangible Value. There
is a new generation of horrendous acronyms, GIPS, TOMAS,
EFQM or BREEAM (Building Research Establishment
Environmental Assessment Method). There are even the new
social auditing standards SA8000, GRI and AA1000. It's a
number-cruncher's paradise. There is even a measure of
culture, devised by North West Water and Manchester School
of Management, with eleven 'metrics' including a measure of

'internalization' – or how much your staff believes all the rhetoric about values.

And behind the measurements there is a vast amount of data, and whole offices full of 'data miners' – with their picks and Davy Lamps – digging through computers to come up with bizarre correlations in the figures. It's done so quickly: 'Every month, I'd receive three cartons of paper that I spread out on the floor in my office,' said Skandia's sales statistics manager Per Kingfors. 'I also received files on disks and faxed reports. It took days, weeks even, to put all the data together. Now we sit and drum our fingers if we wait more than 20 seconds to get a report.'

But behind all these figures, you get the feeling that somehow it isn't working. The more they all measure, the more it all slips through their fingers.

Of course the measurements are not exactly what they want. Screeds of data about customers and how often they buy from you is not the same as a real measurement of 'loyalty'. 'If you want loyalty, buy a dog,' said the chief executive of a UK chain of DIY stores when research showed that most people out DIY shopping didn't know whose store they were buying from.

Even the bottom-line figures are behaving oddly. 'If you want to look at regular stock, you go either to a financial analyst or an economist,' said Michael Bloomberg, the founder of the online information giant, as the value of the website Yahoo overtook that of British Airways. 'If you want to value an Internet stock, you go to a psychologist or a publicist.'

Even the investor magazine *Fortune* has included a rant against the rising tide of measurement. 'If information is a strategic asset, does that mean more and more must be good?' asked columnist Michael Schrage in 1999. 'Just because single left-handed blond customers who drive Volvos purchase 1,450 per cent more widgets on alternative Thursdays than their married non-blond, right-handed, domestic car-driving counterparts does not a marketing epiphany make.'

In a one slightly complicated sentence, Schrage has put the

problem in a nutshell. Measuring is easy these days. But the world is too complicated for figures. 'It's easier to count the bottles than describe the wine,' says Thomas Stewart in *Intellectual Capital*.

It doesn't seem to matter how many figures you have laid out in front of you, they will not interpret. They will not give you cause and effect. For that you have to make a leap of intuition. Which of all the millions of figures that most companies have at their disposal are the ones making them succeed – or is it just the business cycle? Or will they find themselves praised for their astonishing performance one moment, like Marks & Spencer, and the next moment find themselves dropping down the markets like a stone?

Companies now have vast databanks of information about their customers, segmentable in every possible direction. They know precisely how they behave and what they buy. *Why* they behave like that remains as elusive as ever.

Which is one reason why it's so difficult to come to a clear conclusion by calculating a better bottom line. Zadek makes no attempt to add up all the figures in a social audit. 'It would be meaningless,' he says. And how do you balance up the triple bottom line?

'I don't know,' says Elkington. 'The point is that there are at least three different dimensions to valuing performance that we need to address. The best companies can integrate all three and scarcely be aware of it – like walking. For several years I felt it was better to separate them out and give them a bit of oxygen, but sometime over the next five to ten years, all of them must be collapsed back together and integrated.'

This is the great unanswered question, like the search for the Yeti. Is there such a thing as one number at the bottom that really says it all? As far as I know, this is the impossible dream – single numbers don't seem to be able to live up to the complexity of life.

There's an echo here of the days before any kind of auditing. Before Pacioli invented his book-keeping methods, medieval merchants had no books to balance. Instead they kept a kind of diary which listed transactions together with birthdays, battles and other social events. 'The Italians called this a *ricordanze*,' wrote the historian of such things, Alfred Crosby. 'But how does one balance a diary?' Social auditing is simply a return to the ricordanze: you can't balance it.

For the time being, anyway, imposing single numbers seems to distort. Managing by them tends to lead to lower morale, worse service and higher costs. The fact that management has moved a little further on from there is definitely progress. We have come a long way from the 1970s, when fearsome executives would appear with their print-outs in far-flung edges of a corporate empire to grill local managers about figures and nothing but figures. No longer is one of the biggest companies in the world so committed to getting a 20 per cent return on investment that it issues all its executives with underwear bearing the words 'ROI 20%'.

Even old Deming, the total quality guru, got it right years ago when he complained about business people counting too much. 'Accounting-based measures of performance drive employees to achieve targets of sales, revenue and costs, by manipulation of processes, and by flattery or delusive promises to cajole a customer into purchase of what he does not need,' he said.

Need? How can you measure whether a customer needs something? But then, as Deming said – in a wonderfully self-contradictory statement – 97 per cent of what matters in business can't be counted. Maybe this was what Anita Roddick means when she describes business as like her mother's café – about life and people and fun as much as profit.

In the end, even after all those measures and highly paid knowledge managers, the difference comes down to people, their instincts and their intuitions – those business pioneers who can do things automatically like walking. Perhaps that's why the most successful manager in the world, General Electric Chief Executive Jack Welch, spends the vast majority of his valuable time interviewing people for the top 500 jobs in his company. 'My whole job is picking the right people,' he said. And if you wonder how he has time for anything else, he probably doesn't.

Given that, is it possible to run a business successfully without calculating so much? Social auditing suggests that a compromise might be possible. But perhaps the most hopeful sign is the success of the biggest second-hand book chain in the USA, Half Price Books. They have successfully built themselves into a major chain by expanding city by city not according to financial calculations, marketing projections or anything else that requires a calculator. They decided where to open next according to wherever their employees happened to have family reasons for wanting to move.

Bizarre measurement No. 8
Carcel

(Another unit of light, used in France. 1 Carcel = 10 candles.)

....

Proportion of medical columns in Canadian newspapers judged to be giving 'potentially life-threatening' advice: **28 per cent**

Time you would have to yell to produce enough sound energy to heat a cup of coffee: **8 years, 7 months and 6 days**

Chapter 8

Historical Interlude 4:
National Accountant

He keeps a lady in a cage
Most cruelly all day,
And makes her count and calls her 'Miss'
Until she fades away.
G. K. Chesterton, 'Song Against Grocers'

It is astonishing how many foolish things one can temporarily
believe if one thinks too long alone.
John Maynard Keynes

I

It was 5 June 1916. At the River Somme on the Western
Front, the Allied armies were gathering for the battle they
believed would finally cut through the German trenches. To
the north of Scotland, it was a cold, stormy evening as HMS
Hampshire set sail from the anchorage of the British Grand
Fleet at Scapa Flow. Her four funnels belched smoke as she
sailed past the sheer cliffs of Marwick Head, taking the western
route past the Orkney Isles to avoid the worst of the buffeting
wind. At 7.40 pm, a mile and a half from the coast, an enormous explosion almost cut the ship in two. She had sailed
straight through a minefield laid by U475 with great precision,
but in the wrong place. Within ten minutes the ship and crew
had disappeared. Only 14 survived. One of those who was
never seen again was the British Secretary of State for War,
Horatio Herbert Kitchener. He was 19 days short of his sixty-
seventh birthday.

Kitchener had presided over the last cavalry charge of the

British army. He was a national hero for his conduct against the Boers. As Secretary of State for War, he was instantly recognizable from his poster campaign – with a pointing finger and the words 'BRITAIN NEEDS YOU' – which succeeded in recruiting two and a half million volunteers. About 19,000 of them would be killed on the first day of the Battle of the Somme, just 25 days after his icy death. He may not have been a great man, said Margot Asquith, the prime minister's wife, but he certainly was a great poster.

In this sense, Kitchener was the very embodiment of numbers in a society newly alive to the horror of them, when each casualty figure hid a devastated and grieving family. By the end of the war there would be 2,516,014 of them killed, captured and wounded from Britain alone. By December 1915, the official British kill target was 200,000 Germans a month, but they seemed to be suffering similar numbers achieving it. The generals saw no further than the numbers. 'We are like a gambler who must always call his opponent's bluff,' said General Sir Henry Rawlinson about the horrendous casualties. 'Whatever chips he puts down, we must put down more.'

Kitchener's death belongs in this story not just because of the numbers, nor because Lloyd George had been planning to accompany him on the Arctic journey, but had changed his mind at the last minute. It belongs here because Lloyd George – had he joined Kitchener on the ship – would have taken with him a brilliant young Treasury economist, John Maynard Keynes.

The day Kitchener met his end was also Keynes' thirty-third birthday. He was at the time also a fellow of King's College, Cambridge, an active homosexual and a central member of the Bloomsbury set, which was even then conducting its revolution to exorcize stuffy Victorian religion and morality. He was a recognized expert on Indian currency, and his views were increasingly sought by politicians and civil servants alike. If we had lost Keynes on the *Hampshire*, he would not have been there to lay the foundations of modern economics, the world financial system, the IMF – and gross national product, the system whereby we can count up the wealth of a whole nation, and see whether it is rising or falling in one figure.

Although his history-changing *General Theory of Employment, Interest and Money* would be packed full of equations and statistics to prove his contentions, and although he spent eight years before the First World War writing a treatise on probability – pausing on the task during the war years – he didn't like statistics very much. Numbers fascinated him, but then so did myths and fairy tales – especially the story of Midas who could turn anything he touched into gold. He was sceptical of the whole idea of econometrics, which meant applying numbers and statistics to economics. He saw economic problems as basically moral crises – not the old-fashioned kind of morality, urging thrift and careful saving – but all because of people's fatal love of money. Keynes described this love as 'a somewhat disgusting morbidity, one of the semi-criminal, semi-pathological propensities which one hands over with a shudder to the specialists in mental disease'.

'The truth seems to be that numbers were for him simply clues,' wrote his latest and most voluminous biographer Robert Skidelsky, 'triggers of the imagination, rather like anecdotes are for the non-mathematically minded.' Keynes was not, at first sight, one of the great tradition of number-crunchers. How could he be, as a central intellectual figure in the Bloomsbury revolution. There they were, urging a new individualism – urging people to use their intuition and creativity after the dead hand of Victorian stuffiness and pomposity.

And the person he blamed more than anybody else for this stuffiness was the counter-in-chief, Jeremy Bentham, whose tradition he described as 'the worm that has been gnawing at the insides of modern civilization and is responsible for its present moral decay'. Not for Keynes the struggle to understand creativity or poetry because it couldn't be measured. On the contrary, he fell in love with an artist, married a ballerina, and spent part of the Great Depression financing and supervising the creation of the Cambridge Arts Theatre. 'If I had the power today,' he said in 1933:

. . . I would surely set out to endow our capital cities with all the appurtenances of art and civilization on the highest standards . . . convinced that what I could create I could afford – and believing that money thus spent would not only be better than any dole, but would make unnecessary any dole. For what we have spent on the dole in England since the war we could have made our cities the greatest works of man in the world.

Not for Keynes the reduction of the grandeur of human life to money, or to numbers. So how come he is in this book at all? The answer is that it was Keynes' national accounting system, which would sum up everything in the British economy in one gigantic number, that kept Britain alive during the darkest days of the war, consistently outperforming the Nazi economy which everyone thought was so efficient.

As the finest economist of the century, Keynes was wedded to measurement. He used figures every day to win his intellectual battles and conduct his highly successful speculations on the world's stock exchanges. But he never used numbers to pin down life. It was the generation that came later that took his national accounts and turned them into an absolute description, one that reduced whole nations to a single tyrannical figure. By that time Keynes was dead, and the man who claimed the invention of national accounts along with him was having serious doubts.

II

Karl Marx was three months under the turf at Highgate Cemetery, Charles Booth was vaguely wondering about a poverty survey of London, and Robert Louis Stevenson was putting the finishing touches to *Treasure Island*, and on 5 June 1883 – 33 years to the day before the sinking of HMS *Hampshire* – John Maynard Keynes was born at 6 Harvey Road, Cambridge. Like Bentham, he was a sickly child, coming down with rheumatic fever and heart pains around his sixth birthday. For the rest of his life he was obsessed with the idea that he was physically repulsive. He also soon realized he was homosexual – a nervous moment in British history to discover that about yourself. 'Gross indecency' was punishable by a year in prison with hard labour, and had been since he was two years old. As Oscar Wilde discovered so tragically, there was no exemption for genius. At Kings at the age of twenty, he was elected to the elitist intellectual group known as the Apostles, a regular twelve of whom had been meeting since the start of the previous century. They met behind bolted doors on Saturday nights, listening to endless learned papers from each other, eating anchovies on toast.

It was a brand new century, Queen Victoria was dead and a new age seemed to beginning – based on the individualistic ideas of the Cambridge moral philosopher G. E. Moore. They seemed to overturn Victorian religion. Morality couldn't be calculated, he said – it had to come from within. It was 'exciting, exhilarating, the beginning of a renaissance, the opening of a new heaven and earth,' said Keynes. 'We were the forerunners of a new dispensation, we were not afraid of anything.'

The following year he came first in a whole spread of papers in the Civil Service exams, but only eighth or ninth in economics. 'I evidently knew more about economics than my examiners,' he wrote. Soon he was working in the India Office, spending his evenings working on what would eventually become his book on probability – linking it to intuition rather than anything directly measurable – and raging at the way government was run during his day job. It was 'government by dotardy,' he wrote after his first committee meeting. 'At least half of those present showed manifest signs of senile decay, and the rest didn't speak.' He kept the same tone up, inside and outside government, for most of his life.

He was in love with the artist Duncan Grant, much to his friend Lytton Strachey's fury, and was already going to the ballet at Covent Garden twice a week, feeling his way towards his theories of Indian currency. Around him there was a flowering of Edwardian culture. Human nature changed in December 1910, said Virginia Woolf later. From then on the truth was to be found by intuition as well as reason. No more Benthamite calculus. No more tabular data as the source of all truth. No more obsessive collecting of figures. This was the age of Picasso, of leaps of daring imagination.

The Great War broke out over bank holiday weekend. 'Who is this Keynes?' asked Lloyd George the following day. As Chancellor of the Exchequer, he was furious about his interfering memo on the currency, and from that moment on 'this Keynes' would become an increasingly important shadow in Lloyd George's life, sometimes as nemesis – at the peace negotiations in 1919 – sometimes as saviour. Keynes was soon working at the Treasury with a staff of 17 under him.

It was a difficult position for a sensitive man like Maynard Keynes. It made him exempt from military service, which could well have saved his life, yet he found himself increasingly disillusioned with the war and its conduct. After conscription started in 1916, he was constantly battling to get his friends exempted too. As an act of symbolic protest, he even declared himself as a conscientious objector. He agonized about whether to resign his post in protest, only to come home to find an article by a well-known Liberal pacifist on his dinner plate. Attached to it was a note which read:

Dear Maynard, why are you still at the Treasury?
Yours Lytton.

He finally broke down at the Paris peace conference in 1919, resigning from the British delegation and struggled home in despair. Back in London, he denounced the disastrous peace treaty that was to impoverish Europe over the next decade, condemning Lloyd George for threatening the peace of Europe. He described him later, in a more forgiving mood, as 'this goat-footed bard, this half-human visitor to our age from the hag-ridden magic and enchanted woods of Celtic antiquity'. His book on the subject, *The Economic Consequences of the Peace*, made him a world figure but flung him out of his cosy position of influence with the establishment.

Keynes was brilliant, charming, rude and peculiar. He judged people by the cleanliness of their hands and fingernails. He always wore silk underpants, though sometimes until they were so old that they barely held themselves together. He was also staggeringly efficient, holding down a weight of committee work and teaching, with writing laborious articles and newspaper supplements, as well as playing a leading role in a range of other projects from speculation to farming. Even so, he managed to find time to play bridge in college, go riding, spend an hour or so gossiping in the Bloomsbury manner, and his stooping gowned figure would be seen throughout the 1920s dashing across the quadrangles, then ambling around the second-hand bookshops of Cambridge. Or into the little local stores which he described as 'shops which are really shops and not merely a branch of the multiplication table'. To Keynes, life was always more important than numbers.

In London, his life was at the heart of Bloomsbury, where the vermilion front door of his home at 46 Gordon Square proclaimed the fact that no ordinary people lived here. Upstairs the walls were covered by murals by Vanessa Bell and Duncan Grant. Downstairs was the high-pitched sensitive intellectual talk that made Bloomsbury such a powerhouse. Lady Strachey lived at No 51, James Strachey at No 41. Virginia Woolf's brother, Adrian Stephen, lived at No 50. It was all a little incestuous.

It was also a home from home, though his increasing worldliness – and what his friends described as his increasing stinginess – divided him from it as the years went by. Especially when he shocked his friends by marrying the divorced Russian ballerina Lydia Lopokova, the daughter of an usher at the Imperial Alexandinsky Theatre. She shocked Cambridge because she fitted their category of chorus girl. She shocked Bloomsbury because she didn't talk the same language: 'a half-witted canary,' said Lytton Strachey. 'She has no headpiece, poor little parakeet,' moaned Virginia Woolf, complaining that she threw her sanitary towels into the empty fire grate. But it was no marriage of convenience: they loved each other for the rest of their lives.

The world was changing fast. The next generation was embracing extreme politics, and the intellectuals were embracing a whole new philosophy of measurement, known as logical positivism. If you couldn't measure something, they believed it was meaningless. 'What can be said at all must be said clearly, and whereof one cannot speak thereof one must be silent,' said Keynes' mad friend, the philosopher Ludwig Wittgenstein. God was swept away. Mankind could take control by measuring and counting, and by sitting themselves down at the controls of a complex universe. There would be no more original sin, no more old men with their prejudices leading youth to the trenches. And by demonstrating that there were controls for an economy too, Keynes would only strengthen the mood.

Despite his disapproval of figures, counting and statistics, he was also ushering in the world of the technocrat. The idea that an elite of intelligent men (it usually was men) could take control of the forces shaping the world and make it work like a well-tuned machine. He could imagine a world run by a King's College high table all too well, and the generation that came after him clearly felt the same. The elite would run the machine.

But it was an elite who could see beyond numbers. Economic statistics would have to take into account the 'state of employment, the volume of production, the effective demand for credit as felt by banks, the volume of new issues, the flow of cash into circulation, the statistics of foreign trade and the level of exchanges,' Keynes wrote in the early 1920s No wonder at the end of all that, they couldn't count or measure themselves into the right answer but had to allow for what he called the 'the play of judgement and discretion'.

He was about to use his judgement to overturn all the accepted economic rules.

'No Congress of the United States ever assembled, on surveying the state of the Union, has met a more pleasing prospect than that which appears at the present time,' said President Calvin Coolidge in his State of the Union address at the end of 1928. Within less than a year, the Wall Street Crash heralded a worldwide economic disaster. Even Keynes lost a packet.

He hated international crises – they stopped him from sleeping. Throughout the depression he kept up an articulate and fiery bombardment to persuade the world's politicians that simply cutting back wasn't going to work this time. As he scribbled away in his study in Cambridge and unemployment rose, he became more and more optimistic in his public pronouncements – urging that the answer was to unbalance the budget and get life moving again. 'It is often said by wise-acres that we cannot spend more than we earn,' wrote Keynes in a letter to the *Manchester Guardian* in 1932. 'That is, of course, true enough of the individual, but it is exceedingly misleading if it is applied to the community as a whole.'

There would be no more puritanical urgings for self-sacrifice to save the British economy. The whole idea of urging people to sacrifice themselves seemed horrific to Keynes after all those Kitchener posters. But economic sacrifice was the accepted wisdom. One economist back in 1899 who argued (like Keynes) that too much saving was bad for the economy, was told that he couldn't teach, not even to consenting adults in private. Even today, the Treasury copy of Keynes' pamphlet *Can Lloyd George Do It?* has been defaced by a junior mandarin with the words 'EXTRAVAGANCE, INFLATION, BANK-RUPTCY' scrawled over the front.

The crunch came in early 1933. Sidney and Beatrice Webb were hard at work praising Stalin in their final tome *Soviet Communism: a New Civilization*. The Apostles now included the future Soviet spies Anthony Blunt and Guy Burgess. Hitler took power in January, and in March, Franklin Roosevelt took office as president of the USA. It was a moment of supreme crisis. About a quarter of working Americans were out of work, and on the early morning of the day before the inaugur-ation, 4 March, every bank in America locked its doors. Revol-ution seemed almost inevitable. Even Keynes was confused: 'Even I would hardly think that I could know what to do if I were president,' he told his wife. But Roosevelt inspired the world with his speech warning America that 'we have nothing to fear but fear itself', thrilling Keynes as he listened to it on the radio at Lloyd George's country house.

Roosevelt's New Deal owed a great deal to Keynes' influ-ence. So, in their own way, did Europe's dictators, though as a good Liberal, Keynes always recognized Nazism for what it was. When the Blackshirt leader Sir Oswald Mosley provided him with unexpected political support, Keynes warned him that his new economics was intended 'not to embrace you but to save the country from you'. The point was that Keynes believed the First World War had destroyed the social connections that underpinned the economic system. Somehow it had to be rebuilt to 'keep alive the possibility of civilization'. Keynes was no revolutionary in any other sense. He was trying to rescue the capitalist system from itself – it was just that he saw the system differently.

For Keynes, the whole idea wasn't counting things, and it certainly wasn't dictatorship, it was about life. Encouraging people to save doesn't make anybody rich, he said. If we saved everything and spent nothing, we'd all die – leaving us simply 'a peregrination of the catacombs, with a guttering candle'. We are healthy children, he urged, so we should experiment. 'Over against us, standing in the path, there is nothing but a few old gentlemen tightly buttoned-up in their frock coats, who only need to be treated with a little friendly disrespect and bowled over like ninepins. Quite likely, they will enjoy it themselves, once they have got over the shock.'

The shock came with the war, and it shocked Keynes into setting aside his usual dislike of statistics.

III

When Hitler marched into Poland, Keynes was fifty-six and not very well. Battling to rescue the world from depression had seriously damaged his health, and in the month of the coronation of George VI in 1937, he collapsed with coronary thrombosis. He never fully recovered, but like so many others he was raring to help the war effort. He gathered around him a group of friends who had been involved in Whitehall during the First World War (including Sir William Beveridge, who had been in the Ministries of Munitions and Food) and they met once a week in Gordon Square to discuss financial aspects of the war. Keynes called them the 'Old Dogs'. It was a frustrating time.

On health grounds, he turned down the umpteenth offer to stand for Parliament for Cambridge University in a by-election, and set to work spraying his usual trenchant advice. He sent a stream of notes to Roosevelt about how to finance the post-war reconstruction of Europe, and wrote letters to *The Times* criticizing Sir John Simon's budget as 'chicken-feed to the dragons of war'.

But then paying for the war was the most intractable problem of the moment. British finances were in no state to pay for it, and gigantic loans would soon be flooding into the British exchequer from abroad – within the year, for the sake of national liberty, there would be no limit on borrowing at all. By default, the government was doing exactly as Keynes had urged for the past decade – they were unbalancing the budget and spending their way out of the depression because they had to.

The problem was that these vast sums would soon be swirling around the economy and there was no knowing where they might end up. With full wallets after twenty years of near poverty, and a U-boat blockade stopping luxury goods from appearing in the shops, anything could happen. It might not produce what the war effort desperately needed. It might produce rampant, morale-sapping inflation. Prices had more than doubled during the First World War – though they had barely moved before in the century since Waterloo.

What could be done? Precious little without a set of national accounts to sum up the whole intricate complicated web and show where there was spare capacity and when the economy was overheating. But there wasn't one. The Soviets managed their intractable five-year plans by plucking numbers out of thin air and enforcing them with death or Siberia. But Britain had no way of providing any kind of overview of an economy in numbers. In his *General Theory* in 1936, Keynes had complained that the economic figures for Britain were completely inadequate, and it was impossible to manage an economy along the principles he set out without a figure for what he called 'aggregate real income'. The British government in 1939 had no such thing, though Keynes' younger Cambridge colleagues Erwin Rothbarth and Colin Clark were struggling to produce them.

Luckily for the British, some of the work was already being carried out across the Atlantic. The US Congress had called an urgent meeting of economists as they struggled with the depression in 1931, with the sounds of bank crashes in the not too far distance. To their horror, they found there were hardly any of the figures they needed either. The following year – the last year of the Hoover administration – the Senate finally asked the Department of Commerce to prepare a comprehensive set of national accounts. The department called in a quiet and unassuming young economist called Simon Kuznets from the University of Pennsylvania. They set him to work on what turned out to be the start of a lifetime as the international guru of aggregate real income – or, as we call it these days, gross national product or GNP.

National Income means counting money flowing through the economy. At last you could sum up a whole country in one number – one figure on top of a map of a machine called the economy. When the war came, the strategic importance of these numbers was only clear to a few. But at least there did seem to be a possible answer to the critical questions economists ask in wartime – how much can we produce and what impact will it have on the economy as a whole?

Thanks to Kuznets, the American government had the first set of national accounts in the world as early as 1935, the year before Keynes' *General Theory* was published. And by 1939, he had managed to carry out statistical work on 33 other countries – though not Britain. It was Kuznets' idea, but it needed Keynes' special insight for it to be possible in the first place. It was Keynes who realized that money was a flow. One economist was to call Kuznets' work the anatomy for Keynes' physiology. The two bits came together as one of the crucial pieces of the jigsaw that would eventually beat Hitler. But the pieces were not yet in place.

While the 'Old Dogs' were struggling through the winter

streets – with the kerbs and lampposts painted black and white to help navigate during the blackout – Keynes was applying his considerable intellectual resources to the problem. Luckily there seemed to be a breathing space: 'There is still an astonishingly general belief, or hope, or perhaps a mixture of both, that something will happen,' wrote the American columnist Mollie Panter-Downes in the *New Yorker*. Almost nothing did, it was the period known as the 'Phoney War'. So Keynes had time to set out his ideas on war potential to the Marshall Society in Cambridge. Afterwards, he turned his lecture notes into two articles called 'Paying for the War', and a peculiar leak meant that they actually appeared for the first time in a German newspaper, the *Frankfurter Allgemeine Zeitung* of 7 November – an extraordinary mistake given how important it would be for the war effort. *The Times* didn't get round to publishing them until 14 and 15 November. The result was a blueprint for keeping inflation down during wartime.

Keynes' proposal was based on the idea of national accounting, and using the crucial figures to plan how much to spend and where. It also showed how the government could take some of the spending out of the economy, to avoid inflation – but at the same time pay for what people actually needed. He suggested a family allowance of five shillings a week per child up to the age of 15, paid directly to the mother, and a list of the basic necessities of life which would be kept at a level price by subsidizing them. He suggested a top rate of income tax of 80 per cent and he had a brilliant masterstroke – compulsory savings. Part of people's pay packets would not be taxed, but they would be saved for them, and then given back with interest during the post-war slump when they and the economy would really need it.

The articles provoked an excited response. The right-wing Beaverbrook press didn't like it because of the tax rate. The Labour Party and TUC didn't like confiscating people's wages – even temporarily. The National Savings Movement hated it. But then it's all too easy not doing anything about inflation, Keynes complained because then nobody has to take responsibility for it. Next he incorporated the debate into a pamphlet, published in February 1940. It was called *How to Pay for the War: A Radical Plan for the Chancellor of the Exchequer*. At last he was back in the thick of things. There was a discussion in the House of Lords about it on February 28, a meeting with the Chancellor on March 7 and on March 8 a meeting with the Governor of the Bank of England – Keynes' old enemy Montagu Norman. Norman had been the governor during the Wall Street Crash (even the psychologist Carl Jung had pronounced him 'mad') and they had deeply distrusted each other ever since.

Then there was the Norwegian campaign, and suddenly in May, the Blitzkrieg attack on western Europe. Britain was fighting alone and for her life and suddenly money was no object and national counting was really urgent. Keynes shuttled from meeting to meeting, struggling at the same time to get his assistant Rothbarth released from internment – 'the most disgraceful and humiliating thing which has happened for a long time' – and spending long periods resting in his room with an ice-bag. By the time France at fallen, Keynes was suffering from chest pains. By the Blitz, he and Lydia were sleeping in the corridor at Gordon Square.

Chunks of his life seemed to be unravelling. A landmine on the square in September broke every door and window in the centre of Bloomsbury. Virginia Woolf was on the verge of suicide. But he was finally asked by the government to help them prepare the 1941 Budget. On Budget Day 1941, the white paper was published setting out the national accounts and figures on which the Budget was based. 'It was,' said Keynes, 'a revolution in public finance.'

And after all that, they only partially put his ideas into practice. Low interest rates were fixed on both sides of the Atlantic, as he suggested, and family allowances came in towards the end of the war (we have had them ever since). But his deferred pay scheme only saved £120 million, rather than the £550 million he planned, so there wasn't much to plough back into the sickly peacetime economy. It was still a key foundation stone for the postwar welfare state.

If the British adopted his ideas for a wartime economy, that was nothing to the Americans. In the first six months of 1942, Roosevelt's government – urged on by Churchill and his aircraft production minister Lord Beaverbrook when they arrived in Washington – placed orders for more than $100 billion in war equipment, more than their entire GNP. Donald Nelson, the Purchasing Vice President of Sears Roebuck, was appointed to lead the War Production Board and was given unprecedented powers.

To make sure this didn't lead to inflation, the Americans put up their top rate of tax to 91 per cent. The economist John Kenneth Galbraith was drafted in to make sure prices didn't go up – a process, without the powers to enforce it, which became known as 'jaw-boning'. The vast capacity of the USA was brought to bear on the war, and if the contracts were too generous, a fearsome committee of Congress – chaired by Harry S. Truman before his unexpected rise to the Vice Presidency – chased them like terriers. By the end of the war, the figures were staggering: 86,338 tanks had been produced in the US factories, 297,000 planes, 17.4 million rifles, carbines and side arms, 64,500 landing ships. Cargo vessels were being laid down and launched within four days, and the Kaiser Yard in California even once managed to produce a ship in 24 hours flat.

It seemed to be working in Britain too. By 1941, the UK was outproducing Germany in its main military requirements. Despite the fact that the Nazis were using slave labour, and had all the resources of a totalitarian state at their disposal. Keynes' and Kuznets' economic tool had beaten the Nazi efficiency machine where it really mattered – in their productivity. Four years later, Galbraith dashed into Germany ahead of the advancing Allied troops to seize the relevant documents, interrogating Goering and Speer for weeks. He believed by the end that national accounts had been a secret ingredient in the war effort of equal importance to the Enigma Code or the Manhattan Project. Hitler's production targets were far lower because he had not been able to use sophisticated national accounting.

In fact, Galbraith discovered, the Allied bombing campaign

of inefficient German factories in 1944 was the only thing that managed to speed up Nazi production. Military planners are wedded to figures more than almost anyone else, and especially – for some reason – when it comes to aerial bombardment.

By then, Keynes was preparing for the final triumph of his life, the 1944 meeting at Bretton Woods in New Hampshire, to set up a world financial system after the war. He was as charming and as rude as ever at the conference, teasing the American delegation for their jargon (he called it 'Cherokee') negotiating sometimes from 9.30 am to 3.30 am, holding the 730 delegates from 44 United Nations countries spellbound. Although it was not primarily his version of the plan that was adopted for the IMF and other powerful institutions we still have today, Keynes was the hero and it was Keynes who moved the acceptance of the final act. When he finished, the whole assembly rose and cheered him as he walked towards the door, singing 'For he's a jolly good fellow'. 'At such moments, I often find myself thinking that Keynes must be one of the most remarkable men that have ever lived,' wrote the British embassy's economic adviser:

> The quick logic, the wide vision, above all the incomparable sense of the fitness of words, all combine to make something several degrees beyond the ordinary limit of human achievement. Certainly, in our age, only the prime minister surpasses him . . . shot through with something that is not traditional, a unique unearthly quality of which one can only say that it is pure genius. The Americans sat entranced as the godlike visitor sang and the golden light played all around.

A year later, he was relaxing in Cambridge when he heard on the radio that the Americans had ended their 'Lend-Lease' agreement with Britain. Knowing that this meant potential financial disaster for the country, Keynes redoubled his efforts and led the exhausting negotiations in Washington to hammer out some kind of deal. Royal Navy ships that he passed on his way across the Atlantic cheered him as he went, knowing his mission meant the economic survival of Britain. The experience left him utterly exhausted. He died of a sudden heart attack at the age of only 62, at his country home at Tilton in Sussex, over Easter weekend 1946. 'I lost my everything,' wrote Lydia. His father, John Neville Keynes, struggled to his memorial service in Westminster Abbey at the age of 93.

IV

The first attempt at a set of national accounts was made in the 1690s by Sir William Petty, the great anatomist, chemist, musician, Surveyor-General of Ireland and inventor of the copying machine. He was trying to find out how much you could tax the nation – the same motivation which led to the Domesday Book. 'Instead of using only comparative and superlative Words,' he wrote, 'I have taken the course . . . to express myself in Number, Wealth.' The great thing was to count and to sum things up in numbers, he told Charles II. 'By contemplating the universal posture of the nation, its power, its strength, trade, wealth and revenues . . . by summing up the difficulties on either side, and computing upon the whole . . . is what we mean by Political Arithmetic.'

Keynes and Kuznets were not actually the first. Nor were they the first to argue about what should be counted and what should be ignored. When the French kings used to do it, they only measured agriculture as national wealth. It took Adam Smith to include industry and factories, but even he refused to count entertainment, government spending and lawyers because they were 'unproductive of any value'. Alfred Marshall, Keynes' teacher and the founder of neo-classical economics, included both lawyers' fees and car prices for the first time – it was money that counted, after all. Things without a price got left out. They still are.

Even so, Keynes and Kuznets between them ushered in a whole new world. Their bottom line figure for a whole nation meant suddenly that economists could start forecasting the changing pattern. A confusing new world of input-output ratios and linear programming was emerging, with economists – like white-coated scientists – wandering with clipboards through the corridors of power. 'They are to be called wise who put things in their right order and control them well,' wrote Colin Clark quoting St Thomas Aquinas on the first page of his 1940 book on the subject.

The first time the whole counting project was carried out in Britain, it was under the requirements of the Marshall Plan to rebuild Europe. Every country had to write a four-year recovery blueprint for 1948–52. By the 1960s, everyone was doing it. Harold Wilson set up the Department of Economic Affairs under his eccentric sidekick George Brown, and the first National Plan for Britain was published in 1965.

It was the same story in the USA. The new priesthood of number-crunchers no longer preached the gospel of thrift. It was now the duty of consumers to consume, and they measured their ability to do so. Galbraith came back from Europe and joined the staff of *Fortune* magazine. His first job was to prepare a blueprint for American transition to a postwar economy. And with one number that summed it all up, nation by nation, suddenly the economic priests discovered the number could move. If it went down it was recession. If it went up it was 'progress'. 'Progress is our most important product,' said Ronald Reagan week in week out, as the host of the TV show *General Electric Theatre*. But could you really measure something as complex as progress in this way? Who said we should be pleased just because there was more money going through the economy? What about those life-enhancing but priceless aspects of life that never got counted?

The first cracks in the idea of numbering whole nations were beginning to appear. Some of the biggest proponents of GNP were listing what couldn't be counted. Like damage to the natural world: even in 1940, Colin Clark could write in the introduction to his book on the subject: 'It is, unfortunately, as yet impossible to give even the most approximate numerical valuation of the extent of this destruction of natural fertility in different parts of the world . . .'

How right he was. The first meeting of the International

Association for Research in Income and Wealth took place three years after Keynes' death in his old college in Cambridge. Kuznets was there, and one of the key issues was what to count. National accounts were just supposed to measure final products. But what was education? It was free so it didn't get measured. What about taking a walk? What about professional killers? Not included because they were illegal, yet money does change hands. Then there was the question of prices. Are they really a very good measure of what something is worth – especially today? What about housework – an argument which has continued ever since? Not included, but Kuznets reckoned it could make up a quarter of all national income. How could you measure 'growth' in developing countries where the most important products were prayer and monks? It was no idle question – the World Bank needed to be able to compare the 'progress' of countries in the developing world. They were busily measuring their success in Africa using GNP, even though most production there took place for free in the household. It was as if only big industry counted.

There were idle questions too: Kuznets worked out that the average rate of 'growth' since Adam and Eve 500,000 years ago had been about 0.004 per cent a decade. It was the economic equivalent of how many angels you could get onto the head of a pin.

It all seemed so simple when the object was just to win the war, but when it was to make society a better, happier and richer place, then one measurement wasn't very effective. 'Though unable to measure them,' warned Kuznets, as he listed the exclusions, 'we must recognize that their omission renders national income merely one element in the evaluation of the net welfare assignable to the nation's economic activity.'

Kuznets had been having doubts since his first report to Congress in 1934: 'The welfare of a nation can scarcely be inferred from a measurement of national income as defined above,' he warned. Nearly 30 years later, writing in *New Republic*, he went much further: 'Distinctions must be kept in mind between quantity and quality of growth, between its costs and return, and between the short and the long run.

Goals for "more" growth should specify more growth of what and for what.'

But it was too late. The future of Western nations was being bound to GNP and how fast it could grow. Did Keynes have doubts too? He was suspicious of measuring things, or of reducing economics to figures. To find a social system that worked economically as well as morally, he urged people to stop 'counting the money cost at all', telling the future to 'diminish, rather than increase, the area of monetary comparisons'. But then he never liked counting much – his real source of new thinking was intuition and introspection. 'He was not the first of the modern statisticians, but the last of the magicians of number,' writes his biographer Robert Skidelsky. 'For him numbers were akin to those mystic "signs" or "clues" by which the necromancers had tried to uncover the riddles of the universe.'

Theories weren't calculated from piles of figures, said the necromancer. They begin as a 'grey, fuzzy, woolly monster in one's head'. Keynes was on the side of Pythagoras and Plato rather than the modern number-crunchers. He believed that science, art and magic were more similar than they were different. Yet here he was inventing the tools by which his followers would sum up a whole country with one number. So perhaps it shouldn't be a surprise that the man he named as his successor devoted his career to a critique of 'progress' and 'growth'.

When they corresponded during the war, E. F. Schumacher was still 30 years away from writing his bestseller *Small is Beautiful*, but Keynes recognized in him a fellow magician. 'If my mantle is to fall on anyone,' he told a friend in the Treasury just before he died, 'it could only be Otto Clarke or Fritz Schumacher. Otto Clarke can do anything with figures, but Schumacher can make them sing.'

Despite the numbers, Keynes still believed the only purpose of economics was to increase 'the pleasures of human intercourse and the enjoyment of beautiful objects'. And these things, like Keynes' probabilities, weren't really measurable. In April 1933, in front of almost the whole Irish government at

University College Dublin, he delivered a famous and slightly shocking address called 'National Self-Sufficiency'. Reading it seven decades later, it still echoes as a powerful indictment of anybody who thinks that counting money is the same as counting wealth:

> We destroy the beauty of the countryside because the unappropriated splendours of nature have non-economic value. We are capable of shutting off the sun and stars because they pay no dividend . . . Today we suffer disillusion not because we are poorer . . . but because other values seem to have been sacrificed . . . and sacrificed unnecessarily. For our economic system is not, in fact, enabling us to exploit to the utmost the possibilities for economic wealth afforded by the progress of our technique . . . leading us to feel we might as well have used up the margin in more satisfying ways. But once we allow ourselves to be disobedient to the test of an accountant's profit, we have begun to change our civilization.

Bizarre measurement No. 9
Open Window Unit
(The amount of sound absorbed in an open window measuring one square foot: now known as a Sabin.)

. . . .
Length of time 'disposable' nappies take to decompose in rubbish tips: *about 500 years*

Number of guns brought to school each day in the USA: *135,000*

Chapter 9

The New Indicators

If the chief of your local police department were to announce today that 'activity' on the city streets had increased by 15 per cent, people would not be interested. They would demand specifics. Exactly what increased? Tree planting or burglaries? Volunteerism or muggings? Car wrecks or neighbourly acts of kindness.
Atlantic Monthly, October 1995

London is too full of fogs and . . . serious people . . . Whether the fogs produce the serious people, or whether the serious people produce the fogs, I don't know.
Oscar Wilde, *Lady Windermere's Fan*

I

Dickens seems to have foreseen our crisis in counting. Once again in the apparently naive character of Sissy Jupe in *Hard Times*, he set the hard questions about national wealth. Here we are in this nation with fifty million pounds, says the teacher – 'Girl number twenty, isn't this a prosperous nation, and a'n't you in a thriving state?'

But once again, Sissy doesn't know the answer: ' "I thought I couldn't know whether it was a prosperous nation or not, and whether I was in a thriving state or not, unless I knew who had got the money, and whether any of it was mine. But that had nothing to do with it. It was not in the figures at all," said Sissy, wiping her eyes.

' "That was a great mistake of yours," observed Louisa.'

A century after the publication of *Hard Times*, it still seemed a mistake. Armed with GNP, the politicians thought they could see a new era of prosperity stretching before them – all because they could 'count' a nation's wealth in one figure and see how much it was growing. A new phrase entered the political lexicon, 'economic growth'. The idea was introduced during the Conservative Party conference in 1954 to a British public exhausted by wartime rationing and postwar austerity. If Britain can 'grow' by 3 per cent a year, then living standards could double by 1980, said the Chancellor of the Exchequer R. A. Butler. He repeated the message over and over again during the 1955 general election. 'It's not pie in the sky but a sober picture,' he told the crowds that used to go to political rallies in those days. 'Moreover we don't have to wait until 1980. Progress will come year by year if we concentrate on production and investment. The government will help with great new schemes. We will build roads and railways, develop atomic power and help with the re-equipment and moderniz-ation of the whole of industry.'

And so it was that a radical method of measuring which arose out of the battle to rescue the world from depression, and then from Hitler, was embraced by the establishment. And once they had embraced it, they never let it go. It seemed the perfect scorecard. Measure national success by the amount of money changing hands, and before you could say 'Profumo', we had 'never had it so good'.

The mantra of growth has been repeated with growing conviction ever since, and with a kind of manic frustration as real life failed to comply with the figures. Because this count-ing crisis has been the sad story of the postwar world. The growth has been gigantic, the technological innovations aston-ishing, and the living standards – if you measure them in terms of money – have shot up. But real life for most of us has also been less healthy, more stressful and more polluted.

Whatever the technocrats said, you simply couldn't count 'progress' like that. Yet governments fell over themselves to compete for growth, sacrificing their wildlife, nature or people's sanity – and sometimes even their populations – to make way for great dams or motorway projects. Enormous investment flowed as a prize to the countries where the growth was high. And within that, policy-makers battled for supremacy over who had the most mobile phones or computers per head. Anyone who questioned whether it was a good idea to flatten this wetland for a road or that neighbour- hood for a tower block were told, fatuously, that you 'can't stand in the way of progress'. It was an irritating inversion of the meaning of the word.

And life wasn't actually better, as we all knew in our heart of hearts. In the 45 years since Butler painted his hopeful future of growth, there is more ill-health and less creativity, fewer people in sports teams, less amateur dramatics, less learning musical instruments or painting. There are more people with asthma, depression and cancer. There is more crime, more people in prisons. But the key measure of success used by politicians and economists recognized none of these things as important. By narrowing the definition of what con- stituted 'wealth', we ended up narrowing all our lives.

The work we all do bringing up children didn't get counted and planned for; but work flipping hamburgers in McDonald's did. The first was ignored. The second was built into govern- ment policy for single mothers. Only money counted, it was like Jeremy Bentham's calculation, but far narrower. And if the whole of public policy was devoted to improving this one bottom line figure, it was a kind of self-fulfilling prophecy. Things that money couldn't buy were driven out. 'A country that cut down all its trees, sold them as wood chips and gambled the money away playing tiddly-winks, would appear from its national accounts to have got richer in terms of GNP per person,' wrote one economist in 1989. Some of them almost did.

Yet economics was by now firmly wedded to this simplistic measuring system. 'Economic growth is the grand objective,' said Keynes' biographer Sir Roy Harrod. 'It is the aim of econ- omic policy as a whole.' And overwhelmingly the establishment agreed with him – people whose wealth was considerable but whose lifestyles were probably increasingly exhausting. It was the tyranny of the bottom line all over again.

It wasn't a new discovery that wealth meant more than money. 'To my big brother, the richest man in town!' says George Bailey's brother in *It's a Wonderful Life*, even though we know he has very little money. 'When I was a boy, my family had little money, but still we had wealth,' said the businessman Sir Ernest Hall more recently.

But it's a lesson that has to be constantly re-learned. 'The sentence "let's get out of this airy stuff and look at the bottom line" ends with one small phrase,' wrote the American poet Robert Bly. 'And yet a whole civilization can disappear through that small hole.'

II

It slowly dawned on people that there was something wrong with the numbers. Maybe things shouldn't have to 'grow' at all. John Stuart Mill certainly believed that 'it is only in the backward countries of the world that increased production is still an important object'. There might, anyway, be some difference between counting money and counting 'wealth' or 'progress' or 'success'. There *are* other things we want to achieve apart from money. But what could we do instead? The solution was, as always, to measure something else – and preferably a lot of different things: if you want to measure the unmeasurable, this usually seems the best solution. But the backlash to GNP was a long time coming.

It has been a revolution brought about by a long list of people, but four stand out. The first was the economist E. J. Mishan. Mishan's book *The Costs of Economic Growth* came out at the height of flower power in 1967, and four years before the green movement arrived with a fanfare of trumpets and the publication – within a month of each other – of *Blueprint for Survival* and *Limits to Growth*. It was also the year of the *Torrey Canyon* disaster, where an oil tanker split open off the Scilly Isles and covered the beaches of the West Country with oil. It required an enormous clean-up operation – all of which counted as a plus in the national accounts. 'The civilization of the West carries with it the seeds of its own disintegration,' wrote Mishan, whose colleagues at the London School of Economics regarded him as an 'amiable eccentric' as he railed against what he called the 'mass flight from reality into statistics'.

'Our environment is sinking fast into a welter of disamenities, yet the most vocal representatives of the main political parties can't raise their eyes from the trade figures to remark the painful event,' he wrote. 'We have become so preoccupied with the ups and downs of the indices that we fail to raise our sights to the larger issues that confront us.'

Mishan was a prophet, but no revolutionary. Quite the reverse – he prefaced the new editions of his book with long rants about schoolgirl pregnancies, junk-mail, gay hotlines and one-parent families. 'The suburbs were quiet and pleasant,' he wrote nostalgically in 1993 about the days before economic growth. 'Nobody's ears were assailed by low-flying aircraft or the neighbours' stereophonics, nor indeed by screaming chainsaws and long-wailing lawn-mowers. In English seaside resorts it was still possible to smell the salt sea air. The Mediterranean coastline had not yet been wrecked by "development" and the waters were clear and fit to bathe in.'

But as his analysis grew in influence, he became the target for more abuse. What about the costs of not growing, said his critics? What about the poor people who need economic growth? 'Ministerial twaddle,' said Mishan. What about the fact that raw materials haven't actually run out yet? 'A man who falls from a hundred-storey building will survive the first ninety-nine storeys unscathed,' wrote Mishan. 'Were he as sanguine as our technocrats, his confidence would grow with the number of storeys he passed on his downward flight and would be at a maximum just before his free-fall abruptly halted.'

The free-fall continues unabated. But help was at hand for Mishan from a completely different point of view. New Zealand MP Marilyn Waring, whose book *If Women Counted* was published in 1988, used the example of a tree. When it is chopped down and sold as wood it has a measurable economic value. But while it is alive and creating oxygen it doesn't. Surely we should start measuring in such a way that we can include the living trees as well, she said.

It was her time as chairman of the New Zealand public accounts committee that really opened her eyes to the problem. Waring noticed that many of the aspects of life that mattered most were completely ignored by the government, because officials only counted money. And one of these aspects of life was the work done around the world by women, often in the home – which had previously been regarded by economists as an infinite resource. She wrote a paper for the Women and Food conference in Sydney in 1982, and submitted it for comment to Australia's deputy chief statistician. 'His memo of reply to me – a classic of sexist economic assumptions – was one of the major incentives to write this book,' she wrote in the introduction. *If Women Counted* was a brave book to write, and she quoted her fellow New Zealander Katherine Mansfield at the outset: 'Risk – risk anything. Care no more for the opinion of others, for those voices. Do the hardest thing on earth for you to do. Act for yourself. Face the Truth.' It was a risky move for someone with a political career.

She dug out the lists of students who worked under Kuznets in the 1930s to develop national accounting in the first place. The names were all men, but at the bottom was an important note: 'Five clerks, all women with substantial experience and know-how, assisted importantly in this work.' These women – all with substantial experience apparently – had become non-persons. And their invisibility had spread to the system they created which still ignores women's work. In the UN accounting system, farmers' wives and daughters were excluded from the statistics of agricultural labourers because there was no money changing hands. When a man marries his housekeeper, said Waring, the value of GNP goes down.

In 1970, the feminist Lisa Leghorn used a survey by Chase Manhattan Bank to find out 'what a wife was worth'. By multiplying the figure by the number of housewives in the USA, she came up with a total figure of about half of US GNP or twice total government spending. There have been endless studies since, all of them arguing about whether you should value housework at prevailing wages, at the cost of actually getting the hoovering done or the cost of something else.

Strangely enough, however it gets worked out, most studies seem to come up with a figure somewhere around half GNP.

The first step was to come up with an alternative to GNP or GDP. Economists were busy suggesting ones right from the beginning. One of the best known was the Index of Sustainable Economic Welfare (ISEW), which measured money but also subtracted the 'bads' (the pollution, disease or depletion of natural resources) from the total. It was drawn up by the alternative economist Clifford Cobb, whose father – theologian John Cobb – teamed up with the World Bank economist Herman Daly to publish the idea in their book *For the Common Good*.

The ISEW reached a much wider audience as the Genuine Progress Indicator in a long article in the magazine *Atlantic Monthly* in 1994. It was called 'If the GDP is up, why is America down?' The article was written to mark the foundation of a new think-tank in San Francisco called Redefining Progress. It was written by Clifford Cobb, with the journalist Jonathan Rowe and Ted Halstead – the whizzkid founder of Redefining Progress, then still in his twenties – and it had an enormous response.

What's more, the article seemed to hit home. It was the period in the UK when politicians were searching for the elusive 'feelgood factor' which explained why people were so stressed, unhappy and angry with the government even though the numbers said they were wealthy. It was the same in the USA: 'There seemingly inexplicably remains an extra-ordinarily deep-rooted foreboding about the economic outlook,' said the fearsome Alan Greenspan of the Federal Reserve. People had money in their pockets, but they weren't content. It was a mystery to the politicians. They hate that kind of complexity.

The article piled on the evidence against GNP. The *Wall Street Journal* had just worked out that the O. J. Simpson trial had cost the equivalent of the total GNP of Grenada. Was that progress? Then there were the liposuction operations – 110,000 of which take place every year in the USA, each of them pumping $2,000 into the growth figures. GNP seems to win both ways – there is growth making people overeat the least healthy foods, then there's growth operating on them to make them look thin again. There's growth making pesticides that cause cancer and growth selling drugs to cure it – often made by the same company. People in Los Angeles spend a total of $800 million a year just on the petrol they use up in traffic jams. Is that 'progress'? Not only do GNP and GDP ignore the collapse of environmental and social underpinnings to the world, but they pretend it is a gain. Readers reached the end of the article sweating with statistics, but doubting the measurements of success.

Of course this wasn't anything new. A century before, the art critic John Ruskin had urged people to distinguish between wealth and money spent making life worse – what he called 'illth'. But the Genuine Progress Indicator was something fresh. It showed that 'genuine progress' had changed direction some time in the 1970s and was now back to what it had been in 1950. Rab Butler was wrong.

Cobb, Rowe and Halstead attracted hundreds of letters from all over the country. Some of them were supportive and excited. 'Gross National Product is writ; the economists and statisticians its keepers,' wrote one of President Johnson's former ministers in response. 'A tranquillity index, a cleanliness index, a privacy index might have told us something about the condition of man, but a fast-growing country bent on piling up material things has been indifferent to the little things that add joy to everyday living.'

It also attracted the rage of many economists. 'GDP is not, and never was intended to be, a measure of national welfare,' wrote the acting director of US economic analysis, warning that it was not the job of economists to say what was good and what was bad. 'Personally, although I enjoy arguments, that's one argument I'm going to stay ten miles away from.'

Jonathan Rowe popped into the meeting of the American Economic Association, just around the corner from the Redefining Progress offices in San Francisco's Kearney Street. He went to hear the future Treasury Secretary Larry Summers urging the media to distinguish between economic doctors and what he called 'quacks'. Even the great hope of the economic profession, Paul Krugman, described the people behind the article as 'incompetents'.

Rowe introduced himself as one of these incompetents to Krugman on his way out. 'Well I'm sorry, but it's true,' he mumbled, dashing off to do an interview.

III

In 1961, Hazel Henderson was a newly-naturalized American citizen, living in a small flat with her daughter. Like Cary Grant, she had made the transition from Bristol to New York City and found it a thrilling place, bustling with new ideas in the first years of the Kennedy presidency. Unlike Cary Grant, the main thing she noticed was the smog and air pollution. 'I was always getting bronchitis,' she said. 'I found that the city had an air pollution index but that nobody knew about it, and I thought it would be incredible if we could get it on the weather broadcasts.'

So while her daughter was asleep during the afternoons, she started writing letters – to the newly-appointed federal communication commissioner and the heads of NBC, ABC and CBS. When the commissioner wrote to say he liked the idea, she forwarded copies to the broadcasters, and five weeks later, the head of news at ABC phoned up to say they would do it. Soon the air pollution measurements were in the *New York Times* and on the local radio stations, and they have been ever since in most American cities. 'It was my first experience of the power of indicators,' she said.

Soon she was organizing a radical environmental group called Citizens for Clean Air, releasing praying mantises into Central Park to cut down the need for insecticides, and learning about economics in her spare time. Her 1981 book, *Politics for the Solar Age*, made her one of the foremost critics of conventional economic measures in the world – but the air pollution index was an important step towards new ways of measuring success. Maybe we should stop measuring money altogether, she said, and start measuring the stuff that's really important. 'Back then, I really thought that economics could be overhauled if we expanded the framework enough,' she said. 'That we could make all the necessary changes for GNP to reflect all the intangibles. When I finished the book, I realized that didn't work. A multidimensional society can't be measured using one discipline. Using money as the co-efficient would re-anoint economists and use their values to decide how to relate more clean air to more money. Why would we want to re-enthrone economists as philosopher-kings?'

But what should you measure instead? By the 1970s, the most popular alternative to measuring money was measuring 'quality of life'. The phrase dated back to 1939 – about the same year as somebody first coined the phrase 'economic growth' – but in those days it meant 'the good life', luxury, indulgence and fun. It wasn't until President Eisenhower's Commission on National Goals in 1960 that it took on its present meaning, and for the next four decades, policy-makers have been trying to define it and measure it. Quality of life has played the same role in government as intellectual capital has in business – the elusive Eldorado of measurement.

Then suddenly, cities began to wonder whether there was money in quality of life too. Most cities used to think they could attract corporations to set up factories and headquarters by offering lucrative tax breaks or the chance to pollute happily and without fear. But then it became clear that, while the dodgy companies liked the idea of regulation-free zones, these perks were not that high on the priority list of others. Many decisions about where to move headquarters to were often influenced not by money at all, but where the chief executives and their families happened to want to live. Good schools, nice trees and exciting theatres attracted more companies than low taxes.

The US map publishers Rand McNally capitalized on this in 1981 by launching their regular *Places Rated Almanac*, which ranked 277 American cities in terms of their 'liveability'. Atlanta came top the first year. Those at the bottom reached for their lawyers. In the second year, the *Almanac* staggered policy-makers by putting Pittsburgh top. This was a city which had once been so polluted that it had to keep its street lights on all day. At its best, measuring can shock people into realizing that something has changed.

British geographers were not far behind. A group of academics at Glasgow University managed to convince the Scottish Development Agency, and the regeneration body Glasgow Action, that they should try the same idea. But the UK almanac would be measured more accurately. Before anything else, they would do an opinion poll all over the country to ask people what they thought were the most important aspects of city life. Would it be good schools, low crime, cleanliness, high art? Only if you measured that first could you find out how to weigh the data. The public overwhelmingly rated low crime as the most important aspect of the good life.

The academics set to work. Alan Findlay was an expert in migration and believed that it was 'quality' rather than money that was shaping where people were moving. Arthur Morris was interested in where industry wanted to move – and it wasn't a polluted crime-ridden hell-hole with tax advantages. Findlay and Morris took on a geomorphologist Robert Rogerson – an expert in movements of ice and continents – and in the next 18 months, they set about measuring everything.

Often that meant being on the road. Rogerson visited all the 97 places they measured in the next few years, talking to people at random in the streets and at bus stops to get a sense of place. This was no dry measuring project. Just as Charles Booth hit on the idea of asking school board visitors first, Rogerson and his colleagues hit on the idea of asking estate agents. They gossiped to them about house prices and neighbourhoods. Then there were all the other measurements: how long did people have to wait for operations city by city? How long did they get to spend with their GPs? How much violent crime was there? How big were the school classes?

It all went into the pot and their first index was an enormous success. For three days, the university switchboard was

jammed by reporters from all over the world wanting to cover
the story. Birmingham came bottom because of the Bull Ring
centre, but the problem was that Glasgow didn't do very well
either. Worse, their historic rivals Edinburgh came top. It was
the height of the 'Glasgow's Miles Better' campaign which did
so much to improve the city's image, and this was about the
last thing Glasgow's leaders wanted to hear. They had helped
fund the index, after all. The presentation to the city council
was a stilted affair around a large oak table at Glasgow city
chambers. 'They either printed the list of cities upside down
or the interviews were conducted in Esperanto,' the enraged
city provost Pat Lally told the local press.

Rogerson moved the Quality of Life Group to Strathclyde
University and extended the study to cover smaller towns.
Most of them used the findings as the basis for improvement,
but not all. The angriest confrontation was in the worst place
in Scotland, according to their measurements – the notoriously
corrupt district of Monklands. Red-faced with fury, one councillor called Rogerson an 'upstart from Strathclyde University',
shouting 'I don't believe a word you say!'

A decade on, and everyone seems to be putting together
tables of places which measure how good they are to live
in. Most chose somewhere different for the topmost place.
A Reading University study in 1986 put Frankfurt top. The
pioneering 'Booming Towns' studies in the 1980s put Win-
chester top. When they tried again taking house prices into
account, they replaced it with Milton Keynes. *Fortune* maga
zine's best 'foreign' cities for business in 1996 put Toronto
top, followed by London on the grounds that it is safe, friendly
and bustling. *Money* magazine in the USA chose the small
town of Nashua in New Hampshire. The UK marketing group
Mintel even published a European Lifestyles compendium of
quality of life data in 16 volumes costing a cool £2,450 a set.
The London office of the Swiss-based Corporate Resources
Group publishes annual surveys of quality of life in different
world cities, to help companies work out what they have to
pay their executives for working there. Using London as the
base city of 100, their weighted index gives Moscow 52.

It depends how you work it out, of course. Especially when you start counting crime – because people's fears often bear no relation to reality. Two thirds of shoppers from Leicester interviewed in the 1990s revealed that what scared them most was being killed by a terrorist bomb – which even then was pretty unlikely. Go to any city in the world, however safe, and the locals will tell you how careful you have to be. Even if you use the same measuring rod everywhere, local people perceive it differently, define it differently and interpret it differently. Quality of life measures may be better than simply measuring the amount of money changing hands – but they are not exactly definitive.

This same argument was being played out in a series of angry battles behind the scenes at the United Nations. The Chapter 40 of Agenda 21, agreed at the Rio Earth Summit in 1992, had committed all the signatories to measure progress towards sustainable development, using a series of what they called 'indicators' of success. By 1995, they had come up with a working list of 134 of them they hoped all countries would adopt. The trouble was they all chose different ones. They collected data in different ways. They didn't want to subject themselves to some of the indicators – and some of them meant different things in different cultures.

But what should they measure? And who should decide? Would it just be the powerful Western countries all over again? What if one country wanted to measure its success by how energy-efficient they were, but another wanted to measure the progress by health statistics? The OPEC countries fought the environmentalists. The old-style statisticians who wanted scientific indicators fought the new sustainability professionals who wanted thrilling ones. The developing countries fought the developed. There was only one way forward – to let nations and communities choose their own measurements.

It was an important decision, and one of the first to put it into effect – in nearly every district – has been the UK. And so, 160 years since Chadwick sent his assistant commissioners scouring the cities with their measurements and tabular data, their great-great-great-grandchildren set out again – this time by faster modes of transport than the post-chaise – to measure the unmeasurable.

IV

The early twenty-first century looks set to be dominated by the thousand miles or so of the North American Pacific coast. Not so much because of the Hollywood dream machine or the Los Angeles smog, but because of the extraordinary outpouring of wealth and creativity associated with Silicon Valley. So it is no surprise that a book about measuring what is really important should keep coming back there. There was John Vasconcellos, Silicon Valley's representative in the California assembly. There was Ted Halstead, founder of the Redefining Progress and now head of the Silicon Valley's own think tank, the New America Foundation. There was the challenge to accountancy posed by measuring the value of companies like Microsoft.

The next part of the measuring story starts in Microsoft's home town of Seattle, just up the Pacific coast, and also home to coffee bars, Boeing and the good life. Gary Lawrence had been city administrator for Redmond, where Microsoft's headquarters is, before he was head-hunted to be planning director of Seattle – after a nationwide search for a new kind of planner.

The task was to create a plan for Seattle that would cover every neighbourhood, would reflect what people actually wanted, and would not just cover issues like where the shops should be – but health and education too. But since this was in the first flush of excitement after the Rio summit, the new Seattle plan would also measure progress against yardsticks set by the people who lived there. This was a system devised and promoted by the local group Sustainable Seattle, and it has spread all over the world.

It was a tough job and it was going to take years. The mayor was given his own weekly TV show where people were encouraged to phone in with suggestions and views. He and Gary Lawrence appeared on talk radio five times a week – this is after all the city of *Frasier*. Full colour brochures were delivered to every household; teenagers were hired by the city to translate the issues into language that other teenagers might understand. Lawrence himself did 400 presentations over two years. It was a gigantic exercise in local democracy.

Human cussedness being what it is – by the end of this unprecedented consultation, a third of the city had still never heard of the project. Worse, many of those that *had* heard of it said they hadn't been consulted enough. But they overwhelmingly supported the direction the plan was going.

Then there was the job of choosing their indicators of success, along the lines set out by Jacksonville in Florida, with help from Hazel Henderson. Seattle rejected conventional money measurements. They wanted to know how cultured, how educated and how clean the city was. They wanted to measure their success by the number of books sold or lent out by libraries, by attendance at arts events, by participation in sport. They set out to measure the number of latchkey kids, the amount of blood donated, the number of hours people volunteered. They also wanted a series of ratios. They wanted to judge the city's success by the number of vegetarian restaurants as a proportion of the number of McDonald's. Or the amount of bird seed sold at local garden centres as a proportion of the pesticide. They wanted to know the number of therapists per head of population – though I've never been clear if it was considered a sign of mental health if there were more of them or less.

That was 1993. Soon the same idea had spread to the UK, pioneered by the New Economics Foundation and UNED-UK, who set about encouraging a new generation of counters to get out there and measure. Once again, it was a question of how to measure what really matters. If you measure problems you just get depressed. If you measure particular solutions, they might be wrong – they often are. You might for example measure how close the shops or bus stops were to people's homes – forgetting that the food could still be disgusting and the bus service scandalous.

No, you had to find what was most important – and you had to make it inspiring. 'Few people feel passionately about spreadsheets,' said Gary Lawrence. 'For indicators to lead to change, there needs to be emotional content: people need to care in their hearts as well as their minds.'

It was a revolutionary and enjoyably unscientific idea, and it led to the idea of 'hot indicators'. Hot indicators might not have been measuring the most important aspect of life. They might not be exact or scientific, but at least they could catch people's imagination. So Seattle now judges its success on the number of salmon in local streams. In Dundee it was the number of empty houses, and in Fife it was the number of fish landing at local ports. There was the amount of asthma in Leeds, the number of cars with only one occupant in Peterborough, the amount of local produce sold in local shops in West Devon, the number of streets quiet enough to hold a conversation in in Hertfordshire, the number of swans in Norwich, the number of people who have planted a tree in Croxdale, the number of stag beetles in Colchester.

Armed with their equivalent of tabular data, Chadwick's successors stood at street corners collecting figures and bringing them back to the local council to collate. Sometimes it was local people doing the measuring, sometimes local officials, sometimes it was children. And as true followers of Chadwick, the main object of the exercise – beyond science or calculation – was to create change.

Merton people insisted on measuring asthma cases, even though local doctors protested that it wasn't very scientific. Oldham tried to develop an indicator of how beautiful new buildings were, but simply couldn't work out how. Instead they chose to measure the number of local ponds with frogs or newts in. Perry Walker of the New Economics Foundation encouraged the idea because it was something schoolchildren could get involved in. 'These are not scientific indicators,' he said. 'That's not how they achieve their impact. They do so because they're what people care about.'

In another of his projects in Reading, people were puzzling over how they could measure the amount of dog mess in local parks in a way that could excite people. They hit on the idea of planting a little flag by each small brown pile, and then taking a picture of it. There were 900 flags in all, and the pictures were published enthusiastically in the local paper. Two weeks later they did the same, and there were only 250 flags. Counting had worked. Perhaps it should be no surprise that Seattle now has the highest life expectancy in the USA and more books are bought there than in any other US city – you tend to get what you measure, after all.

Alternative indicators were all the rage. The Canadian environmentalist William Rees has pioneered a method of counting the environmental impact of cities in terms of the hectares they need of the earth to satisfy their needs. The UN Human Development Index was ranking countries according to life expectancy, education and purchasing power. The World Bank was working on its improved 'Wealth Accounting System' that included environment and human measurements. Even Standard & Poor, the American financial touchstone, were rating municipal bonds according the quality of life of the city that issued them. And right at the end of the millennium, Hazel Henderson's Calvert-Henderson Quality of Life Indicators – measuring each country by a series of different measures of their environment, health, safety, human rights and much else besides – were being sent out to 1,500 ethical investment brokers instead of their usual Christmas cake.

V

So there they are, Bentham's new generation of counters around the world – peering through the smog in South American cities counting the number of days you can see the Andes. Or scouring the streets of Britain measuring how many people can name their community police. The whole business of indicators began as a radical challenge to governments. One group called Green Gauge even bought the poster site opposite the hideous headquarters of the Department of the Environment in London, and covered it with their own pollution and traffic measurements. But now everyone is doing it. As early as 1991, the Canadian government was measuring its success with 43 new indicators. The OECD was soon counting 150 indicators. A 1993 survey of England and Wales found that 84 per cent of people wanted more environmental information from the government. And heavens – did they get it!

The new-look Department of the Environment, Transport and the Regions announced its thirteen 'headline indicators' in 1999, including the number of unfit homes, adult literacy and more amorphous concepts like community spirit. Behind those 13 was another set of 150 sub-indicators – and they just covered one government department. For some reason, the official mind believes that if indicators are a good idea then we should have too many of them. Soon every department of government was churning out figures of their own, each one backed by a battery of technicians and statisticians, publishing them all in screeds of tables. 'Best value' rules for British local authorities is unleashing a wave of local counting. At the last count, the British government had set itself a total of over 8,000 targets. Chadwick would have been proud.

Why do indicators have such an appeal to modern governments? Partly because of the technocratic thrill of measuring the ebb and flow of cause and effect as if government was a gigantic, though not particularly well-oiled, machine. It is the McKinsey fallacy all over again. Yet cause and effect is the one thing it is quite impossible to measure – interpreting the burgeoning wealth of data to work out what causes what is always a matter of judgement, common sense and intuition.

Yet governments still cling to their other dream – one number to sum up the whole caboodle. GNP and its partner GDP are alive and well. If you look up the policies of the new regional development agencies in the UK, you will see that many of them share the ambition to have the highest growth in Europe. When the Clinton administration tried to add footnotes to the GDP figures that measured the depletion of natural resources, the whole idea was blocked by two representatives from coal-producing states. If national accounts showed air pollution, warned Alan Mollohan from West Virginia, 'somebody is going to say . . . that the coal industry isn't contributing anything to the country'. Quite so.

This fresh outbreak of measuring is one of the defining characteristics of our age. In politics the response to the wider counting crisis – that we need to measure what's really important – is to measure everything. But these bizarre local indicators are different. They are not intended to measure the world, as much as change it. They are about inspiring people. It's the act of measuring that matters. Change happens when children go out measuring stag beetles in their back garden. It probably doesn't happen when the professionals do it with their precision and clever instruments. It happens when they ask people whether they feel well, but probably not when – as in Oldham – they measure the number of babies born less than the official healthy birthweight of precisely 2,499 grammes. This kind of measuring is more likely to suffer the same fate that most official counting suffers from. In alternative economic circles, it's known as MEGO Syndrome. It stands for My Eyes Glaze Over.

What we count is important because it reflects who we are. Or as Hazel Henderson told the first alternative economics summit in London in 1984, 'reality is what we pay attention to'. That explains why Chadwick and his contemporaries spent so much time measuring people's religious feelings and why our own contemporaries are measuring allergies. Strange in a way that both generations counted stag beetles in their back gardens.

But it's more than that. We construct our own reality by counting it. 'Indicators only reflect our innermost core values and goals, measuring the development of our own understanding,' says Henderson. No wonder when we measure what we fear the most – greenhouse gas or child abuse – the figures tend to get worse. At last, an explanation for the Quantum Effect.

Or as one Washington policy-maker puts it at the foot of

all her e-mails: 'We are what we measure. It's time we measured what we want to be.'

Bizarre measurement No. 10

Man hour

(The amount of work done by the 'standard' man, as in 'man year' and 'man day'. The unit is taken to include women, or so it's said . . .)

....

Number of Americans shot by children under six (1983–93): *138, 490*

Number of food shops in Britain (1950): *221,662*
Number of food shops in Britain (1997): *36,931*

Chapter 10

Historical Interlude 5:
The Price of Everything

If it cannot get beyond its vast abstractions, the national income, the rate of growth, capita/output ratio, input/output analysis, labour mobility, capital accumulation; if it cannot get beyond all this and make contact with the human realities of poverty, frustration, alienation, despair, breakdown, crime, escapism, stress, congestion, ugliness and spiritual death, then let us scrap economics and start afresh.
E. F. Schumacher, *Small is Beautiful*

A man who knows the price of everything and the value of nothing.
Oscar Wilde's definition of a cynic

I

'A woman of uranium,' said the French newspaper *Le Quotidien* about Margaret Thatcher. 'Compared to her, how leaden appear most of our leaders.' She may have glowed in the dark, but the great thing about having her as prime minister was that you knew where you stood. With her handbag in constant attendance – even in the kitchen, according to one fly-on-the wall documentary – she could be relied upon to be the Iron or Uranium Lady almost on demand. If it wasn't the Soviets, it was the miners or the Greenham Women, the unemployed, the greens, the Militant Tendency, the 'enemy within'. When it came to the environment, she prided herself as a chemist that she understood the problem – if indeed there was one – a good deal more than those lily-livered, bearded green types.

Yet suddenly on 27 September 1988, and over nine years into her term of office, Mrs Thatcher seemed to turn the world on its head. In her speech to the Royal Society, she deliberately stole the mantle of one of the most famous green campaigns in the world and declared herself a 'friend of the earth'. Politicians had a duty, she said, to 'maintain the planet on a full repairing lease'. And then the most important phrase of all – about global warming – warning that humanity had 'unwittingly begun a massive experiment with the system of this planet itself'.

It was a shocking moment, and for the UK it was the moment the green movement became respectable. It was more difficult to work out the politics of it. Who had actually written the speech? Fingers pointed at Sir Crispin Tickell, the green-tinged British ambassador to the United Nations, for the global warming phrase. Mrs Thatcher had listened to his advice since her visit to Mexico City while he was ambassador there. An earthquake had struck in the middle of dinner and she had admired his stiff upper lip.

But the Thatcher conversion may have had more to do with her regular meetings with Prince Charles. He had enraged her at a crucial moment of inner city rioting by warning (from the distance of Australia) that he didn't want to 'inherit a divided kingdom'. Regular meetings at 10 Downing Street were started to patch up their relationship: Charles was probably one of the few people with decidedly different views she had regular meetings with. By 1988, he was being roundly condemned by one property developer for being 'hi-jacked by the loony green brigade'.

But whoever inspired her speech, ministers and officials who had been expecting the usual rant against hippies and layabouts had to do some quick thinking. The British government was now, at one stroke of a pen, supposed to be firmly in the forefront of the green movement. The trouble is most of them didn't know what that meant. Their attempt to answer the question launched a new twist to the story of measurement, and made the trenchant, cat-loving environmental economist David Pearce into almost a household name – and into a controversial and embattled figure on both sides of the Atlantic.

The most immediate problem was that Mrs Thatcher had

recently appointed the least green of all her ministers to run the Department of the Environment. Nicholas Ridley was a heavy smoker, and clouds of cigarette smoke enveloped his desks and meetings. His main task there had been to abolish the system of local government finance so that everybody in the country – rich and poor – would pay the same amount. This highly-controversial so-called Poll Tax was about to undermine the foundations of her government, but that was months in the future. Ridley also held environmentalists in particular contempt. Even the moderate and well-respected Association for the Conservation of Energy he dismissed as being in the pay of the insulation industry.

Yet the British government was now officially green, and they also had to draft a constructive response to the recently-published Brundtland Report, *Our Common Future*, the most recent United Nations attempt to come to grips with the environment and development agenda. They weren't sure how to do it. The report had introduced the idea of 'sustainability' – which meant making sure development didn't damage the earth for future generations. It also covered everything from poverty to education. Where do you start? Ridley farmed the problem out and commissioned Pearce to write it.

Pearce was then at the top of his chosen profession, one of the best-known and most experienced proponents of cost-benefit analysis in the UK. He was a professor at University College, London – site of Bentham's glass case – and had travelled all over Africa for the World Bank and other UN bodies. If anyone could hold the line between the green agenda and a British government obsessed with markets and costs, it was Pearce.

How could you create a sustainable world in practice? That was Pearce's issue, and his answer was to make the environment expensive. Because it was free to cut down the Amazon rainforest or pollute the atmosphere, everyone just went ahead and did it. Yet there clearly were hidden costs when people did so – damage to the air we breathe causes health problems, for example. Damaged rainforest speeds up global warming, which means freak weather conditions and rising sea levels. There are real costs attached. The idea was to measure these costs and give threatened forests, views and species a monetary value.

Pearce wrote a manifesto for cost-benefit. If the government adopted the idea, it would mean armies of economists measuring every aspect of the environment. It was also a small political breakthrough. At last, a new kind of environmental politics that Conservatives might be able to embrace – it worked not by regulation but by using the market. If there are costs, the polluter should pay. Who could object to that?

When it was ready, Pearce was ushered in to see Ridley in the hideous glass and concrete building that housed the Department of the Environment. They peered at each other though the cigarette smoke and disliked each other on sight. But that didn't matter: Ridley had done his duty and this report was headed for the dusty shelves.

Pearce delivered twenty copies, drafted a press release and the civil servants agreed to host a small press conference. Only two journalists turned up. And that's where it would have ended, had not one of the journalists asked about the green taxes Pearce had hinted at. He had already been careful not to spell these out in the report itself because it was beyond his remit, and not the kind of thing this secretary of state wanted to hear. But in reply to the question he suggested that maybe the government could look at taxes on fertiliser, pesticides and energy. At the back of the room, the Department of the Environment press officer made urgent 'wind it up' gestures with his hands.

Back at home in Bedford with his wife that evening, Pearce was watching the late night current affairs programme *Newsnight*, and was astonished to see a headline on the front of the *Daily Mail* for the next morning which referred to a coming 'pollution tax shock'.

'I can't believe it,' he said to his wife. 'Somebody's stolen our ideas.'

But it wasn't somebody else of course. Pearce's hint that a future government might introduce taxes of this kind swept onto the front pages. 'I literally couldn't believe it,' he said later. 'Anybody's guess is as good as anybody else's. Was this something they wanted or they engineered? To this day I don't know.'

But whoever was pulling the strings, it certainly wasn't Ridley. His main political battle over the Poll Tax was going badly and three weeks later Mrs Thatcher held one of her frequent reshuffles and Ridley was gone. His replacement was the young high-flyer Chris Patten, the future last governor of Hong Kong. At 10.30 am on Patten's second day in office, the phone at Pearce's home in Bedford rang. A civil servant asked him if he could be at the Department of the Environment within an hour. He made it by the skin of his teeth, was ushered in to see the new Secretary of State – whom he had worked with before when Patten had been in charge of overseas aid. 'Patten was an entirely different character,' said Pearce later. 'He had an intellectual and very inquiring mind and a slightly disarming style. He was quite down to earth.'

'Ah, David!' said Patten as he walked in. 'What do you know about the Poll Tax?'

Pearce confessed he knew absolutely nothing about it and couldn't help him on the knottiest political problem of the day. But within an hour or so, he had been appointed to advise him for two days a week on environmental economics. The government would embrace the idea of measuring the price of the environment after all.

It was August 1989, the Thatcher boom was at its height – the day he was appointed, the newspapers were reporting that champagne might have to be rationed because of the enormous demand from British yuppies in their pin-striped suits. Patten's political gamble to embrace the environment was a risk, but it was the silly season and the media were delighted. They described Pearce's trenchant style, his balding appearance, and his strange taste in stripy shirts. They applauded his green credentials, commuting to work every day by train from Bedford. They described him wandering through the forests of Botswana and across Sudan armed with a calculator. They quoted unnamed friends describing him as 'no Maynard Keynes, but very good-humoured for an economist'.

'The tide against the environment has turned,' Pearce told the press. 'But there will be a lot of continuing disasters on a lot of fronts before things get any better.'

It was a hopeful moment. Eastern Europe was on the verge of revolution, the Berlin Wall still stood but only just. And it looked as though ten years of Conservative government had, after all, resulted in senior ministers interested in safeguarding the world for the future. For Pearce, it was also the biggest chance that cost-benefit analysis had been given for decades. If it could be measured – the value of elephants, the cash cost of aircraft noise, the value of the Grand Canyon – Pearce would measure it. And by measuring it, you could set a price to it, and find a way of protecting it.

It was pragmatic in the extreme, but it was also hopeful. Yet within six years Pearce was being condemned by the environmentalists of the world as a pedlar of 'racist economics'. He would have unleashed a torrent of international abuse on his head, and he would face a vitriolic campaign against him – including a public letter signed by leading members of the chattering classes all over the world – culminating in the humiliating rejection of his framework for tackling global warming by the United Nations.

II

David Pearce was born in Harrow on 11 October 1941, in the lull between the Blitz and Hitler's doodlebugs and just as Keynes was turning his mind to rebuilding the world financial system. His father was a glassblower and his mother was a school cleaner at Harrow, the exclusive private school and alma mater to the Prime Minister Winston Churchill.

His life was changed by having a future home secretary as his teacher. Merlyn Rees was then a struggling Labour candidate for the constituency of Harrow East, and it was Rees who persuaded his parents to let him stay on at school into the sixth form. From there it was Lincoln College, Oxford and a Ph.D. at the London School of Economics on the bread crisis of 1795–6. Then via three British economics departments in new universities to be professor of economics in Aberdeen, the centre of the British oil industry.

But Pearce was no dry-as-dust economist. He had enthusiasms. He collected English porcelain. He loved bird-watching in Africa. He loved animals – posters of them are emblazoned around his office at University College, and he has dedicated all his books to his cats. He now owns seven of them, plus two large dogs. At an early stage in his academic career he got interested in making economics kinder to wildlife by adjusting GNP so that the damage to nature and wildlife was accurately reflected in the national accounts. It was the start of his life-long interest in making the economy take the environment into account.

It wasn't a new idea, as we have seen – but it was a technique that had not been developed for some generations. When he moved to Southampton University in 1967, Pearce and his colleagues formed a small group of environmental economists. It had only six members. One of them was E. J. Mishan, whose revolutionary book *The Costs of Economic Growth* was just then hitting the bookshelves.

By then, cost-benefit analysis was back in fashion. The government was desperately trying to work out where to build the third London airport. They had rejected the preferred site at Stansted in Essex, and for the next two and a half years the commission chaired by the senior judge, Mr Justice Roskill, combed the evidence. To make sure there was a choice of sites, the Town and Country Planning Association think-tank put in their own planning application to build an airport at Foulness, on marshland off the Essex coast much frequented by Brent Geese.

Cost-benefit analysis had been used successfully a few years before to defend the idea of extending the Victoria Line to London's poverty-stricken suburb of Brixton. But this wasn't so much a calculation as a way of giving transport minister Barbara Castle an excuse to say yes, which she duly did. The Roskill Commission, on the other hand, were determined to work out the answer mathematically. They would do a cost-benefit analysis on all the possible sites – the biggest analysis of its kind ever carried out. They would put a value on the noise of aircraft, the disruption of building work, the delay of flights, the extra traffic and they would calculate the answer. For the Roskill Commission, there was going to be no value judgement at all. The figures would speak for themselves.

To avoid any chance of judgement and to keep the process completely 'scientific', the measurements were put together in 25 separate calculations. They were only added up right at the end of the process. And to the horror of some of the members of the commission, when the final addition was made, the answer was wrong. The site they felt was best – Foulness – was going to be £100 million more expensive in cost-benefit terms than the small village of Cublington. After 246 witnesses, 3,850 documents, seven technical annexes and 10 million spoken words, some of the planners on the commission felt cheated. In public, they stayed loyal to Roskill. The commission was excellent, said Britain's most famous planner Colin Buchanan – a member of it – 'it just got the small matter of the site wrong'.

The team had managed to measure the exact cost of having too much aircraft noise by looking at the effect noise tended to have on house prices. Doing the same calculation two decades later, Pearce came up with a figure of £250 lopped off the value of each house per extra decibel. But when it came to measuring the value of a Norman church at Stewkley, which would have to be demolished to make way for the runway, things got more confused. How could you possibly put a money price on that? One team member suggested they find out its fire insurance value. The story got out and reached the press. Doing it like that would measure the value of the church at just £51,000.

A fierce political debate erupted. Commission members were accused of being 'philistines'. Pearce's old adversary John Adams, from the University College geography department, drew up an alternative plan. Using similar cost-benefit methods, he showed that the cheapest option would be to build the airport in Hyde Park – but that Westminster Abbey would have to be demolished. The satire didn't work: the *Sunday Times* published a letter from a retired air vice marshal congratulating him for recommending Hyde Park for an airport, and pointing out that he had proposed exactly the same thing in 1946.

Nearly three years after the project had started, the new Conservative government announced in April 1971 that they did not accept the calculation either. The third London airport would not be built at Cublington, as the commission had suggested. It would be built at Foulness, then re-named Maplin Sands, after all. The Maplin plan was scrapped during the energy crisis three years later in 1974 and the airport was built at Stansted anyway, but that is another story.

The residents of Cublington celebrated noisily. Their local MP Timothy Raison wrote to *The Times*, assuring Roskill that people burning his effigy hadn't meant it personally. But the number-crunchers were furious. The first absolutely rational, fair and open system for making a decision had just been dumped by ministers, said the Commission's deputy director of research A. D. J. Flowerdew in a letter next day. But he rather gave himself away when he described the decision as 'a triumph for the ex-urbanites and subsidized farmers of North Buckinghamshire, and engineers who hope to be awarded the licence to print money afforded by the reclamation contract.' The technocrat wasn't quite so coolly rational after all.

But the effigy-burners were nothing to the assault from planning professor Peter Self, who wrote a book about it as a kind of revenge for the mauling he received at the hands of the Commission's planning barristers. 'It struck me at the time as strange,' he wrote, 'that so many intelligent people should apparently accept trial by quantification as the only sensible or possible way of reaching such a decision.'

It infuriated him that the new 'ecor ocracy' – as he called it – were so pompous about numbers that meant so little. Anyone like Buchanan who looked at the competing sites could see that building the airport off the coast was the best plan, he said. You couldn't calculate intuition and experience like that. Yet all the lawyers at the commission did was pick over the measurements: 'The weight placed on cost-benefit analysis was then confirmed by the spectacle of the flower of the English planning bar gargling gingerly and reverently with the cost-benefit figures.'

The whole thing was a 'psychological absurdity and ethical monstrosity', he said. He advised economists to take Dr Johnson's advice and kick a wall hard to convince themselves that the external world exists. His attack destroyed cost-benefit analysis for nearly two decades.

Pearce had been there, of course, retained by Buckinghamshire County Council. Now thirty years on, he emphasizes that the idea of valuing Stewkley church was just a joke. They never did measure what it was worth. In fact the assessors failed to measure a whole range of things. 'They were measuring things that made environmental impacts irrelevant,' he says now. 'They measured the value of even one minute saving time for aircraft, but not the pollution from the road traffic or from the aircraft. There is nothing wrong with cost-benefit analysis, as long as you remember what a benefit and a cost means. If you do it badly, even bad brain surgery might lead you to think that brain surgery is a bad idea.'

III

As a practising Roman Catholic, there were clear moral reasons why Chris Patten wanted to find a new way of rescuing the environment. But there were good self-interested reasons too. Margaret Thatcher had recently embraced the idea, a recent poll had showed that 77 per cent of Conservative voters wanted to protect the environment better, and there was an even more exciting prospect too.

Of all UK government departments, the Treasury is the most senior. It is the Treasury that traditionally scrutinizes all spending plans, and rules Whitehall through the effortless power of tradition and economics. But if spending plans then had to be submitted to the Department of the Environment to cost their environmental impact, things might be different.

Patten had dimly perceived a reversal of roles in government with his own department on top.

Even so, it was a brave decision, also calculated to take attention away from the increasingly disastrous Poll Tax. Patten's influence meant that there was soon a stream of green thinkers through the front door of 10 Downing Street. Mrs Thatcher met the high-profile Friends of the Earth director Jonathon Porritt for forty minutes. The American environmentalist Amory Lovins came away complaining about the waste of heat and light there – especially in the No 10 men's lavatory.

And at the Conservative party conference that year, Patten sketched out a new way ahead, urging that the 'government should regulate on the part of the consumer'. We *can* make a difference, he said from the platform. Pessimism threatened to 'bring down on the heads of our children the darkness that many fear'. Next to him on the platform, Mrs Thatcher, the great deregulator, was seen to applaud.

By 1989, Pearce was one of the Global 500, the United Nations roll of honour for services to environmental protection, and in some demand – he had just completed Botswana's national conservation strategy. But he was still one of only a handful of environmental economists in the country. He reckoned there were only ten at the time, and five of them were working for him.

The first thing to do was to prepare his report for Ridley for a wider audience. It was published swiftly and called after his cat Blueprint. *Blueprint for a Green Planet*, co-authored with his colleagues Anil Markandya and Edward Barbier, quickly achieved bestseller status. It was bought by environmentalists in their tens of thousands thrilled that this kind of thinking could come out of a government. They took it home expecting the usual fuzzy green rhetoric, and were taken aback by the complicated equations and implacable economic theory. But for the time being they were prepared to give him the benefit of the doubt. Hadn't Pearce successfully stormed the Whitehall barricades?

Patten described Pearce as 'my green guru', and as a special adviser he could safely suggest ideas publicly which could be disowned if necessary by ministers. He could and did suggest taxes on carbon and pesticides, or tradable permits to pollute the air or cut down forests. He could and did suggest that the cost of saving the African elephant, paying off ivory traders and equipping game park wardens might be in the order of $100 million a year. He was sufficiently independent to fly in the face of Conservative philosophy in public, telling the press that 'unfettered free markets will not solve environmental problems. They will make them worse'. This was anathema to Mrs Thatcher – but then Pearce had never voted Conservative. He still hasn't.

But the public seemed to respond. A Gallup Poll issued in response showed that people would overwhelmingly be prepared to pay more to protect the countryside. The *Independent* newspaper published a short version of *Blueprint*, looking at how we could measure the value of a diverse range of animals, forest or ancient woodland. A cabinet committee was set up called MISC141, chaired by the prime minister herself, and an environment white paper was promised within the year. It all seemed to be going well.

IV

The first sign that something had gone wrong came only five months later. A speech by Patten raised the possibility that some of these new methods of measuring, and their accompanying taxes, would be postponed until after the general election. The truth was that Patten was facing stiff opposition, as expected from the Treasury – but also from other cabinet colleagues. Transport secretary Cecil Parkinson was trying to push through a massive expansion of road building. Energy secretary John Wakeham was afraid that energy taxes would raise fuel bills in the run-up to the election. And when the civil servant in charge of the whole operation had sent a questionnaire to every ministry asking them about their environmental impact, many of them were livid.

When the white paper was published in September 1990, it was a pale reflection of the hopes laid out in *Blueprint*. There were 356 recommendations, but none of them would change much. Pearce sent a memo to Patten which said simply: 'Is that it?'

Who had spiked the idea, asked the papers? There had been a trickle of damaging leaks from the cabinet, but most fingers pointed at the Department of the Environment permanent secretary Sir Terence Heiser – the equivalent of Sir Humphrey Appleby in *Yes, Minister*. He was said to have taken one look at the book and decided that *Blueprint* would have to have its claws drawn. In fact, the cabinet committee had agreed unanimously that nothing should be done until after the 1992 election, and specifically ruled out a carbon tax or more duty on petrol. They even dumped the simple idea of using more recycled material in government offices. It was a frustrating and disappointing moment.

Pearce was already criticizing the government in public for moving too slowly. Mrs Thatcher was ousted at the end of the year and Patten was promoted to be chairman of the party in the run-up to the election. Pearce concentrated on developing the theory. *Blueprint 2* looked at global threats to the environment in the run-up to the Rio Earth Summit. *Blueprint 3* set out the costs of road transport in Britain. He calculated the real costs, including accidents and pollution, at between £23 and £26 billion – or about twice as much as the road tax brought in.

By 1994, there had still been no action from John Major's embattled government and Pearce was in open revolt. The British government's inertia was 'pathetic', he wrote in *Blueprint 3*:

> I am highly sensitive to the argument that giving a higher priority to protecting the environment can cost industry money. But the government has done no work on how much it would cost, or how it could be paid. It has simply dropped the idea . . . Scandinavia has forged ahead and has demonstrated that it has saved money for industry by introducing environmental levies. The best

the UK can do is point to one such measure in the past five years and a glossy pamphlet telling us what a good idea such taxes are.

By *Blueprint 4* – dedicated to the memory of his cat Dill – he had extended his criticisms to the environmentalists. Without doubt their pressure had brought about the agreements in Rio in 1992. 'Also without doubt, a great many constructive and effective ideas have been ignored or played down because of their desire not just to win but to win in their own way.'

The problem was that Pearce was fighting his battle on two fronts. Governments and industrialists were suspicious of change they simply didn't understand. The Australian miners who threw beer cans at him at one lecture accused him of being 'balmy'. The environmentalists were objecting to the idea of measuring the value of the earth in terms of money. The problem was the idea of 'willingness to pay' or 'willingness to accept compensation' – known to the *cognoscenti* as WTP and WTA. This meant that you could measure the value of something – whether it was grizzly bears or big-horn sheep in America or Amazon rainforests – by asking people what they would be prepared to pay to rescue them.

Using WTP and other measuring techniques, Pearce had come up with a figure of greenhouse damage of twenty dollars per extra tonne of carbon. Cutting down primary forest cost between $4,000 and $4,400 per hectare, said the environmental economists. People seemed to be prepared to pay between $40–48 per person to preserve the entire species of humpback whales – or $49–64 after seeing a video of them.

He and his colleagues were introducing a whole new jargon – bequest values, total user values, option values. Or existence values – what people are prepared to pay for the continued existence of things they may never see – like the Grand Canyon. Grizzly bears seemed to be worth twenty-four dollars per person, under this system. The Grand Canyon's existence he calculated at $4.43 a month.

There were many environmentalists who objected to the idea that you could put any money value on a species at all. Destroying the ozone layer, flattening the rainforest, killing whales was immoral and that was all there was to it. Their loss was of incalculable value, and anyone who said otherwise was immoral too.

The argument between the idealists and Pearce's pragmatism went backwards and forwards. The following year it came to a spectacular head at the international negotiations on climate change. The issue was how to put a price on human life.

V

Pearce now had a bigger team behind him at University College, known as CSERGE – the Centre for Social and Environmental Research on the Global Environment. Their biggest task after the Rio Summit was to put together an economic basis for negotiations to tackle the greenhouse effect. That meant writing a policy paper for the Intergovernmental Panel on Climate Change that would put a dollar value on every possible damage from the greenhouse effect. The trouble was that they valued a human life in the rich developed countries at 15 times the life of someone in a poor country – from $1.5million for Americans down to $100,000 for the poorest peasants. And their ability to pay was similarly lower. A hectare of Chinese wetland was worth just 10 per cent of a hectare of Western wetland. It wasn't what people wanted to hear.

The storm broke over Pearce's head, co-ordinated in an effective campaign around the world by a professional violinist. Aubrey Meyer never looked like an international negotiator, with his trademark pigtail and white T-shirt, but his London-based organization, the Global Commons Institute, successfully drummed up signatures of protest from all over the world. 'Why, if one spotted owl equals one spotted owl, doesn't one human equal one human?' he asked. Even Sir Crispin Tickell criticized the idea. Pearce's adversary John Adams described it as 'the economics of genocide'. Meyer attacked cost-benefit head on as 'racist economics': 'Willingness to Pay embodies the ethics of the protection racketeer,' he wrote. 'It has no place in civilized debate.'

Could you really measure the value of something according to how much people would pay to keep it, they asked? What if they had no money? What if they were poor? Had the researchers travelled across the Third World asking people what they were willing to pay? How can people's rights to a clean environment be proportionate to how much money they had? Surely species have a right to exist even if people are ignorant of them?

But the calculation was simply the basis of an agreement that might work, said the CSERGE team. 'We won't be revising it, and we have no intention of apologizing for our work. This is a question of scientific correctness versus political correctness.'

But Meyer had won. When the representatives of world governments met in Berlin in April 1995, they carried with them a letter from Indian Environment Minister Kamal Nath rejecting the analysis as 'absurd and discriminatory' and urging other governments to do likewise. When they reconvened in Geneva three months later, all the delegates were greeted with a copy of the lead story in the *Independent on Sunday* the previous weekend with the headline 'One Western life is worth 15 in the Third World, says UN report'. As the delegates convened, the *Guardian* in London carried a picture of Meyer playing his violin in the park with the caption 'Who says life is cheap?' Following furious exchanges during the negotiations, delegates threw out the CSERGE analysis.

In Montreal three months after that, the two sides were still yelling abuse at each other. This time, delegates threw out the other figures as well. 'Being alone does not make you wrong,' said Pearce, sadly. Ironically, Kamal Nath's high moral tone was blunted later by his resignation after serious bribery accusations.

VI

It looks like a clear open and shut case. If Pearce was really measuring the value of views, species or human beings according to what people were prepared to pay to protect them, there was no moral defence. And although not everybody is an economist, everyone is an expert in morality. A cursory list of prices shows how bizarre this would be – an Albanian orphan costs £4,000 and a reasonably-sized house in the St John's Wood neighbourhood of London costs over £1 million. Life would be intolerable if people actually behaved as if prices meant real value. But it wasn't quite as simple as that.

'It is a result of poor communication by economists,' says an unrepentant Pearce today. 'Because we were used to using shorthand when we were talking about the value of an elephant, we knew what we mean by it – but it isn't the intrinsic value of an elephant. It's just what someone's willing to pay. We're just measuring people's preferences. But a lot of the opposition was based on sheer pig ignorance. People who couldn't be bothered to read anything or learn anything, thought that in five minutes they can pick up 200 years of economics. To an economist there's no surprise about what's being said. But if you want to discredit it, you don't have to be a master of the media to do that.'

What Pearce and his team were trying to do was to measure the way of the world. It may have looked pragmatic – and that's exactly what it was – but it was designed to create an agreement based on real exchanges of resources. It was just what everyone does in their own homes: 'The rights of individuals are not separate from costs,' he says, and one glimpse around the world shows that, sadly, he's right.

The greenhouse effect negotiations remain bogged down over exactly how the idea of tradable permits will work – nearly a decade after the Earth Summit first carved out the basis of an agreement. So to that extent, Pearce was right too. 'It doesn't necessarily follow that just because you can stand up and shout morally about global warming and all those wonderful phrases, it doesn't mean any of it is correct. One shouldn't be surprised that the rate of deforestation is much the same as it was thirty years ago. Where's the great power in this moral argument? To change something, people have to be better off under the new situation than they were under the old one. If you can't devise a policy which means all the stakeholders are better off, it won't happen.'

Moralists believe it must be done by regulation, and regulation that has to hurt the baddies, claims Pearce. 'The trouble is that the more expensive you make regulation by doing that, the bigger the built-up of hostility to your next piece of regulation. But if you can make a bargain, the Brazilians are better off, we're better off, the world's better off and we've done it more cheaply.'

The greenhouse numbers are one of the best examples of the crisis of counting. It is morally indefensible to work out the money value of human life – especially when it is different according to where you come from. Doing so makes an international agreement politically impossible. Yet without trying to count the real cost, it will be very hard to reach a real bargain.

Still, it may not be impossible. Aubrey Meyer's contraction and convergence model counts human lives equally. You do have to count – the important thing is to realize that you can't succeed in measuring the *real* value of anything.

The difficulty with cost-benefit analysis is that it claims to be a science when it is actually an art. Take the particularly knotty issue of discounting. Goods you can buy immediately are worth more than those you have to wait for, so economists reduce their value by a percentage – the opposite of an interest rate – for every year you have to wait. The British Treasury usually uses 5 per cent a year as a yardstick – but not always. Sometimes they use 7 per cent, sometimes they use 3 per cent. It depends. The truth is that, by changing the discount rate, you can have a dramatic effect on the result. In fact, you can prove almost anything like that. Yet there was the government lording it over road protesters at motorway inquiries, and refusing to let anyone question either their cost-benefit analysis or their resulting forecasts – because they were 'science' and beyond dispute.

There is the problem of actually measuring WTP. About a quarter of people asked what they would be willing to pay to preserve bald eagles, woodpeckers, coyotes, salmon or wild turkeys refuse to reply on the grounds that you can't put a price on such things. And of course you can't. And a Frankfurt woman called Frau Kraus discovered in 1989 that she had a veto over a proposed new skyscraper they wanted to build next door, and refused to play the game at all. She turned down a million deutschmarks, then she turned down 10 million. 'Not even if they were to offer me 20 million would I change my mind,' she told the papers. 'It would block out my sunlight and spoil the place I was born and bred.'

Then there is the usual problem of measuring. Cost-benefits will always have a problem valuing the intangibles. This mixture of careful measuring of the things that can be measured and a vague rule of thumb for the rest led John Adams to call the process a 'horse and rabbit stew'. The rabbit is skinned and dressed with great care. The horse – size unknown – is just tossed into the pot with no preparation at all. 'It is an ethic that debases that which is important and disregards entirely that which is supremely important,' he says.

Valuing 'horses' creates the most peculiar effects. One Washington economist valued the world's population of elephants at $1 million on the grounds that it was an easy figure to remember. The world's largest pharmaceutical company, Merck, actually bought the rights to Costa Rica's entire genetic diversity – plants, seeds and soil – for $1 million plus royalties. It's strange how the figure of $1 million comes up when people don't actually know what something is worth.

Yet cost-benefit analysis is on the increase. Ronald Reagan insisted on an analysis of all major projects within weeks of taking office in 1981. All over the world, the technique is seen as a way of controlling politicians – taking the politics out of decisions. When the *Exxon Valdez* spilled its oil off Alaska in 1989, they had to work out the cost of the damage so that the tanker's owners could pay it. When lorry drivers took to the streets to protest against fuel prices, we needed to have a better idea of the cost of using the roads (probably twice what the tax was raising).

That's the heart of the counting crisis. Measuring is often impossible, but sometimes you have to try anyway.

Bizarre units of measurement No. 11

Median Lethal Dose

(Part of the US Food and Drug Administration's search for measurable standardization. This led to the notorious LD50 test for drugs, which meant new compounds had to be tested as a poison at a concentration which would kill large numbers of experimental animals.)

....

Number of people in the UK visiting accident and emergency departments after accidents involving tea-cosies (1997): *39*

Average time gallery visitors spend in front of each painting (1987): *10 seconds*

Average time gallery visitors spend in front of each painting (1997): *3 seconds*

Chapter 11

The Bottom Line is the Bottom Line

'The other ambassadors warn me of famines, extortions, conspiracies, or else they inform me of newly discovered turquoise mines, advantageous prices in marten furs, suggestions for supplying damascened blades. And you?' the Great Khan asked Polo, 'you return from lands equally distant and you can tell me only the thoughts that come to a man who sits on his doorstep at evening to enjoy the cool air. What is the use, then, of all your travelling?'
Italo Calvino, *Invisible Cities*

Surely there is something unearthly and superhuman in spite of Bentham.
John Henry, Cardinal Newman

I

The man Keynes designated his successor didn't like cost-benefit analysis much either. It is 'a procedure by which the higher is reduced to the level of the lower and the priceless is given a price,' wrote E. F. Schumacher in *Small is Beautiful*. 'It can therefore never serve to clarify the situation and lead to an enlightened decision. All it can do is lead to self-deception or the deception of others.'

Schumacher published this ground-breaking book just four years before he died. It owed part of its immediate popularity to the title, coined by his publisher Anthony Blond, which passed into the language – rather to Schumacher's regret, because he felt it didn't do justice to the message. His claim that the Sermon on the Mount was an instruction manual for economic reform won him enthusiasts all over the world, but enraged many economists and industrialists. When he visited the USA to advise President Carter just before he died, some of his bitterest critics celebrated his visit with death threats.

This extreme reaction was partly because of what his book meant for old-style economics. Measuring everything by price wasn't just self-deception, he said – it was destroying civilization. It did so by concentrating on differences in quantity while suppressing differences in quality. The danger for us all, so wrapped up by numbers a quarter of a century later, is that Schumacher's analysis doesn't just apply to economics. Most areas of life are going the same way. If numbers are not measuring prices, they are measuring something else. And every time they do so, the qualitative aspects of what they are measuring – the least measurable and most valuable – get driven out.

Take education. I was leafing through the autobiography of an old admiral recently and came across a passage that seemed particularly dated. It was only half a century ago, and yet there he was lavishing praise on the headmaster of his son's school because 'his main aim was to develop their character, while ensuring adequate school education'.

Ah yes, those were the days! Nothing about 'excellence', league tables or exams; education was about character, which he went on to define as 'self-confidence and high principles'. Character and just enough education to get by. It's not the kind of phrase a modern educationalist would be seen dead using – probably quite rightly – yet most sane people agree there is much more to education than classrooms, skills and exam results. It's just that they don't tend to get measured, so they get ignored, then they get forgotten by the people who take decisions and those that write about them.

This failure of numbers means we get increasingly blind. Things that can't be measured – love, creativity, awe, religion, altruism – get forgotten by professionals and sometimes get ridiculed too. We are now in a world that is designed to be measured, that praises and promotes people with hard measuring skills, and downgrades those with human imaginative ones. This is one area of life where the feminist revolution has not even sparked. We are increasingly silenced by the number-crunchers – unable to make up our minds or take control of the future in the increasing cacophony of measurements and statistics.

Reading Admiral Lord Chatfield's comments on his son's education made me realize it's impossible to apply modern educational measurements even a generation back. You just can't compare the two with numbers – though, I have to admit, even the admiral and his colleagues tried to measure the success of his kind of education. They did it by sports results, and we all know from watching modern football that this is not a very good way of measuring character.

This is no new problem, yet somehow the measurement of education is where the whole issue is at its sharpest. We have created an equivalent to Jeremy Bentham's fearsome Panopticon for our schoolkids, measured and monitored ever more closely – both for their performance and for the standard of care they are given. Trust is old-fashioned. We don't need it any more now we can measure. Now the government is extending their target-setting and measuring to nursery classes and play groups and urging children to take GCSEs as young as eleven. It's muddling up exams with education, said lecturer Bethan Marshall – a classic case of muddling up the measurements with what you want to measure. 'I want my children and the countless thousands like them to be educated, not simply schooled,' she wrote.

What is it about education that makes it such a special target for the number-crunchers? Because it's just as bad in higher education as it is in primary. The Research Assessment Exercise was introduced in 1986 as a method of measuring the performance of universities. It is now the main way that students, businesses and government funders judge their success – yet it simply measures the number of articles their staff have managed to get published in academic journals. The result? Narrower and narrower research, important articles cut into three, conventional research rather than bold, dangerous new thinking and what historian David Cannadine called 'a large and depressed professoriate . . . with all the frenzied

energy of a battery chickens on overtime, laying for their lives.'
The Research Assessment Exercise is a wonderful example of
what happens when you measure the wrong thing.

There has probably never been a moment in history that
measures as much as we do. Our politicians pack their
speeches full of skewed statistics. Civil servants and businesses
spawn targets with every report. Screeds of data collect on
computer on our buying habits, blood counts, accident rates,
bank balances – and none of it quite gets to the crux of the
matter. There are already six times as many people employed
in accountancy and financial services as there were in the
early 1950s, and that's just a small part of the new auditing
and number-crunching industry. The government has set itself
8,000 new targets at the last count. So many people will soon
be employed monitoring that there will be nobody left to do
the actual work.

We laugh at Dickens' ridiculous character of Thomas Gradgrind and his obsession with facts and nothing but facts. Yet
here we are surrounded by them.

And look what's coming next. Psychiatrists are increasingly
relying on a fearsome numerical system of diagnosis called
the Diagnostic and Statistical Manual of Mental Disorder,
which can have a disastrous effect on your career if you end
up under one of their 'disorder' labels – as almost any of us
would. There have even been moves to force doctors to diag-
nose according to programmable criteria on the grounds that
it would be more 'open and scientific'. A similar number-based
computer programme is being used to write individual reports
in schools. Another one is now used by the Inland Revenue to
spot fraudulent tax returns. The result: the amount of money
recovered dropped by half since the days when inspectors did
the same job by their own judgement.

American companies are now doing such close analysis of
the attitudes of their customers by brand that they were able
to know that those most in favour of the impeachment of Bill
Clinton were consumers of Campbell's Soup (84 per cent),
followed by Oscar Mayer hot dogs, Fantastik cleaner and Tide
detergent. Burger King customers, for some reason, were the

most pro-Clinton. They are also using a special software to help them take decisions called AHP or Analytic Hierarchy Process. It assigns 'intensity' numbers to different options and was inspired by the way the inventor's grandma worked out difficult problems. It's now used by the US army and air force – even by the Egyptian government to work out tough foreign policy issues. But after all that, inventor Tom Saaty doesn't 'recommend using AHP to decide which restaurant to go to,' he told *Fortune* magazine. 'It would spoil my pleasure.' A clue there, perhaps.

A number of British companies are working on the idea of microchip implants for their workforce to measure their timekeeping. Others are pioneering ways of measuring emotional intelligence, or – like one Virginia company – colour-coding staff badges according to a numerical approximation of their personality type. Worse, BT's Soul Catcher project aims to find a way of digitizing every sense and experience in a lifetime so that it can all be held on floppy disk.

Then there are the measuring machines. Panasonic has developed a 'smart' fridge that measures what you eat and orders more milk when you need it. Matsushita has developed a 'smart' toilet that measures your weight, fat-ratio, temperature, protein and glucose levels every time you give it something to work on. Their VitalSigns medical kit then sends this data automatically to your local clinic – probably the last thing they want.

It's hard to object to any of these measurements by themselves, but taken together they represent a massive loss of faith in our own judgement, intuition and our trust in other people.

Measurement as obsessively practised by our society is about standardization and control. It is the by-product of empire, but not the kind of empires we were used to historically. This is *our* empire. The measurements are a reflection of what we believe and what we fear the most. We collect them because we no longer trust politicians, professionals and natural processes. We insist that their ways, methods and progress are measured every step of the way.

'The more strictly we are watched, the better we behave,' said Bentham. Although his Panopticon was never built – the prison where every cell can be watched by a single guard – his calculating has created a world like it, and we live in it.

II

In 1989, the new chairman of chemical giant DuPont Ed Woolard gave two speeches which – without consulting his staff – promised his company would cut poisonous emissions by 65 per cent, carcinogens by 90 per cent and hazardous waste by 35 per cent. DuPont was then the biggest polluter in the USA. 'Well, I've done it,' he told the company afterwards. 'Now you guys have to do it – it's your job.' It was a difficult moment, and there were some in the company who thought he had lost his marbles completely. But when he stood down eight years later, the targets had been all but met. It was a prime example of the power of setting numerical targets and measuring them.

Let's be clear about this. Counting things is a vital human skill. Using numbers can help predict who gets cancer, can show up problems in social or engineering systems and above all – (as Chadwick found) they can shock people into action. They can let us orientate ourselves in our world and – to some extent – begin to compare like with like. They allow us to take the world unawares. All the bizarre measurements scattered through this book fall into that category. They may not be precisely right, but they let us see the world differently for a moment. They are a tool for visualizing problems. Nobody is suggesting that we should stop measuring altogether.

There are also times when we simply have to try measuring the unmeasurable – that is the nature of the counting crisis in education, business and politics. The danger comes when we do nothing but measure, or when we really believe the numbers are measuring something real. Then we will eventually turn round and look at our league-tabled education system and wonder why it's turning out narrow-minded, miserable children who are only good at tests and exams.

The hopeless dream of number-crunchers is still to reach the perfect objective non-political decision, to take all that human prejudice and error out of politics or management. It is a dream from the foundation of the London Statistical Society whose first rule of conduct was 'to exclude all opinions'. It goes right back to the pioneering French statisticians who believed that counting things could abolish politics altogether and usher in a reign of facts. It wasn't true then, and it isn't true now – even if we wanted it to be. Life is just not certain enough.

We can see where it goes wrong all around us. The more politicians urge us to look at the scientific evidence, the more their numbers seem to contradict each other. Red meat has a statistically proven link to bowel cancer in the USA but not in the UK. Tea is statistically proven to be good for you and bad for you – the same with margarine, wine, Q-tips, jogging, breast implants and practically everything on the market. Our overmeasured world has become the victim of some social version of Heisenberg's Uncertainty Principle – that the observer in a scientific experiment affects the result.

By poring over the measurements, we have also convinced ourselves we live in a period of rapid change. We must be because the numbers change all the time. Yet if we step back from them a moment we find that the really important things do not change. Death from disease or highway robbery may be nightmares of the past, but ill-health and crime – as far as we can tell – are with us still. There are no workhouses any more, yet the proportion of the poor and the proportion of national income we spend on eradicating it are comparable with what they were before workhouses were invented. The measurements have blinded us to our greatest failures, just as they have to so much else.

And one of those aspects of life they blind us to is the paradoxical way the world changes. We measure our way to success – money or whatever else we had decided we needed to be happy – only to find that wasn't it at all. Even political success tends to work in the ways we least expect. Change doesn't happen like that: 'Men fight and lose the battle,' wrote

William Morris in *A Dream of John Ball*, 'and the thing that they fought for comes about in spite of their defeat, and when it comes it turns out not to be what they meant, and other men have to fight for what they meant under another name.' You can't measure real progress with figures.

Right back in the 1830s, the philosopher Georg Friedrich Pohl used the metaphor of understanding a journey through beautiful landscape and fascinating people by using a train timetable. The figures were accurate enough, but it left out most of the experience. Now we are all a little like Jedediah Buxton, the eighteenth-century prodigy who tried to understand Shakespeare by counting his words. Buxton probably suffered from autism, and so – in a sense – do we. Not as individuals, but as a society. Like autistic children, we are slow to smile, unresponsive, passive and we avoid eye contact. We find it hard to understand other people's emotional expressions.

It's not surprising that our institutions are being built in this image too. We will soon have a workforce recruited by categorizing aspects of their personalities on a scale of one to ten. We will have our nannies graded for their caring abilities on the basis of some kind of checklist. We will have children who can pass exams but have no judgement. We will measure all our institutions by numerical 'best practice' standards and wonder vaguely why nobody innovates any more. And we will have doctors who translate our symptoms into numbers before feeding them into the computer. We will be turning ourselves ever so slowly into machines.

III

'Tralfamadorians, of course, say that every creature and plant in the universe is a machine,' wrote Kurt Vonnegut in one of his science fiction epics. 'It amuses them that so many Earthlings are offended by the idea of being machines.' Number-crunchers and technocrats are Tralfamadorians, amused that people still resist the idea of being machines or computers – the sum of their parts. The question of whether they're right goes to the heart of the argument about what being human means.

'The human being is the only computer produced by amateurs,' said one General Electric executive, a little scarily, echoing the behaviourist B. F. Skinner. As far back as 1962, another executive, this time from Motorola, wrote the following:

> At birth the infant will be clamped in front of the TV eye by means of a suitable supporting structure, and two sections of tubing will be connected to provide nourishment and to carry away the waste materials. From this time on, the subject will live an ideal vicarious life, scientifically selected for compatibility with the fixed influences of the inherited genes and chromosomes.

This seemed to him a recipe for 'race suicide', but it could so easily have been serious. We have spent the past forty years shaking off these kind of predictions. I can remember when space technologists were predicting that all food would soon come in easy bite-size tablets and tubes – just like in the Apollo capsules. But the futurists had never heard of Elizabeth David. There is a constant human longing for what is 'real' which seems to go beyond the merely calculated. Hence the unexpected survival of live performance, adventure holidays and organic food.

The current front line is over genetics. Can every human characteristic be measured to a specific gene, each with a specific code number, so that every human being could be completely reproducible? Can every human characteristic, good and bad, be numbered according to genes and their combinations? When we can do nothing but count and measure, it sometimes seems that way, especially with highly-educated Tralfamadorians telling us so on the radio and TV every day. The belief that we are more than the sum of our parts is primarily a matter of faith, but the counting crisis is, in this sense, rather a hopeful sign. It means that businesspeople are rejecting the idea that companies are the sum of their measurable parts – worth just what they would be if they were chopped up and sold off. That's why they are struggling to find ways of measuring the intangible core. That's why the boundaries of measuring intangibles are being pushed forward – because individual human beings are more than their constituent chemicals, and that individuality needs measuring too.

It's a hopeful sign and a frightening one at the same time. The problem is not so much trying to measure – sometimes you have to try, as we've seen. The danger is when people or institutions think they have succeeded. That's when the damage is done and when the spirit dies. Every 'bottom line', firmly held, is a generalization that fails to do justice to the individual moment or the individual person, or patient, business or child. Yardsticks are a vital human tool, as long as we remember how limiting they are if we cling to them too closely. The bottom line is the bottom line.

In other words, there are human skills more essential to us than measuring. It's probably time we accepted that computers and machines will always be able to count and measure better than human beings. They can already guide missiles better and play chess better. It is time we looked at those areas of human nature where computers *can't* follow – the world of the non-measurable, non-calculable. Love, intuition, imagination, creativity. There are number-crunchers who say that because they can't be measured, they do not exist. Yet they continue to survive and provide us with the clues for our continued survival despite that heckling from the wings. Perhaps it would be more accurate to say that because they can't be measured, they can't be reduced.

The big problem is what numbers won't tell you. They won't interpret. They won't inspire and they won't tell you what causes what. Statistics have nothing to do with causation, the pioneering number-cruncher William Farr told Florence Nightingale in 1861: 'You complain that your report would be dry. The dryer the better. Statistics should be the dryest of all reading.' But over-reliance on numbers sweeps away your intuition along with ideology. It leaves policy-makers staring at screeds of figures, completely flummoxed by them, unable

to use their common sense to interpret the babble of competing causes and effects – unable to tell one from the other.

If men with long ring fingers are subject to depression – as
they are for some reason – that might alert you to looking for
a causal link. The same is true of other peculiar numerical
links: high stress makes you much more likely to catch colds,
accident rates among children double when their mothers are
miserable. These odd connections might surprise and inspire
you to think about problems in new ways, but it won't tell
you what causes what. You will have to use your intuition to
work out where to look in a massively complex world of
complex systems. 'Scientists try to avoid emotions and
intuition,' says the British biologist Stephen Hardin, 'but it is
exactly those that give them ideas.'

Too many numbers also drives out history – it gives us no
sense of the different ways in which people measured in the
past. It drives out creativity, locking away Keynes' dark woolly
monster of ideas. And it drives out morality too – leaving
our poor beleaguered ethics committees desperately trying to
measure themselves a coherent attitude to the frightening
future of genetically-modified human beings. And to get
through the next few perilous decades, to look after each
other, and solve the looming problems ahead, we're going
to need all the judgement, intuition, history, creativity and
morality we can possibly muster. So we have to make absolutely sure our tidal wave of measurements doesn't drive those
things out.

What can we do to make sure they survive? We could try
measuring more and we could try measuring less. In fact, we
can probably do both.

Measuring more is what many of the pioneers in this book
have been doing. John Vasconcellos measuring the success of
schools and prisons by their ability to give people self-esteem.
Simon Zadek and the social auditors measuring corporate
ethics. Perry Walker and Hazel Henderson measuring salmon,
frogs, vegetarian restaurants and everything else. Measuring
more destroys the tyranny of the bottom line. It undermines
the great importance of the big number. It punctures the

pomposity of the men in white coats and the men in grey
suits.

We can do more than that. We can encourage people to
measure locally what they think is important, not what they're
told to measure. We can de-standardize, get the subjects of
measurement to do their own measuring – the pupils, the
patients, the poor.

But we could also try measuring less. This is a trusting,
conservative approach. Good professional doctors or development economists will tell you that they can know very quickly
what is wrong with the patient or economy – but they then
have to spend a great deal of public money collecting the
figures in order to persuade anybody else. Measuring less saves
money. It also requires considerable faith in other people, and
that's in very short supply these days. It means giving more
hands-on experience to schoolchildren, managers, civil servants, police. It means lecturing less and listening more. It
means decentralizing power. Most of all it means practising
using our imagination and intuition.

Measuring more is the trendy radical solution, but my heart
is probably in the opposite. Measuring less means trusting
enough to lay aside occasionally some of those systems or
policies which ensure we make appointments without dis-
crimination, or decisions without ignoring the people who will
be affected by them. Those are worthy reasons for counting,
but we die a little if we do nothing but count. A world where
we count more is stricter and fairer, but it has less life than
the world where we count less. When we count less and get
it wrong, we risk inefficiency, bigotry, ignorance and disaster.
But when we count less and get it right, we probably get closer
to joy and humanity than we can any other way. Human
beings can deal with a complex world better than any system
or series of measurements.

IV

'There were once eleven generals who had to decide whether to attack or retreat in a battle,' wrote Carl Jung's interpreter Marie-Louise von Franz, introducing the ancient Chinese tale which changed her understanding of numbers. The generals got together and had a long debate, at the end of which they took a vote. Three wanted to attack and eight wanted to retreat – so they attacked. Why? Because three is the number of unanimity.

The story was so shocking, she said, that it woke her up. Suddenly she understood that the Eastern view of numbers was different from the Western one. For us modern Westerners, numbers can only count. Our numbers mount up to cumulative totals – things get bigger, we demand more. In the East, they have significance, meaning and quality. Since Pythagoras' day, it's been hard to bridge the gap between the two, but – with Western figures driving out our sense of such things – we may be at a moment in history when we have to try.

When our decision-makers seem to be able to do nothing but count, you can see in reaction a new longing for significance and complex truth, for poetry – despite Bentham's denial of its existence – and for the sacred. People want rhythms and music rather than bald statistics. We don't want data, we want enlightenment. We don't want numbers, we want meaning. And most of all, we need to stop muddling them all up, to realize where the former stops being helpful in the endless search for the latter. We need to help people disentangle from numbers and connect with the kind of understanding that can help them change – because change, and whether it is possible, politically or personally, is the key issue for our generation. Change without numbers is impossible; change without anything else is impossible too, and we need some Universities of 'Unlearning' to help us find it. In short, we need a Campaign for Real Wisdom.

This is how Prince Charles made the point in his millennium broadcast on the BBC:

Two and a half thousand years ago, Plato was at pains to explain through the words of Timaeus that the great gift of human rationality should not be disparaged. Far from it, he said – it should be exercised to its utmost, but it must not make the mistake of believing it has no limits.

The same is true of counting. Western numbers that split things up, that see only the parts, which are blind to the most important things in life, can only get us so far.

But in case this doesn't convince you, I'll end with an old Scottish proverb which seems to put this point in just nine words, two verbs and thirteen vowels: 'You don't make sheep any fatter by weighing them.'

Bizarre units of measurement No. 12
Foot pound

(A unit of labouring force, applied equally to machines and people, by the engineer William Whewell in the 1840s. A working man could lift water at the rate of 1,700 foot-pounds per minute for eight hours a day.)

....

Average time British people spend on hold on the phone every year:
45 hours

Proportion of people from India who have not heard of the USA:
about 30 per cent

Postscript

We recognize that, in the past, testing has helped reduce unfairness
in allocating opportunities and directing resources to the economically
disadvantaged, and has been useful for making decisions. However,
the growing over-reliance on testing over the past several decades
deprives the nation of all the talent it needs and sometimes conflicts
with the nation's ideals of fairness and equal opportunity.
US National Commission on Testing and Public Policy, 1998

Just as I had finished writing the hardback edition of this
book, and copies were running off the printer, there was suddenly one of those once-in-a-blue-moon moments of global
revelation about counting. It was all a matter of votes. Voting
is a bit like a jury decision: we agree to accept a numerical
verdict, not because it means someone is objectively innocent
or because they are objectively the best potential president,
but because there are no other ways of measuring such things.
The problems happen when the numbers don't work either.

That's exactly what happened in Florida during the November 2000 US presidential election. Despite a political season
where competing statistics were flung over the networks with
ever more abandon, it suddenly became clear just how
muddling, subjective and confused by human error the
business of counting and measurement is. Far from being an
objective assessment of the will of the people, you could count
Florida's votes in any one of a score of different ways.

Like other kinds of statistics in modern life, votes are supposed to be a pretty exact way of finding a new democratic
leader. But, if you insist on them being absolutely *precise*, the
whole edifice starts to unravel. And when the winner hangs
on 300, 327, or 900 votes out of the 6 million plus from

Florida, then every vote counts. But, as the pundits and politicians soon discovered, whether or not a vote was really a vote might depend on how far the ballot had been punched through. It was the constant re-counting in some of Florida's counties that put the little word 'chad' – the tiny bits of cardboard normally knocked out of a computerized ballot card – firmly into the English language lexicon.

Try as they might to recreate laboratory conditions at the re-counts, it just couldn't work. There were rules in Palm Beach that nobody could talk, and anyone whose mobile phone rang would be kicked out, and – in Volusia – they controlled exactly what colour pens the counters were allowed (red) and where they could put their purses (next to the guard). It was no good: any count – even one carried out by machines – was going to be an interpretation. At one stage, sheriff's deputies in Broward County took custody of 78 minute chads as evidence of potential ballot tampering. The police put them into an envelope marked: 'Crime. Found Property'. An official was even accused of eating the stuff. That's what happens when numbers suddenly reveal themselves to be the relative props they really are.

Even so, we have yet to see much resistance to the number-crunchers in the UK, except for the decision to stop publishing school league tables by the new assemblies in Northern Ireland and Wales, but it's a different story in France – especially among economics students. 'It was in the beginning a modest initiative, almost confidential,' wrote the prestigious French newspaper *Le Monde* in September 2000. 'It has now become a subject of an important debate which has created a state of effervescence in the community of economists. Should not the teaching of economics in universities by rethought?'

What had happened was that a small group of students had put a petition on the Web protesting against the 'uncontrolled use of mathematics' in economics. They claimed that the result was that mathematics had 'become an end in itself', turning economics into what they called an 'autistic science' – dominated by abstractions that bore no relation to the world as it really was.

Within two weeks, the petition calling for reconnection with the real world had 150 signatures, many from students at France's most important universities. Soon newspapers and TV stations all over France had picked up the story and even senior professors were starting a similar petition of their own. By the autumn, the campaign had led to a major debate at the Sorbonne and the French education minister, Jack Lang, had promised to set up a commission to investigate the situation, and come up with some proposals to change economics teaching.

Even if they haven't managed such a spectacular turn-around on this side of the English Channel, the UK press had been more vigilant than usual about such matters. The *Independent on Sunday* revealed that Department of Health figures for casualty waiting times don't start when you arrive at hospital, but only measure the gap between when patients are first seen and when they are actually treated. And so it was that one 88-year-old who waited 24 hours before being admitted to hospital was officially recorded as waiting only 30 minutes.

Then there was the story of the government target to cut the time patients are allowed to wait on trolleys to four hours. Hospitals turned out to have circumvented the problem by buying more expensive trolleys and redefining them as 'mobile beds'. Or the tale of the Kent police who promise to answer the phone within two minutes, but actually just do so by switching you through to a call centre that keeps you hanging on the line for ages.

The slow suspicion is dawning on us poor counted and measured people that this kind of stuff doesn't work. The big lies of numerical targets, that they measure something real and that they can be manipulated to create change, are becoming ever more apparent. What isn't yet clear is what we can do instead, how we can retain some of the human complexity that measuring tries to remove, how we can create institutions that build real human contact rather than the fake numerical kind.

Having lived with this problem for some years now – not

to mention being grilled on radio about it, often thrown into the lion's den with statisticians and census managers – I've a feeling it's all about telling stories and asking difficult questions. Telling stories, because they can often communicate complex, paradoxical truths better than figures. Asking questions because they can devastate most political statistics. Yes, the carbon monoxide rate has reduced, but is the air cleaner? Yes, our local university professors have produced a record number of learned published papers, but is their teaching any good? Yes, the exam passes top the league tables, but what about the education? Are the children happy? Can they deal with life? Numbers and measurements are as vulnerable as the Emperor's New Clothes to the incisive, intuitive human question.

The closer any of us get to measuring what's really important, the more it escapes us, yet we can recognize it – sometimes in an instant. Relying on that instant a bit more, and our ability to realize it, is probably the best hope for us all.

Bizarre units of measurement No. 13

Dram

(Ancient unit of measurement for drink. 1 fluid dram – one hundred and twenty-eighth of a pint in the US, or one hundred and sixtieth of a pint in the UK.)

....

Number of Americans injured by supermarket trolleys every hour: **5**

Average duration of sex in the UK: ***21 minutes (compares to 14 minutes in Italy and 30 minutes in Brazil)***

British school children who think Adolf Hitler was British prime minister during the Second World War: ***4 per cent***

Index